Peter Baart

The Roman court

A treatise on the cardinals, Roman congregations and tribunals, legates

Peter Baart

The Roman court
A treatise on the cardinals, Roman congregations and tribunals, legates

ISBN/EAN: 9783337234225

Printed in Europe, USA, Canada, Australia, Japan

Cover: Foto ©ninafisch / pixelio.de

More available books at **www.hansebooks.com**

The Roman Court,

OR

A Treatise on the Cardinals, Roman Congregations and Tribunals, Legates, Apostolic Vicars, Protonotaries, and Other Prelates

OF THE

Holy Roman Church.

BY THE

Reverend Peter A. Baart, S. T. L.,

Author of "Orphans and Orphan Asylums," and "Episcopal Claims Disproved."

FR. PUSTET,
Printer to the Holy See and the S. Congregation of Rites.

FR. PUSTET & CO.,
NEW YORK AND CINCINNATI.

Nihil Obstat.
    CAROLUS O'REILLY, S. T. D.,
                          Censor Deputatus.

Imprimatur.
    JOANNES S. FOLEY,
                        Episcopus Detroitensis.

Die 25, m. Septembris, 1895.

LOAN STACK

COPYRIGHTED, 1895,
BY
P. A. BAART.
ALL RIGHTS RESERVED.

PRESS OF THE STATESMAN,
MARSHALL, MICH.

PREFACE.

IF a reason must be given for writing a book on the Roman Court and presenting it to English-speaking people, it can be found in the fact that there is no other book printed in English on this most important subject. The points which may be gathered from encyclopedias are often vague and not unfrequently misleading. To place before the public a book, which, it is believed, is quite accurate and contemporary, has not been a light task. On a number of points special inquiry had to be made in Rome. It will be noticed that the practice in America on some of these points, particularly in regard to titles, diverges not a little from that accepted in Rome.

The chapters on the Conclave or the College of Cardinals during a vacancy in the Apostolic See, on the Congregations of the Inquisition, the Index and the Propaganda, as well as those on Prelates and Legates may be of special interest to Americans. Regarding the American legation some information is given which heretofore may not have reached the general public. If, however, it is not new, the repetition of it will do no harm.

Throughout this treatise the word Protonotary is spelled without the "h" which is usually inserted.

Protonotary is derived from *protos*, first, not from *prothos*. The Latin, Italian, French, Spanish languages retain *proto* in protonotary, just as in protomartyr and similar compound words. Can any good reason be given for writing *prothonotary*, except that some one else has done it?

Whatever appears in the following pages is cheerfully submitted to the judgment and correction of proper ecclesiastical authority.

PETER A. BAART.

MARSHALL, Mich., August 15, 1895.

CONTENTS.

INTRODUCTORY CHAPTER.—The Roman Pontiff, Primate of the Church.

PART FIRST.—The Sacred College of Cardinals.

	Page.
Chapter I.—The Word Cardinal	10
Chapter II.—Order, Title, Number of Cardinals	14
Chapter III.—Antiquity of the College of Cardinals	22
Chapter IV.—Dignity of the Cardinalate	27
Chapter V.—Mutual Relations of the Pope and the Sacred College	32
Chapter VI.—Creation of Cardinals	42
Chapter VII.—Cardinals in Relation to their Titles	53
Chapter VIII.—The College of Cardinals during a Vacancy in the Apostolic See; The Conclave	59

PART SECOND—The Roman Congregations and Tribunals.

Chapter I.—The Sacred Consistory and its Auxiliary Congregations: The Consistorial Congregation, the Congregation for Choosing Bishops, The Congregation for Extraordinary Ecclesiastical Affairs	80
Chapter II.—The Holy Office or Universal Inquisition	93
Chapter III.—The Congregation of the Index	113
Chapter IV.—The Congregation on Studies	140
Chapter V.—The Congregation of Rites	146
Chapter VI.—The Congregation on Ceremonies	163
Chapter VII.—The Congregation for Indulgences and Relics	165

Chapter VIII.—The Congregation for the Fabric of St. Peter's 170
Chapter IX.—The Congregation of the Council; The Subordinate Congregations for Visits ad Limina, For Reviewing Provincial Synods, For Ecclesiastical Immunity, For the Residence of Bishops 176
Chapter X.—The Congregation of Bishops and Regulars; and the Congregation on Regular Discipline and on the State of Regulars 197
Chapter XI.—The Congregation for the Propagation of Faith 208
Chapter XII.—Certain Rules of the Congregations 228
Chapter XIII.—The Tribunals of Justice; The Rota, Treasury Apostolic, Signature of Justice 235
Chapter XIV.—The Tribunals of Favor; The Signature of Favor, The Datary, The Sacred Penitentiary 243
Chapter XV.—The Tribunals of Expedition; the Roman Chancery, The Secretariate of Briefs, The Secretariate of State, The Secretariate of Memorials 256
Chapter XVI.—Advocates, Notaries, Agents in the Roman Court 266

PART THIRD—Prelates, Legates, Vicars Apostolic, Protonotaries.

Chapter I.—Prelates of the Roman Court 271
Chapter II.—Legates of the Apostolic See 280
Chapter III.—The Power of Apostolic Legates 297
Chapter IV.—Vicars Apostolic 316
Chapter V.—Protonotaries Apostolic 325

INTRODUCTORY CHAPTER.

The Roman Pontiff, Primate of the Church.

1. The Pope, the Bishop of Rome, is the visible head of the Catholic Church throughout the world. He is the vicar of Christ and the successor of St. Peter, who died Bishop of Rome and primate of the whole Church. This primacy, not only of honor but also of jurisdiction, which Christ conferred on St. Peter, is essential to the constitution of the Church; and because the Church, according to the promise of Christ, is to last to the end of time, the primacy also shall ever remain with the successor of St. Peter in the See of Rome.

2. By virtue of this primacy the Roman Pontiff has full and supreme power of jurisdiction over the whole Church, not only as the infallible teacher in questions of faith and morals, but also as the ruler in what pertains to the discipline and government of the Church throughout the world. Moreover this power is ordinary and immediate over all churches and over both pastors and people. Hence in the

universal Church the Roman Pontiff is the supreme teacher, lawgiver and judge. He can therefore make laws which bind the whole Church; he can abrogate the general laws even of œcumenical councils; he can convoke, preside at and confirm œcumenical councils; he can examine and decide all ecclesiastical causes and receive appeals from any and every ecclesiastical tribunal. To him exclusively belongs the right of treating what are called major causes. Such are questions regarding faith, the erection of episcopal sees, the division of ecclesiastical provinces, the cononization of saints, the trial of bishops.

3. It is evident that the Pope requires assistance in performing the many and onerous duties of the primacy. The collection of assistants who participate under the Pope in ruling the universal Church is called the Roman Court. Those who assist the Pope in administering the diocese of Rome or in ruling as a temporal sovereign are also considered part of the Roman Court, but only in an accessory or secondary way. Of this secondary part of the Roman Court we shall not treat, for only indirectly does it concern the universal Church.

4. Considered then in its stricter sense, the Roman Court is composed of the Sacred College of Cardinals, of several congregations of these same cardinals, of some other ecclesiastical tribunals, and finally of those legates, vicars, administrators and prefects who are called apostolic, that is, sent by the Apostolic See and fortified with its authority and jurisdiction.

Through all these councilors, judges and officials

combined, the strong and yet mild rule of the Supreme Pontiff in spiritual affairs reaches throughout the world; and thus he fulfils the obligation imposed upon him of feeding and guarding the whole flock of Christ.

5. We shall divide this treatise into three parts. In the first we shall treat of the cardinals of the Holy Roman Church or the Sacred College; in the second, of the Roman Congregations and Tribunals, and of their authority; and in the third part we shall write of prelates, legates, vicars apostolic and certain other ministers or officials of the Apostolic See.

PART FIRST.

The Sacred College of Cardinals.

CHAPTER I.

THE WORD CARDINAL.

6. It is interesting and profitable to note the use of the word CARDINAL in earlier church history; for not a few writers formerly endeavored to maintain that this title was peculiar to parish priests, that in the earlier ages cardinals were only parish priests, and that consequently the pre-eminence of the cardinals of the Holy Roman Church over bishops, archbishops and even patriarchs was introduced through the ambition of the Roman Court.

7. Marius Lupus in his work, *On Parishes*, says that in all the more celebrated dictionaries which he consulted the word cardinal is derived from *cardo* which means a hinge; but he adds that it was used metaphorically by the ancients with the meaning of primary, principal. Thomassin, Muratori and others interpret the word to mean, fixed, stable,

irremovable. Gothofred in his *Notes on the Theodosian Code*, writing in the year 1625, says: "To this day we do not know what the word cardinal means."

8. The first use of the word in church writings is found in a letter which Gratian in his compilation of canon law under the heading of *Can. Sacrosancta, dist. 22*, ascribes to Pope Anacletus, who reigned in the year 84, in which letter the Pontiff calls the Roman Church "the hinge," cardo on which other churches depend. This letter, however, is rejected by the learned as unauthentic.

In the same way, according to Labbe, we must reject the "Second Roman Council under Pope Sylvester" which is ascribed to the year 324, and from which is gathered the following explicit mention of the cardinals of the Holy Roman Church: "Let not a bishop be condemned unless with seventy-two witnesses; let not a cardinal-priest be deposed unless with sixty-four witnesses; let not a cardinal-deacon of the city of Rome be condemned unless with twenty-seven witnesses." This quotation is found in *Cap. Praesul. 2. quest. 4. causa 2;* but whatever legal weight, because of being inserted in canon law, the passage itself may have, historians now admit that the whole council known as the "Second Roman Council under Pope Sylvester" is fictitious; therefore as a matter of history it is not certain that the word cardinal was used at the time of Pope Sylvester. Hence Dr. Smith in his *Elements of Ecclesiastical Law* is in error when, following Craisson and Ferraris, he quotes from the apocryphal Second Council of Rome to show the early use of the word cardinal.

9. Coming to documents which are authentic, it may be said that the word cardinal is found first under Pope Damasus I. in the year 366. Volterran, a writer of great authority, relates that he himself saw a charter by which Zenobius, a Roman senator, made a certain donation to the church of Arezzo in the time of Pope Damasus I. This charter, preserved in the church of Arezzo, has the following endorsement: "I, John, cardinal-deacon of the Holy Roman Church, on the part of Pope Damasus praise and confirm the grant." *In Antropol. 1, 22, in Vit. Innoc. IV. pag. 255.*

Under Pope Gelasius, who began his reign in the year 492, the word cardinal was freely used, and evidence of the fact is found in ancient parchments now preserved in St. Mary's beyond the Tiber. Even before him, Pope St. Leo frequently mentions the priests and deacons *cardinis nostri*, "of our church". In fact during the fifth century it may be said the word cardinal was in common use. Its meaning, however, was quite different from that given it at the present day.

10. In the sixth century, especially in the writings of St. Gregory the Great, to incardinate or make a cleric a cardinal, meant the same as to assign him at least temporarily to some church in which he was to perform the duties of his order and thence also derive his support. Whether other than cathedral churches were called *cardines*, hinges, is uncertain; though several passages in the letters of St. Gregory tend to show that all churches and even oratories were called *cardines*. It is certain, however, that the title of cardinal was not confined to any

one cleric assigned to a church, but was used indiscriminately of all connected with it. Hence it can never be proved that parish priests had the peculiar title of cardinal in the ancient discipline of the Church.

11. In the Middle Ages, at least from the eighth century, it is certain that the chief clerics of cathedral churches and especially of the Apostolic See, were called cardinals. They constituted the college which was first called the presbytery and later the chapter, and which, associated with the Bishop as head, participated in the government of the churches.

How the transition was made from the general use of the word cardinal as we find it in the time of St. Gregory, to the restricted use of the Middle Ages, extant documents will not help us discover.

12. Cardinal Petra in his work *Ad Const. 15, Eugen. IV., No. 15*, says that Pius V., by his Constitution of February 15, 1568, took away from all except the cardinals of the Roman Church the privilege of using the name cardinal. Cohellius, however, and Tria object that no such constitution can be found. As a matter of fact, also, the canons of some churches still retain the name of cardinal. In the cathedral of Naples there are fourteen canons who are called cardinals, and in Soissons until very lately there were eleven cardinal-priests among the canons. For a long time, however, the name has been the peculiar property of the cardinals of the Holy Roman Church.

CHAPTER II.

THE ORDER, TITLE, NUMBER OF CARDINALS.

13. Cardinals are divided into the three orders of bishops, priests and deacons. This classification, though now well known and fully recognized, was of gradual development. First in chronological order was the institution of cardinal-priests; then came cardinal-deacons and lastly cardinal-bishops.

There have been also cardinal-subdeacons of the Holy Roman Church; but since the time of Alexander III. we find no mention of them. Thomassin in his work, *Old and New Discipline of the Church, part 1, bk. 2, ch. 116, 6*, says that in the Roman Council held in 963 under the Emperor Otho I., a cardinal-subdeacon named John was present. Tomagna, *Origini de Cardinali, vol. 1, pg. 147*, and Cohellius tell us that in the year 1057 a certain Fredericus Lotharingius was decorated with the cardinalitial dignity under the name of cardinal-subdeacon. Likewise under Nicholas II., Hildebrand a Soana was made a cardinal-subdeacon. Baronius in his annals of the year 1177 relates that the cardinal-deacon of the title of St. George and a certain cardinal-subdeacon of the Apostolic See were sent as legates by Alexander III.

14. The order of cardinal-priests seems to have originated in this manner: St. Cletus, who was the second successor of St. Peter and began his reign in

the year 78, according to *Liber Pontificalis* divided the city of Rome into districts and assigned to each its own priest. Pagius says there were twenty-five such districts, others mention seven, but Antonelli says the exact number is not known. Pope Evaristus later confirmed this division of the city of Rome into parishes or titles and the priests who were incardinated or entitled in these churches were afterwards called cardinal-priests. It is more than likely that not until the time of Pope Dionysius, A. D. 259, was a similar division made of the territory outside the city of Rome; for in *Cap. Eccles. I, Causa 13*, we read the words of Dionysius himself regarding the institution of parishes: "We have given churches to priests, one to each. We have divided parishes and cemeteries among them, and have ordained that each shall have his right, in such a manner that one may not infringe on the limits or rights of the parish of another, but that each may be content with the limits assigned him and thus guard the church and the people committed to his charge."

15. How the word TITLE originated is not clear, for there are four opinions concerning it. The first is that of them who think that any building converted unto sacred use and devoted to the gatherings of the faithful was called a title. But this is unsatisfactory, for no reason is given why such buildings were called titles. The second is that of Baronius, who by learned testimony shows that to houses belonging to the royal fisc, a banner ornamented with the image of the emperor was affixed, and by this banner the house was entitled or known as the emperor's. In the same way, according to him, the buildings con-

verted to Christian worship had the cross affixed to them and were thus entitled to Christ and called titles. The third opinion, also proposed by Baronius, is that which Thomassin favors. According to it, churches were called titles because the priests who served them took their title and name from them. The fourth opinion is proposed by Tomagna. He deduces the word title from the well-known history of the patriarchs and prophets of the Old Testament, who called stones and altars erected for the worship of God, titles. The heathens also used the same appellation for their altars. What then, he asks, is more natural than that the Christians should continue the use of the word title to signify their places of worship. Every church, however, is not now called a title, but only those which are assigned to the cardinals of the Holy Roman Church.

16. In the time of Pope Dionysius there were twenty-five such titles, and under Pope Marcellus there were twenty-eight, according to Cohellius. In the year 1410 when John XXII. began to reign, there were thirty-one cardinal-priests. But the Council of Constance in 1414 and that of Basle in 1429 determined that the number of cardinals should be restricted to twenty-four. Pope Paul IV. issued a bull prohibiting a greater number than forty cardinals, but nevertheless he himself as well as Pius IV. in 1559 and Gregory XIII. in 1572 increased the number to seventy-six. This is the greatest number ever reached, according to Ferraris, and there is no good authority for the assertion of Dr. Smith, *Elements, Vol. 1, No. 492*, that under Pope Pascal II. there were ninety cardinals.

Pope Sixtus V. in 1587 fixed the number at seventy, which is the rule at the present time. He also assigned fifty titles to cardinal-priests, abolishing some previously existing and creating other new ones. Finally Clement VIII. in 1602 re-arranged the churches of the cardinal-priests and his action was confirmed by Paul V. in 1618. Following are the presbyteral titles according to the present discipline of the Church:

- S. Lorenzo in Lucina.
- " Agnes fuori le Muri.
- " Agostino.
- " Anastasia.
- SS. Andrea and Gregorio.
- " XII. Apostoli.
- S. Balbina.
- " Bartholomeo all' Isola.
- " Bernardo alle Terme Diocleziane.
- SS. Bonifacio ed Alessio.
- S. Calisto.
- " Cecelia.
- " Clemente.
- " Crisagono.
- " Croce in Gerusalemme.
- " Eusebio.
- " Giovanni a Porta Latina.
- SS. Giovanni e Paolo.
- S. Girolamo degli Schiavoni.
- " Lorenzo in Panisperna.
- SS. Marcellino et Pietro.
- S. Marcello.
- " Marco.
- " Maria degli Angeli.
- " Maria della Pace.
- " Maria della Vittoria.
- " Maria del Popolo.
- S. Maria in Aracœli.
- S. Maria Transpontina.
- " Maria in Trastevere.
- " Maria in Via.
- " Maria sopra Minerva.
- " Maria Nuova et S. Francesca.
- SS. Nereo ed Achilleo.
- S. Onofrio.
- " Pancrazio.
- " Pietro in Montorio.
- " Pietro in Vincoli.
- " Prassede.
- " Prisca.
- " Prudenziana.
- SS. Quottro Coronati.
- " Quirico e Giulitta.
- S. Sabina.

SS. Silvestro et Martino ai Monti.	S. Tommaso in Parione.
S. Silvestro in Capite.	SSma. Trinita al Monte Pincio.
" Sisto.	
" Stefano al Monte Celio.	SS. Vitale, Gervasio e Protasio.
" Susanna.	

17. The origin of cardinal-deacons is more obscure than that of cardinal-priests. Undoubtedly there were in Rome deacons ordained to perform work similar to that of the seven deacons mentioned in the Acts of the Apostles. Pope Clement in the year 92 according to *Liber Pontificalis*, appointed seven deacons to preside over the seven districts or regions into which he divided the city of Rome; and to their care he confided the *diaconiæ*, that is, hospitals or houses where widows, orphans and the poor in general were received and supported out of the patrimony of the Church. About the year 240 Pope St. Fabian divided the city into fourteen districts and assigned two to each deacon. But as the number of Christians rapidly increased and donations to the Church were larger and more frequent, the seven deacons found it impossible to properly attend to the consequent work, and the number of deacons was therefore increased to fourteen. These were incardinated or assigned to the fourteen *diaconiæ* and later were known as cardinal-deacons of the Holy Roman Church.

18. To these fourteen deacons Gregory III. in the year 731 added four others who were assigned to the Basilica of St. John Lateran and were to assist the Sovereign Pontiff when celebrating. Hence they

were called Palatine cardinals. In the year 1410 there were nineteen cardinal-deacons, but Sixtus V. reduced the number to fourteen. Following are the *diaconiæ* at the present time:

S. Maria in Via lata.	S. Cesario in Palatio.
" Eustachio.	" Maria in Cosmedin.
" Maria ad Martyres.	" Angelo in Piscaria.
" Maria della Scala.	" Georgio in Velabro.
" Adriano.	" Maria in Portico.
" Nicola in Carcere Tulliano.	" Maria in Aquiro.
	SS. Cosma e Damiano.
" Agata.	S. Vito in Macello.
" Maria in Domnica.	

To these is added the title of St. Lawrence in Damaso, intended for the cardinal vice-chancellor, whether he be a cardinal-priest or cardinal-deacon.

19. The admission of cardinal-bishops into the College of Cardinals seems to have taken place not earlier than the year 731. Before that time the bishops of the dioceses surrounding Rome may have been consulted by the Supreme Pontiff in affairs regarding the universal Church; but they were not considered part of the presbytery or chapter of the Roman Church, nor were they called cardinals.

20. Gregory III., however, who reigned from 731 to 741, devoted special attention to the splendor of religious worship. He enriched St. Peter's with numerous works of art, and to his own cathedral, the Basilica of St. John Lateran, it is certain he gave much care. He increased the number of cardinal-deacons by four whom he assigned to St. John Lateran and on whom he imposed the special duty of assisting the Roman Pontiff when celebrating the

divine mysteries. This same Pope Gregory, it seems quite probable, appointed seven bishops to officiate by turn in the cathedral of St. John Lateran, and thus he instituted the order of cardinal-bishops.

21. A confirmation of this supposition may be found in the writings of the librarian Anastasius. Speaking of Pope Stephen IV., who reigned from 768 to 772, he says: "This Pontiff was a strict observer of church tradition; hence he renewed the former practice of the Church regarding the various honors given the clergy. He ordained that every Sunday Mass should be said at the altar of St. Peter by the seven hebdomadary cardinal-bishops who serve in the church of the Saviour." Since, therefore, these seven bishops were assigned to the church of the Saviour and were called cardinals, and since Pope Stephen IV. only renewed their honors and re-appointed their duties, it may rightly be concluded that these honors and duties originated with Gregory III., about forty years before the reign of Pope Stephen.

22. In the *Capitularies of Charlemagne, bk. 5 ch. 34*, we find mention of these bishops when he says: "By the advice of Leo and the other bishops of the Roman Church;" and in the letter which the Emperor Otho I. sent to Pope John XII. in the year 963 we find these words: "While we ask your children, namely the Roman bishops, the cardinal-priests and deacons and the whole people concerning your absence." Undoubtedly the bishops mentioned in these texts are the ones appointed to the Lateran Basilica. St. Peter Damien when he was created cardinal in the year 1058, addressed them in these words: "The ven-

erable, holy cardinal-bishops of the Lateran church;" and Baronius, ad annum 1057, quoting from an ancient Vatican codex distinctly explains their titles and their duties. He says: "There are in the Roman church, that is in Rome, five patriarchal churches. The first is the Lateran church, which is also called the church of Constantine and the basilica of the Saviour. This has seven cardinal-bishops, and they are called collateral and also hebdomadary bishops, because each week by turn they fulfil the duties of bishop. The cardinal-bishops are these: The bishops of Ostia, Porto, Santa Rufina or Silva Candida, Albano, Sabina, Frascati, Palestrina."

23. The suburbicary churches or dioceses to which the cardinal-bishops of the Holy Roman Church are assigned, according to the designation of Clement VIII., are the dioceses of Ostia, to which Velletri had been annexed by Eugene III., Porto, to which Santa Rufina had been annexed by the Callixtus II., Frascati, Sabina, Palestrina, Albano, making six in all. The bishops of these dioceses, and they alone, are cardinal-bishops of the Holy Roman Church. Bishops of other dioceses may be cardinal-priests or cardinal-deacons of the Holy Roman Church, but the appellation of cardinal-bishop is reserved to the incumbents of the above mentioned suburbicary sees.

According to the present discipline of the Church, there may be in the Sacred College, six cardinal-bishops, fifty cardinal-priests, and fourteen cardinal-deacons; but the full number is hardly ever reached.

CHAPTER III.

THE ANTIQUITY OF THE COLLEGE OF CARDINALS.

24. Whatever meaning in early-times may have been attached to the word cardinal, it is certain that for many years past and at the present time by the College of Cardinals is meant, a body of clerics whose peculiar office is to assist the Roman Pontiff in ruling the universal Church, and in case of vacancy in the Apostolic See, to assume the guidance of the Church in necessary affairs until the election of a new Pope. Though the cardinals have other prerogatives, still this one of assisting and supplying the place of the Roman Pontiff in ruling the whole Church seems the principal and essential. These duties are performed by the cardinals as a body, not as individuals, so that the collegiate or corporate form seems of the essence of the cardinalate.

25. The exclusive right which the cardinals now possess of electing the Sovereign Pontiff is not essential to the cardinalate, for others formerly participated in this election. Nor is it distinctive of the College of Cardinals that it participates with the Pope in ruling the diocese of Rome, *sede plena*, and supplies his place during a vacancy; for this office it holds in common with every other cathedral chapter in respect to its own bishop and diocese. The essence then of the cardinalate, is that which has been its constant, peculiar and distinctive office or charac-

teristic; and this is none other than the right and duty of assisting the Roman Pontiff in ruling the universal Church and in case of vacancy in the Apostolic See of supplying his place until the election of a new Pope.

26. The body of clerics now known as the College of Cardinals dates its origin back to the time of the establishment of the Apostolic See in Rome. The name, privileges, and even the various accessory duties of the cardinals, it is true, may have undergone great changes in the course of ages, but the essence of the cardinalate is surely of apostolic if not of divine institution. This is expressly taught by Pope Eugene IV. in his *Nineteenth Constitution* when he says of the cardinalate: "Although the name of this dignity was not expressed from the beginning of the primitive Church as it now is, still the office itself you will find evidently to have been instituted by Blessed Peter and his successors." He goes further, and following his predecessor Innocent III. teaches that the cardinalate is prefigured by the seventy ancients of Israel who were to assist Moses in judging and ruling the people of God. "Indeed, as Innocent III. says, the cardinalate draws its origin from the command of God in the Old Testament. For he (Innocent III.) asserts that what is said in the seventeenth chapter of Deuteronomy, (viz., that for a doubtful and hard matter of judgment recourse should be had to the priests of the levitical race and to the judge who should be at that time, and obedience should be given to the judgment of those who preside in the place which the Lord shall choose) is to be understood of the Roman Pontiff and his breth-

ren, that is, the cardinals of the Holy Roman Church, who also by levitical law perform the sacerdotal office."

27. The doctrine that the cardinalate is of divine institution is maintained by so many and such prominent doctors that Cohellius after quoting their words thus sums up their teaching: "Therefore from the writers cited above and others quoted by them it seems satisfactorily proved that the origin of the cardinalate can be said to be of divine right from both the Old and the New Testament." The celebrated Gerson, of the Sarbonne, said to the œcumenical Council of Constance in 1417: "The state of the supreme and sacred College of our Lords the Cardinals was founded in the ecclesiastical hierarchy on earth immediately by Christ, and it cannot be destroyed by any human institution or presumption." Likewise Peter de Aliaco in his treatise *On Ecclesiastical Power* which was presented to the Fathers of the same council, beautifully and succinctly lays down the common teaching of that age: "Although the names of the papacy and the cardinalate were not in use in the Church in the time of Peter and the other apostles, still the ecclesiastical powers designated by these names shone forth at that time in the apostles, viz., the papal dignity in Peter and the authority of the cardinalate in the other apostles. · To understand which it should be known that, (as appears from the history of the Acts of the Apostles, from ecclesiastical histories and from the decrees of the Holy Fathers,) before the division of the apostles by which they were dispersed into different parts of the world, the apostles exercising the ministry of the

cardinalate assisted Peter who bore the papal office; just as now the cardinals assist the Pope, as his principal assessors and councilors and co-operators in the government of the whole Church. But after the apostles, having separated from Peter, obtained special dioceses, from that time they exercised the episcopal office. From this it can be inferred that the apostles were cardinals before they were bishops; that they were cardinals of the world before they were of the city of Rome. To the senate of the apostles succeeds the sacred College of Cardinals in as much as the apostles assisted Peter before they became bishops of particular churches; but to the state of the apostles in as much as they were bishops, the order of bishops succeeds."

28. This doctrine was made of obligation in the year 1413 on all who received the doctorate or licentiate in the University of Prague, which was founded with the sanction of the Holy See. For in the formula of faith to be pronounced by the candidate, among other things, he was to profess: "That he thought and believed as the Roman Church wishes us to think and believe and not otherwise; of which Roman Church the Pope is the head, and the College of Cardinals the body; the manifest and true successors in ecclesiastical office of the Blessed Peter, prince of the apostles, and of the college of the other apostles of Christ.

29. This doctrine, however, while generally received, is nevertheless not of faith, for the words of Innocent III. and Eugene IV. are not considered an explicit definition of the matter by the Apostolic See. Hence, too, the question whether the College of

Cardinals may sometime be suppressed by the supreme power of the Church, may well be left among doubtful matters. For if the cardinalate is of divine institution, as Gerson says, then no power of the Church can suppress it or change its essence; but if it is only of ecclesiastical or apostolic origin, then, absolutely speaking, it may be modified or even suppressed. The matter can be settled only by a definition of the Church and her practice is not to make definitions except for some great and urgent need. As long as there is a doubt, things will be left as they are. Rightly then may it be said that the cardinalate will last as long as will the Church, which is, to the consummation of the world.

CHAPTER IV.

THE DIGNITY OF THE CARDINALATE.

30. The dignity of the cardinalate is, after that of the Pope, the highest in the Church. It is greater than that of bishops, archbishops, primates or even patriarchs. Whether this precedence was obtained by cardinals only in the eleventh or twelfth century or whether by right and in fact they always held it, is a controverted question.

31. Cardinal Belarmine epitomizes the former opinion when in his work *De Clericis* he says: ."I confess indeed that formerly all bishops were preferred before cardinals who were not bishops; yes, even the cardinalate was a step to the episcopacy, as Onuphrius rightly teaches in his book *On Cardinals* and as is clearly gathered from the seventh chapter of the first book of the life of St. Gregory. Afterwards, however, the order was changed, and cardinals began to be preferred to bishops and the episcopacy to be a step towards the cardinalate. For this change a twofold reason may be given: One, that to the cardinals alone the election of the Supreme Pontiff was reserved; for at the time the emperors or the clergy and people chose the Pontiffs, it is not strange that cardinals were not highly considered; but when afterwards they alone began to choose and also for the most part to be chosen for the papacy, not without cause was the cardinalitial dignity more

highly considered. The other reason is because the cardinals began to be the sole councilors of the Supreme Pontiff; for before, the cardinals were neither the only nor the chief councilors of the Pontiff. In the first six or seven centuries the Supreme Pontiffs convoked national councils of the bishops of Italy to judge the more important affairs of the Church; and at these councils the cardinal-priests were indeed present, but the bishops held the first place. Wherefore there was no reason why at that time cardinal-priests should be preferred to bishops, since the bishops did not help less, but in fact helped the Pontiff more than the cardinals in the government of the universal Church. Later, however, when the business of the Roman Church became greater, particularly with the accession of the temporal power under Pepin and Charlemagne, the Sovereign Pontiff needed the help of his advisers more frequently than before. Still he could not convoke councils of the bishops as often as was necessary. Taught then by utility and urged by necessity, in the next six or seven centuries the episcopal councils began gradually to be omitted and all affairs to be referred to the senate of cardinals. Such a legitimate change of the pontifical council from the bishops and cardinals to the cardinals alone, being brought about, it is not to be wondered at that a change in precedence also took place."

32. Baronius maintains the same doctrine and so does Thomassin. Natalis Alexander claims that only under Innocent IV. in the year 1243 did the cardinals obtain the right of precedence in session over bishops. Cohellius and Cardinal Petra, Ferraris

and others, all of whom are strenuous advocates of the cardinalate, give their adhesion to the theory that the precedence of the cardinals of the Holy Roman Church over all other dignitaries except the Pope, was only of gradual development. They allege among other reasons that in ancient diplomas of the Roman Pontiffs and of synods, bishops who were not cardinals are found to have signed before cardinal-priests and deacons, and from this fact they conclude that the episcopal dignity had precedence over the cardinalitial. But to this Pagius and Tomagna reply that no proof can be deduced from the order of signing, for according to ancient custom, bishops, whether cardinals or not, signed according to the date of their consecration; then priests, then deacons.

33. Similar are the other reasons advanced, but none seems to be based on positive historical testimony and much less on any dogmatic teaching of the Apostolic See. On the other hand, to prove that the cardinalitial dignity always had precedence over the episcopal, the constitution which Pope Eugene IV. prepared on this very subject gives strong testimony. The Archbishop of Canterbury had denied precedence to a certain cardinal who was Bishop of York and to determine the matter the Pope issued his celebrated constitution *Non Mediocri*, in which he says: "You will easily see how sublime is this dignity of the cardinalate and how much more excellent than others it has up to the present been considered in the Church, if you diligently examine its office and the statutes of the Holy Fathers and the custom which has always been observed both in this See and in general councils." From the beginning of

the Church just as to-day they have assisted the Supreme Pontiffs in guiding and ruling the whole Church. The Supreme Pontiffs call the cardinals, because of the greatness of their honor and dignity, a part of their own body. From which without any doubt it is shown that after the head of the Church, who is the Pope, the contiguous members of the body, who are his brethren the cardinals, are to be honored before the other members and parts of the Church.

"Who also does not see that the dignity of the cardinalate is greater than that of the archiepiscopate, because while the latter looks after the private good of one country, the former attends to the public good of the whole Christian people? The one rules only one church; the other with the Apostolic See, governs all churches. And while cardinals are judged by no one except only the Pope, they on the other hand with the Supreme Pontiff judge both patriarchs and archbishops and the other grades in the Church. Rightly also does their very name agree with their office; for, as the door of a house turns on its hinge, so on the cardinalate does the Apostolic See, the door of the whole Church, rest and find support. You should be convinced also by the long-continued and universally observed custom, which, were other proofs wanting, would have to be held for law, because it is so ancient that no memory of its beginning exists to the contrary; especially since this occurred while not one Sovereign Pontiff only, but as many as the Church has had, knew and approved of the custom. For in all nations and kingdoms the honor of this pre-eminence has been given to the cardinals, which indeed is to be considered not so much given to themselves as to Us, whose members they are. You should be convinced also by the custom of the Roman Church, which is the head, the rule and the teacher of other churches, according to which the cardinals *always* and without any objection in all acts have been honored above all other prelates. The same was done in the ancient general councils, especially in the two of Lyons, at one of which Innocent IV. presided and at the other Gregory X., the acts of which are still extant."

They who maintain that the cardinalitial dignity was always greater than the episcopal, point with special emphasis to the passage wherein the Pope says that the cardinals as a matter of fact *always* were given this pre-eminence and always were entitled to it for the reasons he gives. Likewise they note the passage wherein the Pope says that the custom of giving the cardinals this pre-eminence is so ancient that no memory of its beginning exists. They conclude that in view of this positive teaching of Pope Eugene IV. it will require proofs much more conclusive than any yet adduced, before we are forced to admit that a change was brought about in the eleventh or twelfth century and that only then was the dignity of the cardinalate made the greatest in the Church except only that of the papacy.

Whichever opinion is adopted as more tenable, no one can deny that at the present time the cardinals of the Holy Roman Church as a matter of fact have the right of precedence over bishops, archbishops, primates and patriarchs. They are inferior only to the Pope.

CHAPTER V.

THE MUTUAL RELATIONS OF THE POPE AND THE SACRED COLLEGE.

35. Because of the antiquity and dignity of the Sacred College, and because it is for the Apostolic See a senate similar to the chapters of the various dioceses throughout the world, false notions may possibly be deduced concerning the mutual relations of the Supreme Pontiff and the College of Cardinals. That these false notions may be warded off, it may be allowed with all deference to examine whether the consent of the cardinals is of necessity required for the Pope to perform certain acts; and again whether the Pope is bound to ask at least the advice, or consult with the cardinals in undertaking certain difficult affairs.

36. No one will contend that either for the validity or the licitness of his action in affairs of lesser moment the Pope needs the consent of the cardinals. Neither can it be maintained that in arduous affairs their consent is necessary for the validity of his acts. For in such a supposition, the Pope would not have the full power of guiding and governing the universal Church; since his acts would be null and void without the consent of the cardinals. Thus also we should have practically not one but two heads of the Church; both of which conclusions are against Catholic faith. Further it is of Catholic faith that the

cardinals, just as other faithful, are sheep and subject to the supreme shepherd of the Church; when he speaks and teaches, they like others are bound to hear and obey; hence the absurdity of the supposition that the supreme pastor depends on the consent of the cardinals for the validity of his acts.

Again if such consent is necessary for the validity of pontifical acts, it must be because of some law, natural, divine or ecclesiastical; however, no such law is in existence and therefore the Pope has full and absolute power without any limitation as to certain difficult matters or dependence on the consent of the Sacred College. Who in fact could determine what affairs are to be considered so difficult as to require the consent of the cardinals for the validity of pontifical acts? The Council of Florence defined as of Catholic faith that the Pope has *full* power to feed, guide and govern the universal Church. Hence it is not only a gratuitous supposition, but also a doctrine opposed to faith to say that the Supreme Pontiff needs the consent of the cardinals for the validity of his pontifical acts.

37. Neither does he need such consent even in arduous affairs for the lawfulness of his acts. Some, it is true, would maintain that as often as the Pope uses the fulness of his power, not as he ought, but against the good of the Church, his act would indeed be valid because of his supreme power which can be judged by no one, but nevertheless he would grievously sin, and would be held to an account for the authority which he abused. Whence they conclude that in certain difficult matters the consent of the cardinals is necessary that the Pope may not sin,

but not for the validity of his acts. But who does not see the consequences of such a theory? If the Pope has received from Christ the full and unlimited power of feeding, guiding and governing the universal Church, he must be able to exercise this power to its full extent without sin. The contrary supposition would be blasphemous. However, in the theory mentioned above, the Pope could exercise this power fully and without restraint only by committing sin in acting without the consent of the cardinals. Hence the theory should be rejected as unsound.

38. Apparent difficulties are presented by various enactments of the Sovereign Pontiffs which seem to require the consent of the cardinals for the validity of certain pontifical acts. One of these regards the alienation of church property. Pope Symachus in a synod held in the year 499 decreed that, "It is not licit for the Pope to alienate the land of the church for any necessity;" and Gregory IX. in the year 1234 more specifically determining the law of Symachus, decreed that, "any and every alienation of the patrimony of the Apostolic See shall be null and void unless it is done with the advice and assent of our brethren," the cardinals. There are many similar decrees; but nevertheless it must be said that the pontifical authority is not bound by them in any way, nor is the consent of the cardinals thereby made necessary for the validity of pontifical acts. The reason for this, Cardinal Petra thus explains: "Against the above mentioned enactments of Symachus and Gregory rises the living and convincing reason, that they could in no way compel or comprehend the suc-

ceeding Pontiffs; since the Pope is above canon law, and since an equal has no authority over an equal, as was expressly stated by Innocent III., *De Electione:* 'Because he could not create any prejudice in the matter for his successors, who would enjoy an equal power after him, yes, the very same power, since an equal has no authority over an equal.'" All canonists admit the same; hence the adage 'The Pope is above canon law.'

39. These decrees, then, can at most be considered advice, or counsel founded on experience, which a Pope gives other Popes who succeed him. No Pope can bind his successor; for by divine right each Sovereign Pontiff has the plenitude of power which cannot be restricted, and against which no custom to the contrary can prescribe. Whatever power the cardinals have is from man, not from divine right, even though we admit the divine institution of the cardinalate. "The power of the cardinals," says Fagnan, "flows from the Pope alone." And again: "But the power of the lord cardinals is from man, for whatever they have of power, they receive from the Pope."

Herein, then, we see the difference between the cathedral chapter and the College of Cardinals. The bishop of a diocese in certain things requires not only the advice but the consent of his cathedral chapter for the validity of his acts. The power of the bishop is limited in this respect by canon law, for he is not above the law, but subject to it. Both the bishop and his chapter must follow the law, for on it both depend. The bishop does not give nor can he take away from his chapter its power of restricting his acts in certain affairs. But not so the Pope, for he both gives and can take away power from the College of Cardinals, because he has full power and has it alone.

40. Hence too, notwithstanding the bull of Sixtus V. limiting the number of cardinals to seventy, the Pope, if he so desires, may exceed this number; and such is the common teaching according to Cohellius: "It is asked whether the Supreme Pontiff, notwithstanding this constitution of Sixtus V., can exceed the number of seventy; and all without an exception reply affirmatively, saying that the number of cardinals is left to the free will of the Pope." In the same way it must be concluded that the Sovereign Pontiff can depose any cardinal from the cardinalate, and that too without the consent or even the advice of the other cardinals. Likewise of his own free will he can elevate anyone to the cardinalate, nor does he need the advice or consent of the other cardinals for that purpose. It is true, that in the consistory creating the new cardinal the Pope asks the cardinals, "What do you think?" but this is merely a ceremonial form. In fact any inquiries concerning the proposed cardinal are always made before the consistory is held, and usually in private. Thus as Cardinal Petra says on the constitution of Pope Eugene IV.: "It should be remarked that the consent of the cardinals in this as in other matters is asked from a certain indulgence of the Supreme Pontiff rather than from necessity; since by many reasons it is shown that the Supreme Pontiff can decorate with the sacred purple of his own power without having asked any suffrage."

41. Many canonists however, and chiefly Cardinal Palaeotus in his work, *De Sacro Consistorio*, have adopted a distinction, and teach that the Pope depends on the advice and consent of the cardinals if he proceeds with his ordinary power, but not so if he acts with the plenitude of pontifical jurisdiction. Thus they believe they will not offend on the one hand against the supreme power of the Vicar of Christ, nor on the other will they detract from the dignity of the cardinals, as they fear they might, should they say that their consent or advice is never necessary. But it must be confessed that the Pope is the judge of whether he shall proceed with his ordinary or so-called extraordinary power, and also whether the exigencies are such as to warrant him, according to these canonists, in proceeding with his extraordinary authority. Thus the theory practically and finally resolves itself into this: The Pope is obliged to proceed with the consent of the cardinals whenever he wishes to proceed with it, or in other words, the Pope is never obliged to obtain the consent of the cardinals.

42. In so delicate a question it may be well to quote the very words of Cardinal Palaeotus when he explains the difference between the ordinary and the extraordinary authority of the Supreme Pontiff. He says: "While the Pope has supreme and full authority in the Church, nevertheless when he wishes to reduce it to exterior acts and to certain use, he does this in a twofold way, viz., using the faculty which is called ordinary or using the faculty which is called extraordinary. Whence his power is said by doctors to be twofold, the one absolute, the other

ordinary, which however refers to the use of the power rather than to the proper and natural force of it, since intrinsically it is always full, *plenissima*. Just as God could make laws for the things of nature according to which they are to act, but the same God nevertheless of his own power can act beyond the laws of nature, which act is then called a miracle; so in the Church it pertains to the Supreme Pontiff to make moral laws and prescribe the law for all ecclesiastical persons and the whole Church, but nevertheless he himself is not always obliged to keep these laws, but may act beyond them. When therefore the Pope wishes to observe those things contained in the laws, then he is said to use his ordinary power; but when he wishes to do something above what is laid down in the laws, then he is said to exercise the plenitude of his power."

43. As to whether it is lawful for the Pope to use his absolute or extraordinary power according to his judgment and as often as he wishes, the same cardinal says: "There are others, who, on the one hand seeing that this plenitude of power is necessary in the Church of God, on account of the many accidental occurrences for which the general provisions of law cannot suffice; and on the other, foreseeing the great dangers which could threaten the Christian world, if at any time the Supreme Pontiffs should abuse this power, have said that recourse is to be had to this plenitude of power, like to a sacred anchor, only in extreme cases, since even the canons rarely mention such a power. Whence, as the omnipotent God himself, to whose power everything is rightly

subject, nevertheless almost always keeps to the common order and nature of things, and does not perform miracles except in very necessary circumstances; so, they say, ought the Pope to use this plenitude of power as an extraordinary remedy only for the highest good and necessity of the Church." The cardinal then maintains that the Pope in using his ordinary power is obliged in arduous matters to have the consent or advice of the cardinals. "For," he says, "the use of the ordinary power in the Pope is considered nothing else than to do what the canons, decrees and constitutions have declared. Since, therefore, by old establishment and common observance, the memory of whose beginning does not exist, it is received that the Pope administers the affairs of the Church with the advice of the cardinals, and the same has been approved by canon law and the perpetual practice of the Supreme Pontiffs, as the monuments of authors attest; therefore, in order that he may be said to act according to his ordinary power, it is necessary that he perform his actions according to constituted laws and usual custom, and that by the usual course of the laws he proceed together with the cardinals."

All this, however, seems only to say that when the Pope follows a certain method, then he is said to use what is called his ordinary power; but it seems no proof that he is bound to follow a certain method. The fact that he does something does not prove that he is bound to do it. In view then of the plenitude of pontifical power, it may safely be stated that never and in no case does the Pope require the *consent* of the cardinals for the validity or even the lawfulness of his pontifical acts.

44. But another equally delicate question arises as to whether the Pope is bound to ask the *advice* of the cardinals. That seems to be the common opinion which frees the Pope from any such necessity; but adds nevertheless, that it is proper and honorable that the Pope should not act without consulting the cardinals in difficult matters.

Some doctors, however, maintain an opinion contrary to the common teaching even to the extent of declaring that the acts of the Pope are null if the advice of the cardinals is not asked. But as Cardinal Palaeotus says: "Let no such false opinion enter our mind, for it would weaken the supreme power of the Pope, would debilitate his primacy, would subject his most eminent authority to human laws, and finally would confuse the divine authority with merely secular power."

45. But the kernel of the difficulty seems to be, whether for the *lawfulness* of his acts in arduous matters the Pope is obliged to ask the *advice* of the cardinals; or in other words whether he would sin if he did not ask their advice. All admit that if asking the advice of the cardinals might be hurtful to the Church, because of the delay thus experienced in an urgent matter, or because some important business might thus be divulged, the Pope would not do wrong to omit requesting such advice. But, it may be asked, do they not admit thereby that the Pope is the sole judge whether or not he should seek advice? How then do they who admit the above, and Cardinal Palaeotus especially, maintain that the

Pope in order to act lawfully, or without sin, should in difficult matters ask counsel of the cardinals? The texts of scripture, "Son do nothing without advice," "There shall be safety where there is much counsel," and others are adduced by them to show that by divine law all, even the Pope, should seek counsel. They add that the cardinals are of the number of advisers whom the Pope is bound to use; and that this is true even though it is not admitted that the cardinalate is of divine institution.

There is great propriety in this assertion, but it must be confessed that the argument itself does not seem so conclusive as to force us to say that it is unlawful for the Supreme Pontiff to act without consulting the cardinals; since he himself may understand thoroughly certain difficult matters, and since if he wishes, he may consult with others than the cardinals; thus sufficiently fulfiling the scriptural injunction of seeking counsel.

Whatever view we may take of the necessity of the Supreme Pontiff seeking advice, as a matter of fact it is well known that the Roman Court is most tenacious of traditional customs and that very few matters of importance are treated without at least some of the cardinals being consulted. And judging from their character, their learning and their experence in ecclesiastical affairs, it may well be doubted if better councilors can be found.

CHAPTER VI.

THE CREATION OF CARDINALS.

46. For the creation of a cardinal all that is required is the will of the Sovereign Pontiff sufficiently expressed. Neither a certain form nor any special ceremony is essential, because the whole substance of the cardinalate consists in the power of jurisdiction, and its consequent prerogatives, which depends simply on the will of the superior. The cardinalate is not, like the priesthood, a sacrament imprinting a character and requiring sacramental matter and form divinely instituted; and hence the unanimous teaching is that the form of promoting a cardinal depends entirely on the will and word of the Supreme Pontiff.

47. It is true that Pope Eugene IV. in his Constitution, *In Eminenti*, decreed and declared, "That the cardinals announced in secret consistory, although they are to be considered as possessed of the beginning of the cardinalate, can nevertheless claim no right in fact or in name, and are not to be considered cardinals until the insignia of the cardinalate have been given them, that is, until the giving or sending the red hat, the assigning a title and the placing of the ring on their finger have all been done; and that the cardinals thus announced, even after they have received the insignia, shall not have an active voice in the selection of the Supreme Pontiff, until that faculty is expressly given them by the Roman Pon-

tiff, or, to use the ordinary phrase, until their mouth has been opened."

But this constitution of Pope Eugene could not bind the succeeding Pontiffs and as a matter of fact his immediate successors by merely promoting in consistory conferred all cardinalitial rights even before the insignia were given the new cardinals, or their mouth was opened. At first this was done with special mention of derogating from the constitution of Pope Eugene IV., but later no mention of it was made at all, and a doubt arising as to the rights of cardinals thus promoted, Pope St. Pius V. on January 26, 1571, decreed as follows: "Since it has been doubted whether the cardinals whose mouth has not yet been opened, would, if the See became vacant, have a vote in the election of the Supreme Pontiff; His Holiness decrees that, since the chief faculty of the cardinals consists in electing the Roman Pontiff, which surely should not be taken away from them because of a defect of insignia or ceremonies, for that reason His Holiness decrees that after anyone has been created a cardinal of the Holy Roman Church and has accepted the honor and given his consent, he shall immediately have a voice and right in electing the Roman Pontiff, even though the insignia of the cardinalate have not yet been given him, nor his mouth been closed, or if closed, opened again."

48. Since the publication of this decree of St. Pius V. it is certain that cardinals obtain all cardinalitial rights the moment they are appointed in secret consistory, unless the Sovereign Pontiff makes special mention of the contrary intention. Thus

after the death of Clement VIII. and in the election of Innocent X. the decree of St. Pius V. was put into execution. Hence as Cardinal Luca says in *Relatione Romanæ Curiæ*: "The opening of the mouth, the oath and the conferring of the insignia are ceremonies or solemnities which do not affect the substance or perfection of the act; since by nomination alone they are true and perfect cardinals; and therefore, whatever doubt there may have been formerly, they have a vote in the conclave in the election of the Pope, and also all the other cardinalitial jurisdiction and pre-eminence, as modern practice teaches."

49. That the cardinals might have a stronger voice in the creation of new cardinals, certain agreements were made and sworn to in the conclave before the election of a new Pope, by which all bound themselves, that, if chosen Pope, they would not select any new cardinals without the consent of the Sacred College or at least of a majority of its members. This happened before the election of Eugene IV., of Pius II., of Sixtus IV. and of other Popes. But it must be remarked that such an oath is null and void, because it attempts to limit the divinely constituted supremacy of the Sovereign Pontiff. Hence too the practice has become extinct.

50. At times the Sovereign Pontiff creates some cardinal in consistory, but does not mention his name, and, as they say, keeps that name in his breast, *in petto*, intending to publish it in another consistory. This practice the Roman Pontiffs usually follow, when someone deserves the dignity of the cardinalate, but reasons of prudence and especially the office

which the person holds suggest that the publication should be deferred. Thus, if an apostolic nuncio residing at some court, has merited promotion to the cardinalate, but in the meantime it is very expedient that, as a prelate only, he should continue discharging the duties of his office, he may be created a cardinal *in petto*. The effect of such creation is that when the publication is made at a later consistory it has a retro-active effect, and goes back to the day of creation *in petto*, thus giving the person a seat and a place before those who were afterwards created and published. But the publication of the name of the new cardinal in consistory is absolutely necessary in order that he may obtain the rights and privileges of the dignity. Hence, although the promotion may be made known to the person, nevertheless if the Pontiff dies without publishing his name in consistory, such a person will not be admitted into the conclave, and the new Pontiff is not obliged to ratify the creation and publish the name in consistory.

51. An act of Pope Pius IX. in creating cardinals seems to merit special attention. In a consistory held on March 13, 1875, among others he created five cardinals whose names he reserved *in petto*. But concerning these five cardinals he decreed: "Besides these six aforementioned cardinals, to the glory of the omnipotent God We intend to create five other cardinals, whom nevertheless because of good reasons We keep *in petto*, at some time according to our judgment intending to publish them; and if, God so disposing, the Holy See should be widowed before they are published, they are made known by letters attached to our last will, and in the plenitude of our

apostolic power We wish, determine and decree that they shall have a right, both active and passive in the election of our successor."

In this case, as is evident, Pius IX. plainly receded from the customary and solemn form of publishing cardinals and ordered that the publication should be made by his last will. No one will deny that the Supreme Pontiff can recede from the solemn form of publishing cardinals and choose either the way of a testament or another less solemn form of making known his intention of creating certain cardinals. But, as Santi says, there may be a question of the advisability of receding from the ordinary and public form of creating and publishing cardinals, and especially of making them known through a document attached to a last will. For the creation of cardinals is an affair of great moment, since the questions which can arise concerning it, may affect the very election of the Supreme Pontiff. Facts, too, are not wanting to show the practical working of a departure from the ordinary form. Pope Paul II. created four cardinals who were to become known immediately after his death, and he supplied every defect from certain knowledge and the plenitude of his power. These clauses, as is known, have a full and wide interpretation and therefore derogate from all laws to the contrary which would require special mention. Nevertheless these four ecclesiastics, who produced the documents of their promotion, were not admitted into the conclave, nor were they considered cardinals until several years later when in different consistories they were promoted and published.

Likewise Pope Paul III. created a cardinal who after the death of the Pontiff showed his brief of promotion. But the cardinals did not only not receive him as a brother, but indignantly tore up the brief itself. "And thereafter," says Corradus, "up to the present time, this method of creating cardinals went out of use; and indeed it could bring great danger and extreme scandal into the Church of God."

And truly questions might arise in this matter which would be difficult to answer. If for instance, the authenticity or integrity of the document naming cardinals should be called in question, who would be a competent judge? Especially in the present condition of Rome, with the Holy See deprived of civil dominion, who would be a competent judge of the validity of the Pope's last will? Doubts thus might arise against the election of a new Pontiff because of the participation of these cardinals named in an extraordinary way. Pius IX. himself seems to have appreciated these difficulties, for while on March 13, 1875, by an implicit naming he had completed the promotion of these cardinals, nevertheless on September 17, of the same year, he called another consistory and therein published the names of the five cardinals whom he had reserved *in petto*.

52. The form and ceremonies for creating a cardinal in the usual manner may be thus summarized: The Roman Pontiff calls a secret consistory, and the other business having been transacted, he addresses the cardinals who are present in these or similar words: "You have brethren." Then he mentions the names of those whom he has determined to promote to the cardinalate and asks: "What do you

think?" As a sign of assent the cardinals uncover and reverently incline their heads. Then the decree concerning the promotion of the new cardinals is drawn up and at once published out of consistory.

If the newly-appointed cardinals are in Rome they proceed in their usual dress and without any attendants, to the apostolic palace, where one of the old cardinals presents them to the Holy Father who gives them the red cap or biretum. And from that time to the public consistory in which they receive the insignia, they are not allowed to make or receive any public visits, neither may other cardinals call on them without the previous permission of the Holy Father.

If a newly-appointed cardinal is absent from Rome, one of the attendants of the Sovereign Pontiff is at once dispatched to carry him the red biretum, in receiving which the new cardinal must promise on oath, under pain of deprivation of the cardinalate, that within a year he will proceed to Rome to visit the Holy Father. It is customary for a cardinal who receives the biretum in this way, to give the one who brings it certain favors or offerings to be divided among the private chamberlains of the Pope.

53. A public consistory is then called for the purpose of giving the insignia to the new cardinals. All the cardinals being assembled in the apostolic palace, the Sovereign Pontiff wearing his precious mitre, orders the new cardinals to come forward. They, bowing profoundly, are placed with uncovered head in the sight of the Pontiff below the last cardinal-priest. The Pontiff then makes a short address on the office and greatness of the cardinalate. Then

the new cardinals approach and kneeling kiss the feet and then the hand and lastly the mouth of the Sovereign Pontiff. After this they go to receive from the other cardinals the kiss of peace. This being done the Pontiff confers the red hat on them and says: "For the praise of Almighty God and the ornament of the Holy See receive the red hat, an emblem of the singular dignity of the cardinalate, by which is signified that even to death and the shedding of blood inclusively for the exaltation of our holy faith, for the peace and quiet of Christian people, for the increase and preservation of the Holy Roman Church, you are to show yourself intrepid; in the name of the Father and of the Son and of the Holy Ghost. Amen."

In another consistory the Supreme Pontiff closes the mouths of the new cardinals, prohibiting them from speaking in consistories and other meetings until their mouths are opened again. Then, again in another consistory, the Roman Pontiff orders the new cardinals to retire while he asks the older cardinals whether they think the new cardinals should have their mouths opened. And all assenting, the new cardinals are called back and kindly admonished by the Holy Father, who then opens their mouths with these words: "We open your mouth both in conferences and in councils and in the election of the Sovereign Pontiff, and in all acts which both in and out of the consistory pertain to cardinals. In the name of the Father and of the Son and of the Holy Ghost. Amen." Then finally the ring is given and the title assigned to each new cardinal.

54. Besides the red hat and biretum the cardinals

wear a *solideo* or calotte of the same color. This privilege was granted them by Pope Paul II. who also prohibited all others from using one of red color. Cardinals wear purple. This was the distinctive dress of the emperors; but after the time of Boniface VIII. all cardinals were entitled to wear it. Cardinals who are chosen from religious orders retain in their dress the color of their own order, except the red biretum and calotte. Those, however, of the Jesuit order dress like secular cardinals. The coat of arms of a cardinal should be surmounted by a cardinal's hat and fifteen tassels, but not by a secular crown even though the cardinal is a member of a royal or imperial family.

The privileges of cardinals are many, but chief among them is the precedence all of them have over bishops, archbishops, primates and patriarchs. They also have the exclusive right to the title, "Eminence," and are considered equal in rank to kings. In fact some kings even have yielded precedence to cardinals. Everywhere they rank with princes of the royal blood. Hence, too, as princes of the whole Church they take personal precedence over apostolic delegates in church ceremonies and social gatherings. Moreover the word of a cardinal is to be believed when he asserts that something was done in presence of the Holy Father; also when he says that some mandate was given him verbally by the Pope; also when he asserts that he is a legate, for then the ordinary power of a legate is to be acknowledged in him even without his showing any letters of delegation.

That the cardinals may have decent support in their proper state, they are to have benefices which will give them an annual income of at least $4,000; if their income is less, they are to receive each month $100 additional from the general treasury. The cardinals who attend the consistories and the congregations participate in a certain sum of money set aside for that purpose, which is distributed to each by the cardinal-camerlengo of the Sacred College. A peculiar privilege, flowing from their office of assisting the Roman Pontiff in ruling the universal Church, and in case of vacancy in the Apostolic See of supplying his place until the election of a new Pope, is that the cardinals may convoke a general council in case of schism when two candidates are contending for the papacy.

55. Because of the office and the eminent dignity of the cardinalate, it is evident that only those who are conspicuous for virtue, learning and experience should be chosen for cardinals. Hence by way of direction the Council of Trent decreed that all the qualities required by the canons for the episcopal dignity should be required in the creation of cardinals of the Holy Roman Church, even if they are only deacons in holy order. Again those who are born illegitimate, even if legitimized by a subsequent marriage of their parents, should not be promoted to the cardinalate. Also a person who has an uncle or a nephew a cardinal, cannot himself be made cardinal; or to be more exact, Pope Sixtus V. in order to ward off all danger of factions or rivalry absolutely forbade that two persons related in the first or sec-

ond degree of consanguinity should be in the Sacred College together, and decreed that the selection of the second should be entirely null and void.

Among the cardinals there should be at least four from the regular and mendicant orders, for Sixtus V. says: "Among these seventy cardinals, besides doctors celebrated in their knowledge of law and the decrees, there should be some men who are masters in theology, and especially should they be taken, not less than four of them, from the regular and mendicant orders."

And finally, according to the mind of the Council of Trent, the cardinals as much as can be, should be selected from all the nations of Christianity. There is good reason for this desire and counsel; for the business transacted by the cardinals and particularly the election of the Roman Pontiff, pertains to all Christian nations. Hence that a balance may be preserved among nations and that their circumstances and needs may be better known to the Holy See, it is very advisable that every nation should have defenders and judges in the senate of the Roman Pontiff. Following the wish of the Council of Trent the Roman Pontiffs unto our own day, have promoted to the dignity of the cardinalate select men from various regions, but particularly from Catholic nations.

CHAPTER VII.

CARDINALS IN RELATION TO THEIR TITLES.

56. The title of a cardinal is the church in the city of Rome to which he is appointed. Cardinals of the Holy Roman Church who are at the same time ordinaries of dioceses are obliged to reside, not in their titular churches in Rome, but in their dioceses, and in every respect are subject to the laws regarding the residence of bishops. It is indeed true that such cardinals cannot assist the Sovereign Pontiff as their office requires; but nevertheless they assist somewhat, giving from a distance what help they can; and it has long been the custom that quite a number, sometimes reaching nearly half of the seventy cardinals, are selected from among such bishops as are obliged to reside in their own dioceses.

But the six cardinal-bishops, that is, the bishops of the six suburbicary sees are not obliged to reside in their own dioceses; for these dioceses being near Rome can easily be ruled from that city. These bishops are therefore specially exempt from the law of residence which requires every bishop to live in his own diocese.

With the exception, then, of the bishops who rule dioceses, all the other cardinals are obliged to reside at the Roman Court, that is, near the Supreme Pontiff, that they may give him the assistance their office requires. Wherever the Pope is, there is the

Court. Moreover the cardinals may not leave the Court without permission of the Roman Pontiff under pain of forfeiting their privileges; and this applies also to those cardinals, who being ordinaries, wish to return home after a visit to Rome *ad limina* or for any other reason.

57. The appointment of a cardinal to a title or church in Rome necessarily gives him certain rights and jurisdiction in that church, even though he is a bishop of a diocese away from Rome. Jurisdiction in his diocese is concurrent with that in his title. The six suburbicary cardinal-bishops have no titles in the city of Rome, but they have churches or dioceses near Rome, and in them they have full episcopal jurisdiction. The cardinal-deacons, strictly speaking, also have no titles, but have deaconries in Rome. But since these deaconries are also churches and since their jurisdiction in them is the same as that of cardinal-priests in their titles, both cardinal-priests and cardinal-deacons may be said to have titles or churches in Rome.

58. Formerly these titles had each of them a separate territory with a clergy and people subject or belonging to them, and the cardinal-priest or cardinal-deacon consequently had quasi-episcopal jurisdiction in his title. They could therefore dispense their subjects from vows, could validly assist at their marriages or appoint others for that purpose. They were, to use an illustration, parish-priests of these churches with quasi-episcopal jurisdiction. The cardinals, though only priests, were also entitled to pontifical insignia in their own churches, and, like bishops in their dioceses, could solemnly

bless the people. In fact these honors so clearly and fully belonged to them that without their permission no one could pontificate in their titular churches.

59. But a change was made by Pope Innocent XII. in the year 1692, and while all the honors were left them, the quasi-episcopal jurisdiction of the cardinals over the clergy and people of their titles was taken away and given to the cardinal-vicar who has real jurisdiction over the whole city. Thus as Pitonius says, *De Controv. Patron.*, "By the constitution of Innocent XII. not only is their jurisdiction over their clergy and parishioners taken away, but also they are given only a *domestic* jurisdiction in those things which concern the service of the church in regard to discipline and the correction of morals, (which jurisdiction is common to all chapters of churches or their vicars) in an extra-judicial way. But this faculty does not extend to grave offenses and contentious trials."

60. In regard to conferring orders it may be remarked that the cardinals who have titles in Rome may, if they themselves are priests, confer tonsure and minor orders in their titular churches, but only on those who are in the service of their church. But even though they themselves are bishops, they cannot confer major orders in their titles. The cardinal-vicar of Rome is the only one who has the right to confer major orders in Rome, excepting of course the Pope whose vicar he is.

Likewise the suburbicary cardinal-bishops cannot ordain in Rome, though to their own diocesans they may give tonsure in the chapel of their palace.

Further, if they themselves or their coadjutor-bishops do not ordain in their own sees outside of Rome, then they are obliged to send their candidates to be ordained only by the cardinal-vicar of Rome.

61. From a very recent decision it is certain that only the titular cardinal has a right to pontificate in his title even to the exclusion of the cardinal-vicar of Rome. In the year 1877 a doubt arose as to whether a new altar erected in the Eudoxian basilica should be consecrated by the cardinal titular of that church or by the cardinal-vicar of Rome. Pope Pius IX. delegated four suburbicary cardinal-bishops to examine the case. In the meantime, because the day for consecration was at hand, it was agreed that for that time the titular cardinal, because he was in possession, should perform the consecration. When Leo XIII. succeeded to the pontifical throne, he instructed the cardinal-dean of the Sacred College to have the question settled as soon as possible. Various consultive opinions were asked, and when they had been prepared, the four cardinal-bishops together with the cardinal-prefect of the Sacred Congregation of Rites who had been added to the commission, met on January 25, 1879, and having discussed the reasons advanced on both sides, unanimously voted that "the right to consecrate altars in churches of a cardinalitial title belongs to the most eminent cardinals of those titles and not to the cardinal-vicar of the city." This decision was confirmed on January 30, 1879, by His Holiness, Leo XIII., and a decree made to that effect.

62. Cardinals retain the title assigned to them in the public consistory at which they were created,

until by right of option, with the consent of the Sovereign Pontiff, they acquire a higher one. The right of option consists in this, that cardinals of a lower order have the right to ascend to a higher order. Concerning which it should be noted, that cardinal-deacons after ten years, if they are priests, can choose a cardinal-presbyteral title, and then they immediately take precedence over all cardinal-priests who were created cardinals after them. Again, the oldest cardinal-priest present at the Roman Court when one of the suburbicary sees becomes vacant, has an option on that see, except it be that of Ostia or that of Porto which are reserved for the dean and subdean of the Sacred College. Hence the cardinal-bishops, because they assume the administration of the suburbicary churches by option and by the disposition of the law itself, ascribe their promotion to the divine mercy which prolonged the days of their cardinalate; and sign themselves thus: "Francis, by the divine mercy, Bishop of Frascati, cardinal of the Holy Roman Church." Other bishops insert in their signature, "and by the favor of the Apostolic See," thus attesting that they depend not on the law itself but immediately on the Holy See for their appointment. Lastly, according to the constitution of Clement XII., the oldest cardinal-bishop who is present at Court becomes the dean of the Sacred College as soon as a vacancy occurs. This seniority is reckoned, not physically nor yet from episcopal consecration, but it is reckoned from the time of promotion to one of the suburbicary churches.

63. The cardinal-dean of the Sacred College has a number of special prerogatives. He becomes the

Bishop of Ostia, than which dignity, excepting the papacy alone, there is no greater in the Church of God. As Bishop of Ostia, taking the place of a metropolitan, he consecrates the newly elected Pope if he is not yet a bishop, and wears the pallium during the consecration. The cardinal-dean is always the prefect of the Sacred Congregation of Ceremonies and generally also secretary of the Sacred Congregation of the Holy Office over which the Pope himself presides.

. In the absence of the Pope and during a vacancy in the Apostolic See, the cardinal-dean presides over the College of Cardinals. Hence Pope Alexander IV. frequently said that after the papacy there is no greater dignity in the Church of God than that of the Cardinal-bishop of Ostia, the dean of the Sacred College.

CHAPTER VIII.

THE COLLEGE OF CARDINALS DURING A VACANCY IN THE APOSTOLIC SEE.

64. The selection of the Sovereign Pontiff is a most important event for both the Church and the secular world. Our Lord himself selected the first Pope, St. Peter; but nowhere in Scripture or tradition can any law be found by which he determines by whom or in what manner the succeeding Pontiffs are to be chosen. Since, however, we must suppose the Saviour builded his Church wisely and carefully, we must also conclude that he left the necessary power of selecting a Supreme Pontiff with the Church, and that to it he also left authority to arrange the method of selection.

From this it follows as a necessary consequence that to the Supreme Pontiff, the Vicar of Christ, has been given the power of determining the method of selecting his successors; for he alone is supreme in the Church and without him as head, no decree of the Church as the body is of any force. Moreover, the constant practice of the Church confirms this view, because time and again the Roman Pontiffs have enacted laws regarding the selection of their successors and these laws have always been observed.

65. Whether the Pope can choose his own successor is a controverted and difficult question. For, while all the learned unanimously agree that the

Pope has the power of determining by whom and in what way his successors shall be chosen, nevertheless when they come to the question whether he can choose his own successor, they maintain very divergent opinions. Cardinal Petra thus sums up the question: "Descending to this arena the doctors, forming three armies, vehemently fight among themselves. For some absolutely speaking teach that the Pope can select his own successor. Others absolutely deny this power to the Sovereign Pontiff. And lastly some, holding the middle course, affirm that only in some urgent necessity or for the great utility of the Church, but not as an ordinary matter can the Pope select his own successor."

As a matter of fact some Popes have pointed out those whom they deemed best fitted to succeed them, but church history has no record of any Supreme Pontiff choosing his own successor, if we except Pope Boniface II. in the year 529. This Pope, in order to prevent a recurrence of the scandalous contentions which took place at the time of his election, when the Ostrogoth king set up an antipope, adopted the extraordinary measure of issuing a decree by which he appointed the deacon Virgilius his successor in the papacy. But the next year in a council held in Rome he recalled his decree and declared it annulled.

On the other hand it is of record that Pope Celestine III. wished to resign the papacy in favor of Cardinal John de St. Paul, but because such an action was unknown in the Church, he determined not to do it. Pope Paul III. was asked by Cardinal Francis Pisana Veneto to choose his own successor, but positively declined. And under Pope Paul IV. the question whether the Pope can choose his own successor was discussed in consistory, and he, with the majority of the cardinals, thought the affirmative opinion should be rejected as false, but no decree was issued on the subject.

66. The method of selecting the Roman Pontiff has been different in different ages. In the beginning of the Church, the election pertained to the priests and deacons of the city of Rome. But from the time of St. Sylvester when the Christian religion began to be publicly professed, the whole Roman people had a certain part in his election by bearing testimony to his life and character. Throughout the first four centuries, while the Roman Pontiff was selected in this way, the greatest liberty prevailed. But from the fifth to the eleventh century, emperors and kings usurped great authority in the matter, so much so that at times the election ruled by them was clearly injurious and invalid, and was so declared by those who had the right of suffrage.

It is true, that in these centuries, the Roman clergy to whom the election pertained, could so elect as to make their choice depend on the confirmation of some king or emperor; and history teaches that owing to the calamitous times and the necessity or policy of satisfying temporal princes such elections sometimes were held.

But all such interference on the part of temporal authority was revocable at the will of the Church, and if too long continued could end but in her destruction or complete subjection. Hence in the year 1059 Pope Nicholas II. with great prudence prescribed a certain form and method for filling the Roman See, which was published in the Lateran Council, and by which the cardinal-bishops were declared the electors of the Sovereign Pontiff, while to the other cardinals, the clergy and the Roman people it was left only to consent to the election made by these cardinals.

67. In the year 1178 in another Lateran Council Pope Alexander III. decreed that the election of the Sovereign Pontiff should pertain to all the cardinals but to them alone; and that he who received two-thirds of the votes of all the cardinals participating in the election should be the Pope. This decree has proved of incalculable good to the Church from that time to the present; for by it the turbulence of the populace and the violence of temporal rulers, which interfered throughout so many ages, were entirely eradicated from the election of the Sovereign Pontiff.

But it required still other precautions to ward off the dangers which could result from too tardy an election and the chance of interference with the liberty or integrity of the cardinal-electors. Hence in the Council of Lyons in 1274 the use of the secret conclave was introduced by Pope Gregory X., and it was further prescribed that if the cardinals could not make a choice within three days, thereafter until a Pope was elected they should be allowed but one meal a day. And if within five more days no choice was made, thereafter they should be allowed only bread and wine or water until they should finish the election. These regulations were somewhat changed and additions to the method of election made by succeeding Popes, until, under Gregory XV. in 1623 and

METHOD OF ELECTION. 63

Clement XII. in 1740 the laws now in use were perfected.

Finally Pope Pius IX. of blessed memory, to preclude all chance of controversy, on December 4, 1869, a few days before the solemn opening of the Vatican Council, issued a decree, determining that, "If the Holy See becomes vacant during the holding of an œcumenical council, the election of the new Pontiff does not devolve on the council, but remains wholly and exclusively with the cardinals." Moreover the council itself becomes adjourned until re-convened by the new Pontiff.

68. Thus it will be seen that the right which the cardinals have of electing the Sovereign Pontiff is not of divine origin, for no trace of it can be found in Scripture or tradition; but it is rather of apostolic institution, for from apostolic times the Roman clergy, that is, the priests and deacons of the Roman Church, who to-day are called cardinals, have exercised this right. Whatever part the Roman people afterwards had in the election was but secondary, and in subjection to the right of the clergy. The taking away this right to participate from the Roman people and the inferior clergy and confining the election to the cardinals of the Holy Roman Church is of ecclesiastical institution and is founded on decrees of the Sovereign Pontiffs.

69. Likewise on the decrees and will of the Sovereign Pontiffs is founded all the jurisdiction which the College of Cardinals has during a vacancy in the Apostolic See. In the earlier centuries the College of Cardinals, the presbytery of the Roman See, succeeded to the jurisdiction of the deceased Pontiff,

just as other cathedral chapters obtained jurisdiction by the death of their respective bishops. Moreover this ordinary jurisdiction of the College of Cardinals extended to the whole Church. But in the year 1274 at the Second General Council of Lyons Pope Gregory X. decreed that during a vacancy in the Apostolic See the College of Cardinals can neither validly nor licitly exercise any pontifical jurisdiction or power; the only exception being some imminent danger, which, in the unanimous opinion of all the cardinals present, demands immediate action on their part.

In this respect the College of Cardinals is in a worse position than inferior chapters; for unto these the episcopal jurisdiction is transferred by the death of the bishop; but not so to the College of Cardinals. In case of a vacancy in the Apostolic See, it acquires none of the ordinary powers of the Supreme Pontiff. Hence it cannot create new cardinals, nor restore to their rights and a vote in conclave any cardinals who have been deprived of their office; neither can it give the insignia to newly created cardinals. It cannot create bishops nor confirm those chosen; it cannot confer benefices nor execute decrees of favor or justice granted by the deceased Pontiff.

70. However the jurisdiction of the Sacred Congregations continues during a vacancy in the Apostolic See, because their faculties are perpetual, and do not expire with the death of a Pope. They have ordinary jurisdiction founded on law and statute, as is plainly evident from the constitution of Sixtus V. on the subject. But although the faculties of the Congregations of Cardinals do not expire with the

death of the Pope, nevertheless during a vacancy, the cardinals being in conclave, they should be allowed to lie unused, particularly in regard to those affairs which are transacted with the signature of the cardinal-prefect or the seal. The business, however, that is usually transacted by the secretary can be done also during a vacancy; and in case there is reasonable cause, business requiring the signature of the prefect may also be transacted, and the documents be signed by him in conclave.

71. It will be noticed that there is a very great difference between the College of Cardinals and the Sacred Congregations to which the cardinals residing at the Roman Court are assigned. Each of these Congregations is composed of several cardinals and other learned clerics, but the College of Cardinals is made up of all the cardinals of the Holy Roman Church and of them alone. The College of Cardinals is a corporation, and as such has various officers. It is presided over by the dean of the Sacred College, who is the senior cardinal-bishop, and whose suburbicary see is that of Ostia and Velletri.

The cardinal-camerlengo of the Sacred College administers its revenues and each year distributes to the cardinals the portion assigned them. He is assisted by several subordinate officials; and during a vacancy in the Apostolic See continues discharging all the duties of his office. While he is in conclave, he does not personally attend to external business, but only through his ministers and officials. His appointment does not expire with the death of the Pope, and if he should die during the vacancy the cardinals may fill the office temporarily.

The secretary of the Sacred College is an Italian cleric elected to the position by the votes of the cardinals. His duty is to care for the books and documents pertaining to the Sacred College. Pope Urban VIII. decreed that he should be also secretary of the Sacred Congregation of the Consistory. He has a substitute who is also chosen by the cardinals. The term of office of the substitute is one year, and he is chosen by turn from the German, French, Spanish and English nations. Hence he is called the "national cleric."

It should be mentioned, that, although the cardinal-dean presides over the Sacred College, still, except in a vacancy of the Apostolic See, he may not call a meeting of the College without previous permission of the Sovereign Pontiff.

72. A vacancy occurs in the Apostolic See when the Sovereign Pontiff resigns or dies. The *Roman Ceremonial* prescribes that as soon as the Pope is dead, all the officials are to leave the palace except the cardinal-camerlengo, whose office does not expire with the death of the Pope. The secretaries, immediately after the camerlengo has declared the Pope to be dead, bring the ring of the fisherman and the seal of the deceased Pontiff to this cardinal who breaks them with a hammer. The dean of the Sacred College, the senior cardinal-priest and the senior cardinal-deacon together with the camerlengo then assume the administration of the affairs of the Apostolic See. Notice is sent immediately by the secretary of the Sacred College to all the absent cardinals informing them of the death of the Sovereign Pontiff; but they are not summoned or convoked by the secretary

BEGINNING OF CONCLAVE.

or any one else to attend the election of his successor. The law itself is their guide.

The cardinals who are at Court when the Sovereign Pontiff dies, await the arrival of the absent cardinals for the space of ten days and no longer. But if before the expiration of the ten days they should hold an election, or if they should wait longer than ten days, the election nevertheless would be valid. During these ten days funeral services are held daily in St. Peter's for the deceased Pontiff; after which the body of the Pope is deposited in its provisional tomb. If the Pope should die away from Rome or its vicinity, the conclave is to be held in the place of his death. But to avoid this difficulty, before leaving Rome on any journey, the Pontiffs usually decree that in case they should die away from Rome, the conclave is nevertheless to be held in Rome.

73. The funeral services of the deceased Pope having been completed, and the ten days, including the day of the Pope's death, having expired, on the morning of the eleventh day the cardinals gather in the basilica of St. Peter and the cardinal-dean there celebrates the Mass of the Holy Ghost. After this is finished, while the *Veni Creator* is being sung they proceed to the conclave in the Vatican palace. Here when they reach the chapel of the conclave the dean of the Sacred College recites the prayer, "*Deus qui Corda.*" Then the pontifical constitutions concerning the election of the Sovereign Pontiff are read and the cardinals promise under oath to observe them. Once having entered the conclave they cannot leave until after the election of the new Pope. If any cardinal should leave the conclave because of

sickness or other cause, he cannot return again even if he recovers, nor can he have a voice in the election.

When Dr. Smith in his *Elements*, *No. 330*, says the contrary and claims that Craisson is in error, he seems to overlook the consequences of his assertion. What would be the use of a conclave if any cardinal could go out and in according as he *felt* the state of his health? The whole intention of the conclave would be nullified, and through such a claim of sickness a constant communication with the exterior world might be kept up. Craisson, Bouix and the *Roman Ceremonial* are right and Dr. Smith must be considered in error on this point even if he quotes the learned Philips.

During the first day, according to Cardinal de Luca, there is free access granted to the representatives of princes, to magnates and prelates, and in fact to nobles, priests and people generally. All who wish may visit the cardinals in their apartments and offer good wishes and testimonies of respect. But when evening comes all but the conclavists are rigorously excluded. The cardinals remain in their cells which without any acceptation of persons have been assigned by lot; and the cardinals who may have been detained then also enter the conclave and proceed to their apartments. Over the entrance to the cell of each cardinal is placed his coat of arms, covered with green serge, or with purple if he has been created by the deceased Pontiff.

74. The windows of that part of the Vatican palace or other place which is set apart for the conclave are walled up and all doors leading to the conclave are likewise closed, except one which is doubly locked

and only opened to permit a sick cardinal to leave, or a late-arriving one to enter. A cardinal just arriving may enter the conclave up to the time of the election. The key of the inside lock on this door is kept by the cardinal-camerlengo; that of the outside lock by the governor of the conclave who is a prelate chosen for the position by the cardinals before they enter the conclave. Food and whatever else may be nesessary is introduced through a turning-box which is also doubly locked, the key to the inside lock being kept by the master of ceremonies and that of the outside by the prelate appointed for that purpose.

That a strict watch may be kept over the food and that no letter or message of any kind may be transmitted to or from the cardinals or any of the conclavists, guards stationed on the outside of the conclave are appointed to watch the entrance and the turning-box, and to examine thoroughly everything that is sent to or from the conclave. These guards are prelates of various grades and are changed twice a day, morning and evening. An exact order is followed in the assignment, so that of the prelates present in Rome at the time of the conclave, the patriarchs serve first, then archbishops, bishops and other prelates according to the order of their promotion. Under pain of perjury and suspension they are to use the greatest diligence in examining the food and other things, as well as the persons who enter or leave the conclave, that no letters, or other signs may be transmitted either way. If any of the servants or other conclavists are found delinquent in this respect, they are subject to most severe punishment and no cardinal is allowed to intercede in their favor. On the inside of the conclave, the cardinal-dean and the camerlengo make a tour of inspection every evening to see that all is in proper condition.

75. Inside the conclave and subject to its restrictions, each cardinal is allowed to bring two servants, who cannot be merchants, ministers of princes or temporal lords, nor brothers or nephews of cardinals, but who must be real servants of the cardinals themselves and in their employ for at least one year previous to the conclave. If aged or infirm cardinals need a third servant, the concession may be granted by the College of Cardinals. Besides these personal servants, there are several other officials and attendants who serve the cardinals in common. They are, one sacristan and his assistant, two masters of ceremonies who assist the cardinal celebrating, one religious to hear confessions, one secretary of the Sacred College with one servant only, two physicians, one surgeon with two assistants, two barbers with two assistants, one carpenter, one mason and eight or ten servants for general work. All these are elected by ballot by the College of Cardinals and paid from the public treasury; but none of them can be chosen from the household of any cardinal.

76. The day after entering into conclave the cardinal-dean says a low Mass of the Holy Ghost, at which all the cardinals receive Communion. Then a scrutinium or vote is taken for the new Sovereign Pontiff. During the balloting everyone is excluded from the chapel. A cardinal who may not have received deacon's orders is not admitted to the con-

clave; but all the cardinals in conclave, and they alone, have a vote. No one can vote by proxy. No cardinal, even though excommunicated or without the insignia, can be deprived of a vote. This regulation was made to preclude all dissensions.

If in the course of the election a considerable number of cardinals should withdraw from the conclave refusing to participate in the election, the right of choosing the Pontiff would remain with the cardinals in conclave, even though but two, yea, even though but one were left. Likewise if all the cardinals but one should die, he would have the right of electing the Pontiff; but he could not choose himself. If all the cardinals should die before the election of a Sovereign Pontiff, it is disputed who would have the right to elect. Some say an œcumenical council should elect, but the more common and safe opinion is that the election would still pertain to the Roman clergy, that is, to the canons of the Lateran basilica, the cathedral of the Pope.

Any man, even a layman and a married person may validly be elected Sovereign Pontiff, and as soon as he is elected and consents, he has full jurisdiction as the supreme pastor of the Church and Vicar of Christ. For some centuries, however, none but cardinals have been elected to the papacy.

77. The election of the Sovereign Pontiff may be accomplished in three ways; by quasi-inspiration, by compromise or by vote which in Latin is called scrutinium. That an election by quasi-inspiration may be valid it is required that, after the conclave has begun, every cardinal unanimously and at once should agree on the same person, without

there having been any previous deliberation on the subject. An election by compromise occurs when the cardinals commit the right of choosing the Pope to a few specified persons. As soon as these persons make a choice, the one chosen is validly elected Pope. This method of election is rare and that by quasi-inspiration is still rarer. The usual method is by the scrutinium or ballot, which is conducted with great solemnity.

Before the voting begins three cardinals are chosen by lot to act as tellers. A large vase, made in the shape of a chalice, is placed on the altar of the chapel wherein the cardinals are assembled, and near it is the form of oath which each cardinal takes before depositing his ballot. The oath is: "I call upon God who will be my judge to witness that I choose the person whom before God I judge ought to be elected, and that I will do the same in the accession." The ballot is prepared thus: Each cardinal writes the name of his candidate on a specially arranged ballot or ticket using the words: "I choose for Supreme Pontiff the Most Reverend ——." He then affixes his own name in a specified part of the ballot. This ticket is then folded so that the name of the candidate may be read at the first unfolding, but not the name of the cardinal who cast the ballot until it is opened out in full. After the ballot has been sealed by the voter with his own seal, it is deposited by him in the vase on the altar. The three tellers meanwhile stand by the altar and superintend the voting. When all the cardinals have voted, the tellers at once begin to announce the votes in this manner: The first teller takes one of the ballots out of the vase and, partly unfolding it, simply looks at or ascertains the name of the candidate voted for; he then hands the ballot to the next teller who having looked at the name, passes it to the third and he audibly announces the name to the cardinals.

78. When all the ballots have been counted by the tellers and it is found that no candidate has received two-thirds of all the votes cast, then what is called the accession may begin. The accession consists in this, that the cardinals by balloting as before may, if they wish, go over to one of the candidates who has received at least one vote in the previous balloting. All are obliged to vote, though they are free to go over to some candidate or to stand by their previous choice. A cardinal who wishes to change his vote writes on his second ballot: "I go over to ——;" but one who wishes to stand by his previous choice writes, "I go over to no one." After all have voted in the accession the tellers first sort the ballots in such a way that they place each ballot of the accession along-side the ballot of the previous vote which has the same marks and seal. When a ballot in the accession shows the same marks and seal as a ballot in the previous vote, and the candidate voted for is also the same, then the ballot in the accession is not counted; for a cardinal might thus vote twice for the same candidate. But if the marks and the seal on the ballot of the scrutinium and of the accession are the same, and a different name is found on the ballot of the accession, then this ballot is considered valid and the vote is added to the number cast in the previous balloting.

When all the ballots have been compared and the

valid votes of the accession allowed, then the tellers count all the votes of the original ballot together with the added votes of the accession, and if no candidate has received two-thirds of all the votes cast, that is, those of the scrutinium and the accession, then there is no election. If some one of the cardinals has received just the two-thirds of all the votes, then his ballot is entirely unfolded so that also the name of the voter as well as that of the one voted for is apparent. If it is discovered that he has voted for himself, that one vote is invalid and therefore he lacks just one of an election. It is then declared that as yet there is no election. All the ballots are burned forthwith, and the cardinals return to their cells, where they remain until the next balloting which takes place about two o'clock in the afternoon of the same day.

79. During the balloting it may happen that a certain candidate, who is objectionable to one of the great Catholic powers, receives such a large number of votes as to appear likely to be elected. Those cardinals, therefore, who are charged with protecting the interests of temporal princes anticipate the accession which might give the requisite number of votes, and if the election seems' tending against the wishes of their country or its sovereign, rise to exclude such an objectionable candidate. Any such objection or pacific removal, as it is styled, must be made before the election is complete, that is, before the votes have been cast. The governments of Austria, Spain and France claim the privilege of each excluding one candidate who is objectionable. Whence this privilege originated or at what time is

unknown; but a diligent examination fails to reveal any trace of it in canon law or in any concordat granted by the Holy See. Many writers claim that it is wholly a usurpation.

An instance, however, occurred in the conclave in which Innocent XIII. was elected in the year 1721; for when the name of Cardinal Paolucci was pronounced by those who were announcing the votes, and it was noticed that he received a great number of votes, Cardinal Althan, minister of the Emperor Charles VI., rose up and in his master's name pronounced exclusion against Paolucci. Meanwhile the tellers continued to announce the ballots and three votes were wanting to make the required two-thirds in favor of Paolucci.

Regarding which incident Ottieri says: "Most assuredly, had the cardinal received the required number of votes, he would have been proclaimed, for the exclusions pronounced by the courts of Austria, France and Spain, are admitted, not as a definitive compact, but by way of prudent consideration, in order to avoid a schism in the Church in case the princes should refuse to acknowledge a Pope whose election has been displeasing to them."

80. Some writers assert that the privilege of exclusion enjoyed in the conclaves by the three courts of Vienna, Paris and Madrid, took its rise in the Council of the Lateran held by Pope Nicholas II., in 1059. But the question debated in this council was the coronation of the Sovereign Pontiffs, for which the emperor's consent may have been necessary at this time, and not their election. The Popes at this time had temporal power and needed a protector.

The right of exclusion which we have just seen exercised in the name of Austria against Cardinal Paolocci, dated no further back than one century. It sprung, as Ottieri perfectly expressed it, from a kind of provident connivance, from a prudent deference which would not have the Sovereign Pontiff personally disagreeable to the great Catholic powers, for the Pope is pastor and father of them all. There have been nearly thirty schisms, all occasioned and fomented by the spirit of distrust existing between the Pontiffs and the secular rulers. It is proper then to have some regard for the repugnances of certain courts; otherwise the peace of the Church is imperiled and the Pontiff is deprived of the respect and friendship of the most powerful princes. Such were the reasons advanced in the year 1644 by the learned Cardinal de Lugo, in favor of maintaining the exclusions. The conclave of 1721 respected these considerations, and as Darras says, expressed to Paolucci its deep and sincere regret and elected Cardinal Conti who took the name of Innocent III.

A later instance of pacific removal took place during the conclave of 1831 which elected Cardinal Capellari, known as Gregory XVI. Spain filed a formal protest or exclusion against Cardinal Guistiniani, who had been nuncio at Madrid, and while there had, it seems, opposed the plans of the prime minister in certain complicated ecclesiastical affairs. His conduct at the time was satisfactory to Ferdinand VII. of Spain and to the Holy See; but this did not prevent the Spanish court from instructing its ambassador to protest against his election to the papacy. Hence on January 6, 1831, the twenty-

OBJECTIONS TO CANDIDATES.

second day of the conclave, Cardinal Marco-y-Catalan, a Spaniard, received the following formal note from Labrador, the Spanish ambassador to the Holy See, bearing date December 24, 1830:

"The undersigned Ambassador Extraordinary of his Catholic Majesty to the Holy See, presents his distinguished reverence to his Eminence and prays him to make known to the Sacred College united in conclave that he, in the name of his august sovereign, and by the express orders of his Catholic Majesty, gives the exclusion to the Most Eminent Cardinal Giustiniani.

PEDRO GOMEZ LABRADOR."

In the scrutinium of the following morning Cardinal Marco, seeing that there were twenty-one votes recorded for Cardinal Giustiniani, sixteen of scrutinium and five of accession, and that four more of accession would suffice for his election, hastened to communicate the exclusion to Cardinal Pacca, dean of the Sacred College. The cardinal-dean, having first informed Cardinal Giustiniani thereof, before the midday scrutinium read out the note of exclusion to the assembled cardinals. The conclave lasted twenty-six days after the exclusion of Cardinal Giustiniani, until on February 2, after fifty days of conclave Gregory XVI. received the requisite number of votes.

Whether the changed conditions of the papacy, now that it no longer has temporal power, will relieve it of any claim on the part of these powers to interfere in the conclave by way of pacific exclusion, is a question to be determined by the conclave itself. Since there is no law or agreement on which the claim of these three courts is founded, the College of Cardinals need not respect any such pretended privilege. If, on the other hand, as a matter of prudence or good policy it wishes to accept the objection of these powers against a candidate, there is nothing to prohibit the cardinal-electors from dropping that candidate and voting for some one else who is generally unobjectionable.

81. If no choice is made at the morning session, another is held in the afternoon, and thereafter twice a day until a Sovereign Pontiff has been canonically elected. Meanwhile in all the churches of Rome, and throughout the world, special prayers are offered that a proper choice may be made. As soon as the tellers find that some candidate has received two-thirds of the votes, his name is declared. The junior cardinal-deacon then rings a bell, and the master of ceremonies and the secretary of the Sacred College enter the chapel. If, as is now usually the case, the newly-elected Pope is one of the cardinals, the cardinal-dean with two others, advances before the elected cardinal and asks him if he accepts the papacy. When he consents, all the baldichinos over the seats of the cardinals are taken down, except that of the new Pontiff, and the cardinals on either side of him leave their places. The cardinal-dean then asks the Pontiff what name he intends to take, and of his choice and the other events the secretary makes proper record. Two cardinal-deacons then conduct the Pontiff behind the high altar where he puts on the pontifical vestments. He is then placed before the high altar, where seated in the chair of state he receives the salutation of all the cardinals.

They each kiss his foot, his hand and his mouth. The cardinal-camerlengo places on his finger the ring of the fisherman, which the Pontiff then gives to the master of cermonies to have his name engraved on it. Then the first cardinal-deacon, preceded by musicians and the choir singing *Ecce Sacerdos Magnus*, goes to the balcony over the entrance to the palace to declare to the people the election of the Pontiff. "I announce to you a great joy. We have as Pope the Most Eminent and Most Reverend (mentioning the Christian name and the title) Cardinal of the Holy Roman Church (then he mentions his sirname) who has taken the name of ——."

At this announcement the crowds utter shouts of joy, the castle of San Angelo fires its guns and the bells of the city are rung. Ordinarily, the Pontiff is brought to St. Peter's, where seated before the high altar, he again receives the homage of the cardinals. After this the *Te Deum* is solemnly sung, and while its echoes are still resounding in the glorious cupola and ascending to the throne of God, the Pope is carried back to the Vatican palace and the memorable ceremonies of the papal election are ended.

PART SECOND.

The Roman Congregations and Tribunals.

CHAPTER I.

THE SACRED CONSISTORY AND ITS AUXILIARY CONGREGATIONS: THE CONSISTORIAL CONGREGATION; THE CONGREGATION FOR CHOOSING BISHOPS; THE CONGREGATION FOR EXTRAORDINARY ECCLESIASTICAL AFFAIRS.

82. The primacy of the Roman Pontiff entails immense labor, because from every part of the world questions are referred to him for settlement. As he is the supreme pastor, legislator and judge, it is necessary that these questions, whether of justice or of favor, should be thoroughly examined and satisfactorily adjusted; for against a papal decision there is no appeal. For this purpose various Congregations and Tribunals have been established in Rome,

to the study of which we shall devote this second part of our treatise.

83. First among all the assemblies for the transaction of business in the Roman Court is the CONSISTORY. Consistory in a general sense means any assemblage or congregation of men gathered together for public affairs. But when we speak of the Sacred Consistory of the Roman Pontiff we mean that solemn assembly or congregation which is made up of the Pope and the College of Cardinals gathered together as a senate in the apostolic palace. In olden times the Consistory was the only congregation and tribunal in the Roman Court; and in it the Roman Pontiffs used to decide all causes which are now examined and decided by the various Congregations of Cardinals. Hence, too, it met nearly every day, and with its other work, heard also contentious causes. But later, because of the mass of business, many cases were assigned to various committees and officials, and a number of permanent congregations and tribunals were instituted. Thus it was brought about that only certain kinds of important business were reserved for the Consistory itself.

84. The origin and antiquity of the Consistory may be traced back to the very beginning of the Roman Church. Hence in the Roman Ceremonial we read: "The senate of the Roman Church was instituted by Peter through divine inspiration, that with it he might determine all difficult affairs in the Church." Catalanus says the clergy and especially the priests were called the "Senate of the Church." St. Jerome makes frequent mention of this senate or gathering of priests, and St. Ignatius calls it a sacred gather-

ing, a council, the assessors of the bishop. Likewise St. Cyprian says that it was a most ancient custom of the Church that the bishop should do nothing without the meeting and advice of his clergy. According to this custom, we find Pope Siricius in the year 384 in a synod of his priests and deacons, which he calls his presbytery, condemning Jovinian and his heresy. Later we find Pope Felix III. in his fourth letter, written about the year 485, deposing Peter Cnapeus, the pseudo-bishop of Antioch, and promulgating his deposition in these words: "Let this your deposition be firm, pronounced by me and those who with me rule the Apostolic Throne." From this it is evident that the Roman priests and deacons, together with the bishops who happened to be in Rome, were present at the councils of the Pontiff and together with him decided all causes which were referred from every part of the world to this primary and principal Church. This too was the rule of all metropolitan and cathedral churches; all causes, temporal and spiritual, being decided by the bishop on the advice and judgment of his priests and deacons. The great antiquity and dignity of cathedral chapters is herein manifest, and so also is the practice of the Supreme Pontiff of holding meetings with his presbytery or senate and with it deciding the important affairs of the Church throughout the world.

85. At the present time a Consistory is either ordinary and secret or solemn and public. In the solemn and public, which is also called an extraordinary. Consistory, very little actual business is transacted. It is rather a ceremonial affair. During it the

reception of kings and princes or their ambassadors takes place; the red hat is given to newly-created cardinals; a legate *a latere* is solemnly received on his return from his mission.

The ceremonies of the papal Court are most elaborate and to a public Consistory are gathered not only the cardinals but also prelates and princes in large numbers, so that an ordinary spectator feels lost in wonder and admiration of the quiet dignity and venerable appearance of what is undoubtedly the most august assembly in the world. Public Consistories are called at the will of the Pontiff and in our times are celebrated but once or twice a year.

What may be termed a semi-public Consistory is held when the canonization of a saint is in progress. To it all the bishops and archbishops, titular and residential, who may be in Rome at that time are admitted. They may also vote. Such a Consistory takes on the appearance of a general council and in a manner represents the universal Church.

86. The ordinary or secret Consistories, according to present custom are held twice a month, and the usual time is Monday forenoon; though the day and hour of meeting as well as the Consistory itself depends entirely on the Sovereign Pontiff. Notice is given the cardinals of the Court the day before the Consistory. At the proper time they proceed solemnly and in regal state to the appointed place, where vested in cappa magna, rochet and biretum they sit on wooden benches awaiting the Pontiff. When he arrives, dressed in ordinary cassock, rochet, mozzeta and pontifical biretum, he takes his accustomed seat, which is somewhat elevated and covered

with a baldachino, and, the doors being still open so that access is given to nobles, prelates and other qualified persons, he gives private auricular audience to each cardinal who may wish to speak with him concerning business in the settlement of which he is interested, or concerning favors which he wishes for himself or friends. In this function is the majesty of the Pope especially recognized; for, although the cardinals sit in the presence of the Pope having their head covered with the cardinal's biretum, nevertheless when any of them thus publicly speaks to the Pope, he stands before him with head uncovered and with great attention and reverence, even though he be the son of a king, or a cardinal of great power and worth.

This private audience being ended, all but the cardinals are excluded from the hall and the business of the Consistory is begun. In an adjoining room the secretary and national cleric of the Sacred College with the various assistants remain so that they may be at hand when wanted; but they nevertheless are excluded from hearing the secrets of the Consistory. The Pope lays various matters before the cardinals and asks the vote or opinion of each of them. Decrees are made, and the cardinal-vice-chancellor, who acts as notary or secretary to the Pope and the Consistory, records them. From this it will be noticed that although there is a prelate who has the name of official secretary of the Sacred College, still his office is rather a private one and he is not the secretary of the consistorial acts.

87. The matters usually treated in secret Consistory are: Promotions to the cardinalate; promo-

tions to metropolitan, cathedral and other important churches; the transfer of bishops from one see to another; the appointment of coadjutor-bishops, with or without the right of succession; the creation, union or dismemberment of dioceses; the granting of the pallium; and generally important ecclesiastical affairs which are to be adjusted with kings or princes, unless the Supreme Pontiff judges it better not to make mention of them to the Consistory.

In secret Consistory the Pontiffs are also accustomed to address the Sacred College on the general condition of the Church, or on some storm which has arisen against it in a certain part of the world. At times also they point out errors and dangerous doctrines, separating what they approve from what they reject and condemn. Such allocutions are given with the intention of having them published throughout the world, to the end that bishops, priests and people may be warned against the efforts of irreligious men, and against the latent danger of pernicious doctrines; to the end also that Christian people may be shown the path which they can safely follow in the peculiar circumstances whereby they find themselves surrounded.

88. The Consistory no longer has the appearance of a court where contentious matters are tried; for all such matters are referred to certain congregations or committees whose duty it is to thoroughly examine and practically determine the decision which ought to be rendered, and then report to the Supreme Pontiff before the matter is brought up in Consistory.

There are several congregations instituted for this purpose, which may therefore be called preparatory and auxiliary to the Consistory itself. Chief among them is the CONSISTORIAL CONGREGATION, which was establishd by Pope Sixtus V. in January, 1588. It is composed of cardinals, eight to twelve in number, and the Pope himself is its prefect. The secretary is one of the Roman prelates, the same who is secretary to the College of Cardinals. His tenure of office is not for life, but he must be re-appointed or confirmed by the cardinals each year. The secretary has a substitute who is also the minutante of the Congregation. An archivist and a scrittore are the other officials.

The work which Sixtus V. assigned to the Consistorial Congregation is: 1° To examine the reasons for establishing new churches of patriarchal, metropolitan and cathedral rank and to inquire concerning their endowment, chapter, clergy and people; and further to examine all the difficulties incident to the proposed changes and all controversies between the newly-established churches and those by whom they are surrounded; 2° To examine the reasons for union, dismemberment, cession, change, translation, assignment of pension in the revenues of churches, dioceses and monasteries; 3° To examine causes concerning nominations and the confirmation of those elected or postulated for churches; 4° To examine causes concerning plurality of monasteries and incompatible dignities; 5° To examine causes concerning the assignment of suffragans and the appointment of coadjutors with or without the right of succession.

Questions such as these not unfrequently are contested, and the opposing parties may be heard before the Consistorial Congregation but not in the Consistory itself, whence all form of contest has been eliminated. But not only in contentious affairs but also in others which are treated extra-judiciously and in a summary way does this Congregation prepare the matter to be laid before the Consistory. Thus also it examines the process which is prepared when bishops and abbots are to be appointed in Consistory, and makes a summary of the whole matter which is printed and handed to the cardinals before the meeting. The office of the Consistorial Congregation is in the Palazzo della Cancelleria Apostolica.

89. Pope Benedict XIV. on the seventeenth of October, 1740, established a special Congregation composed of five cardinals, whose office was to inquire and suggest persons who might properly and usefully be promoted to episcopal or archiepiscopal sees; to help the Pontiff by their advice so that when a vacancy occurred he could know and promote the more worthy; to examine the causes for proposed transfers of bishops, and in a word to offer what advice they thought proper regarding the selection of bishops. The auditor of the Apostolic Chancery was made secretary of this CONGREGATION FOR CHOOSING BISHOPS. Soon, however, it was merged into the Consistorial Congregation so that when an informative process regarding promotion to vacant sees was to be prepared, the whole matter was arranged by the Consistorial Congregation together with the auditor of the pontifical chancery. The reason of this change was the many difficulties which were thrown in the way of the Congregation for

Choosing Bishops, as it was called. In fact the cardinal-protectors of different kingdoms who were accustomed to propose in Consistory the bishops of their respective countries, rose up and protested against the new Congregation. Thus the duty of gathering for the Consistorial Congregation and the Sovereign Pontiff the necessary information regarding the candidates and the vacant churches was transferred to the apostolic nuncios.

90. But Pope Leo XIII. restored this Congregation at least as regards Italy, and nominated for it five cardinals with his auditor as its secretary and two other officials as assistants. He imposed upon them the obligation of strict secrecy and approved practical regulations for gathering the necessary information regarding the character and qualities of various persons suggested or thought fit for promotion to the episcopate. This information is gathered even before a choice is made by the Sovereign Pontiff and in this respect the present Congregation for Choosing Bishops differs from the Congregation for the Examination of Bishops. This latter was established by Pope Clement VIII.; but because of difficulties has now practically ceased to exist, even though theoretically and canonically it remains in full vigor.

91. The Council of Trent and the canons among other qualities require competent knowledge in one who is to be made a bishop. Hence, according to the Fathers of Trent, the simple owning a degree of doctor or licentiate in theology or in canon law is not deemed sufficient, but it is required that the one to be promoted to the episcopate shall have obtained

this degree meritoriously as the result of work and examination. Following this canonical regulation, Pope Clement VIII. established for Italy and the adjacent islands a special Congregation whose duty it should be to examine a person chosen for bishop and find out his knowledge of theology and canon law. This Congregation was composed of one or more cardinals and examiners in theology and of other cardinals and examiners in canon law. It had also a secretary chosen from the prelates of the Court. Practically, however, as was said above, the Congregation for the Examination of Bishops has ceased its work, but, as Santi says, its place is well filled by the re-organized Congregation for the Choosing of Bishops.

92. There is still another Congregation which may be called auxiliary to the Consistory. This is the CONGREGATION FOR EXTRAORDINARY ECCLESIASTICAL AFFAIRS. It is a development from the various particular Congregations or Committees which were appointed by the Sovereign Pontiff to consider and report on certain matters which it was not advisable to treat in Consistory, but concerning which it was nevertheless prudent to make inquiries and obtain special information. Similar Congregations or Committees even in our day are appointed to consider and report to the Sovereign Pontiff on special questions; but the cardinals thus specially appointed are usually selected from those who belong to the Congregation on Extraordinary Ecclesiastical Affairs.

The origin of this Congregation may be traced back to the particular committee which Pope

Pius VI. in the year 1793 instituted CONCERNING THE AFFAIRS OF THE FRENCH KINGDOM. Pope Pius VII. shortly after he ascended the throne ordered that this Congregation should have charge also of extraordinary ecclesiastical affairs in other kingdoms and gave it the more general name by which it is now known. The Congregation lasted until the year 1809 at which time the Sovereign Pontiff was dragged away from Rome. While he was a prisoner it became extinct, but after his happy return in 1814 it was re-established. And indeed at that time it was most necessary; for the disturbed condition of all Europe had so affected ecclesiastical affairs that many important and intricate points had to be settled at once and the ordinary Congregations were too slow to meet the emergency.

The Congregation as arranged by Pope Leo XIII. consists of fourteen cardinals with a secretary and eight consultors. The secretary, as was specially declared by Pius VII., has a vote as well as the cardinals. The Cardinal-secretary of State is always a member of this Congregation, and so intimately is the business of the Congregation connected with the business of the Secretary of State that the offices of the Congregation adjoin the offices of the Secretary in the Vatican palace. There are five officials employed in the secretariate of the Congregation, besides scrittori or copyists. To obtain an appointment as an official when a vacancy occurs, it is necessary for the applicant to show diplomas certifying to university degrees obtained through examination in theology and canon law. When appointed the official receives the sum of thirty dollars a month, and is required to be at his desk between the hours of 10 a. m. and 4 p. m. The scrittori or copyists, whose work is merely clerical, in many cases receive three times the salary of the officials. Surely this arrangement seems anomalous, and the salary of the officials meagre indeed.

93. The competency of the Congregation is not limited to a certain kind of business but affairs of any kind which can be treated in this way better than in the ordinary Congregations are assigned to it. Especially all matters pertaining to concordats and other relations of the Holy See with the various governments of the world are committed to this Congregation on Extraordinary Affairs.

All members of the Congregation are bound to secrecy by oath and the sanction of most severe punishment. Meetings are held, not on specified days, but whenever called, sometimes before the Sovereign Pontiff, at other times in the office of the Secretary of State. At these meetings of the cardinals, the secretary, who is a prelate, is present and votes; but the consultors are not admitted.

The duty of the consultors is to prepare, each of them, a written opinion on the matter in hand, which opinions are presented to the meeting or to the Supreme Pontiff as the case requires, by the secretary of the Congregation.

94. Such a Congregation is of great utility in the spiritual government of the Church, for it points out and explains to the Sovereign Pontiff the way and the means of treating, according to the dictates of truth and prudence, the more important affairs which may arise. It also affords the Sovereign Pontiff a

convenient method of following out a certain predetermined line of action in state affairs without the annoyance of delay. Hence Pope Pius IX. used to call this Congregation his "right hand."

Furthermore this Congregation on Extraordinary Affairs treats all the church business of the countries subject to the Russian Empire; and it also exclusively attends to the business of the countries of South America, in the same way as the Congregation of the Propaganda attends to the affairs of North America. Hence among other duties it grants all faculties and indults that may be required in the ecclesiastical affairs of these countries, and examines into the merit of those proposed for episcopal or archiepiscopal sees situated therein.

CHAPTER II.

THE CONGREGATION OF THE HOLY OFFICE OR OF UNIVERSAL INQUISITION.

95. Chief among all the Roman Congregations is that of the Supreme and Universal Inquisition. It is also called the Holy Office, for the reason, that, as heresy is designated the crime of rebellion against God and a most pernicious danger to Christian society, to seek out heretics and labor for their conversion and thus preserve nations in the faith and protect them from internal contention has justly been considered a holy office. The Sacred Congregation of Universal Inquisition should not be confounded with the tribunal of the Inquisition. For the former was established by Pope Paul III. in 1542, whereas the latter is nearly 400 years older and owes its beginning to the Eleventh Ecumenical Council held at the Lateran in the year 1179. So much that is false or perverted is found, especially in English works, concerning the Inquisition, that we may be pardoned for inserting an extensive review of it, for many points of which we are indebted to Alzog, Balmes, Bouix and Hefele.

96. Innocent III., because he ordered heretics to be looked after in southern France, and to be either instructed and brought back to the Church, or if obstinate, prevented from doing harm by consigning them to perpetual imprisonment, has been generally

credited as the author of the Inquisition. But previously to his time, the Eleventh Ecumenical or Third Council of the Lateran, held in 1179, had published a decree declaring that, "though the Church thirsts not for blood, a fear of corporal punishment is nevertheless frequently salutary to the soul of man, and that therefore such heretics and their abettors as would not be content to act silently and in private, but *boldly* insisted on *preaching* their errors *publicly*, thus *perverting* weak and silly people and inflicting cruelties upon the faithful, sparing neither churches, widows, nor orphans, should be denied all intercourse with the orthodox and that an indulgence of two years should be granted to those who would wage war against them."

The Council of Verona, in 1184, presided over by Pope Lucius III. and at which Emperor Frederick I. was present took measures to comply with this decree. Such, according to Alzog, was the true origin of the Inquisition. It was not till much later, when heretical fanaticism, spurning all overtures of the Holy See, and exciting public indignation by the cruel assassination of Peter of Castelneau, that Pope Innocent III. resolved upon vigorous measures for its suppression; not, as has been asserted, to give a sanction to tyrannous and arbitrary measures, but in some sort unwillingly, fearing in his paternal solicitude that the good grain might be plucked up with the tares, that some might manifest a stubborn spirit, and the weak be driven into heresy. The Twelfth Ecumenical or Fourth Council of Lateran, in 1215, laid down instructions for inquisitors, among which we find: "The accused shall be informed of the charges preferred against him, that an opportunity may be given him of defending himself. His accusers shall be made known to him, and he himself shall have a hearing before his judges." In the Council of Toulouse, held in 1229, during the pontificate of Gregory IX. the Episcopal Inquisition was formally established and received definite organization. Its courts were raised to the dignity of regular tribunals, the methods and duties of which were laid down in an instrument embracing fifteen chapters. Lest bishops might be tempted to spare their friends, Gregory IX. in 1252, sent foreign monks, chiefly Dominicans, to perform the duties of inquisitors.

97. The Inquisition thus established was no longer as formerly a local tribunal, but one having general jurisdiction. The heretics against whom it was established were equally dangerous to Church and State. The consequences of the teaching of the Cathari, Waldenses and Albigenses reached out until they embraced all the relations of political, social and commercial life, and were subversive of them all. For they declared marriage fornication, thus sundering the most sacred of social bonds and sloping the way to the most revolting immortality; they set fire to churches built by the generous devotion of the faithful and endeared to them by a hundred ties; they sought out and destroyed objects of Christian worship which every Catholic regarded with feelings of love and reverence. It would have required a heroic exercise of patience in Catholics of any age to remain indifferent or peaceful spectators of such outrages, and patient endurance was not a

characteristic of those sturdy and uncompromising ages of faith. It is doubtful if in our own day sectaries as dangerous and malignant as the Albigenses and Cathari would be treated more leniently. Hence their treatment is not surprising in times when Church and State were so intimately united and when heresy was associated in the public mind as a crime equally offensive and dangerous to both, and apostasy from the faith an evil more heinous and not less menacing to social order than larceny and murder. Therefore, once a person indicted for heresy had been found guilty, he was handed over to the civil authority for punishment, with however, the invariable prayer that he might be spared and not condemned to death. It should be observed that princes of very different character like the Emperor Frederick II., Raymond VII., Count of Toulouse, and Louis IX., king of France, enforced the inquisitorial laws with extreme severity, enjoining their faithful execution upon the magistracy. "We should bear in mind," says the Protestant Bluhme, in his *System of Canon Law*, "that these things happened under an Emperor (Frederick II.) who had made himself odious to the Catholic Church and that the worst horrors of the Inquisition were first perpetrated after it had passed into the hands of the Spanish kings."

98. It is to be noted that the Inquisition was at first nowhere established as a permanent tribunal such as it became later in Spain. Gregory IX. and Innocent IV. confined its jurisdiction within narrow limits in southern France, and Boniface VIII. and Clement V. considerably modified the rigor of its

-rules. After these changes had been made and partly in consequence of them, the Inquisition was established in the whole of France, in Italy, Germany and Poland, and by act of parliament in 1400 in England. One cannot help deploring the fate of these heretics, who like the "witches" of a latter day expiated their offenses by the penalty of death, and regretting with St. Augustine in a similar case, that efficient and progressive disciplinary enactments, sufficiently severe but stopping short of extreme punishment, had not been employed to reclaim them from their error and bring them back to the Church; but still we cannot agree with Protestants in condemning the Inquisition and its methods of dealing with heresy, as inducing mental servitude and affording a pretext and a means of taking a bloody revenge. To be just to the Middle Ages they should be judged by the principles and ideas of those times and not of our own. Protestants boasting of superior mental freedom have affected to ignore the weight of reason based upon contemporaneous circumstances and while arraigning Catholics have passed in silence over the policy of Luther, Calvin Melanchthon and Beza. Did not these men support by arguments at once solid and decisive the lawfulness of coercive measures against heretics? Did they not make a signal and terrible application of their principles to a vast number of persons? Did not these Protestant reformers punish witchcraft and sorcery as capital crimes at the very moment when Catholics like Cornelius Loos at Mentz in 1598, and, still later, the Jesuits Adam Tanner and Frederick von Spee were earnestly protesting against the policy as absurd; and when Catholic sovereigns at the request of Catholic priests were abolishing these tribunals?

99. To instance a few: Felix Mans, the Anabaptist, was drowned at the instigation of Zwinglius; Servetus was burned by the advice of Calvin, because he held heretical doctrines on the Trinity; Gentilis was beheaded; Sylvanus of Ladenburg was put to the sword in the market place of Heidelberg; Chancellor Crell after suffering inhuman torture to the demoniacal amusement of his persecutors, was finally beheaded for embracing Calvinism; Henning Brabant after being frightfully mutilated was executed because of his pretended familiarity with the devil; Carlstadt and Hesshusius were cruelly persecuted; Kepler, the celebrated astronomer, by his scientific teachings provoked the wrath of the reformers; and last but not least were the victims of the star chamber in England. In the small district of Nuremberg alone, between the years 1577 and 1617 three hundred and fifty-six persons suspected of heresy and witchcraft were executed, and three hundred and forty-five flogged or mutilated. Such is a partial record of Protestant Inquisition and punishment of heretics. Melanchthon praised Calvin's action and in *Consilia II.* has left us an elaborate defense of the practice of inflicting capital punishment on heretics. Beza went so far as to insist that the Antitrinitarians should suffer capital punishment even after they had retracted their errors. *Crenii, Animadversiones XI. 90.*

100. Although it is notorious that the Spanish Inquisition was wholly different in character and

aim from that established by the Holy See, numerous and strenuous efforts have been made to identify the two for the sole purpose of aspersing the Catholic Church. After the kingdoms of Castile and Arragon had been united into one by the marriage of Isabella and Ferdinand, no efforts were spared to consolidate the new monarchy, increase its power, and curb the overbearing insolence of the nobility. To secure these ends and fill the depleted exchequer by fines and confiscations, the two sovereigns determined to establish the Inquisition, whose special office from the year 1484 was to oppress the Jews and Moors, two numerous, wealthy and influential classes, the implacable enemies of Catholic Spain. From this time forth the Inquisition became a national institution in Spain, and not only the lower and illiterate classes, but the nobility, men and women, might be seen in crowds at the *Autos da Fe*, the scenes, not only of bloody executions, but of solemn retractions. Those who abjured their errors were immediately granted their freedom. The sword and olive branch on the armorial bearing of the Inquisition had a deep significance. Neither atheists nor infidels, however, were persecuted in Spain unless when they attempted to proselytize. The "Holy Office" of Spain was therefore a *purely political institution* against which Popes sometimes exerted their full influence and power. Thus Sixtus IV. wrote indignantly to the Spanish monarchs when he learned to what extent he had been trifled with by their abusing his authorization of the establishment of the Inquisition, and rejected their petition for the establishment of the tribunal in other cities than Seville. (Llorente Vol. IV.) Ranke says: "The Spanish Inquisition was above all things in its spirit and object a political institute." "The Inquisition," says Guizot, "was at first more political than religious, and destined rather for the maintenance of order than the defense of faith."

If the government condescended to appoint churchmen to some of the offices of the Inquisition, it did so of its own accord, and their presence not unfrequently softened to clemency the rigor of this terrible tribunal. Such was the influence of Thomas Torquemada and Diego Deza, from 1483 to 1506, both of whom held the office of Grand Inquisitor The number of victims of the Spanish Inquisition has been grossly exaggerated; but as the English historian, Gibbon, remarks, and de Maestre re-affirms, even admitting the accuracy of the figures, when compared with the thousands slaughtered in the bloody conflicts occasioned throughout Europe by the introduction of Protestantism, the advantage is on the side of Spain.

101. The tribunal of the Inquisition in the city of Rome was ruled by the Sovereign Pontiff himself, who was assisted by several ministers and advisers. Chief among these assistants were the members of the Order of Preachers, or Dominicans, one of whom under the name of Master of the Sacred Palace, performed the duty of assessor or special adviser to the Pope in matters of heresy. Another of the same order filled the office of Commissary of the Inquisition. In time, however, one of the cardinals was assigned to take the place of the Pope as head of the tribunal, and he was called the Prefect of the

Inquisition. The Inquisition in Rome was noted for its leniency compared to similar tribunals existing in other countries; and it had no connection whatever with the Spanish Inquisition, except to receive complaints and as a rule mitigate the severity of the Spanish tribunal. Thus we learn that two hundred and fifty Spanish refugees were found in Rome at one time, and convicted of having fallen into Judaism; yet there was not one capital execution. Some penances were imposed upon them, and when they were absolved, they were free to return home without the least mark of ignominy. This took place in Rome in 1498.

102. It is a remarkable thing, says Balmes, that the Roman Inquisition was never known to pronounce the execution of capital punishment, although the Apostolic See was occupied during that time by Popes of extreme rigor and severity in all that relates to the civil administration. We find in all parts of Europe scaffolds prepared to punish crimes against religion; scenes which sadden the soul were everywhere witnessed. Rome is an exception to the rule; Rome which it has been attempted to represent as a monster of intolerance and cruelty. It is true that the Popes have not preached like Protestants, universal toleration; but facts show the difference between the Popes and Protestants. The Popes, armed with a tribunal of intolerance, have not spilled one drop of blood; Protestants and philosophers have shed torrents. What advantage is it to the victim to hear his executioners proclaim toleration? It is adding the bitterness of sarcasm to his punishment. The conduct of Rome in the use which she

made of the Inquisition, is the best apology of Catholicity against those who attempt to stigmatize her as barbarous and sanguinary. In truth, what is there in common between Catholicity and the excessive severity employed in this place or that, in the extraordinary situation in which many rival races were placed, in the presence of danger which menaced one of them, or in the interest which kings had in maintaining the tranquility of their states and securing their conquests from danger? It is not necessary to enter into a detailed examination of the conduct of the Spanish Inquisition with respect to Judaizing Christians; none will think that the rigor which it employed against them was preferable to the mildness recommended and displayed by the Popes. What is claimed is that that rigor was the result of extraordinary circumstances, the effect of the national spirit and of the severity of customs in Europe at that time. Catholicity cannot be reproached with excesses committed for these different reasons. Still more, if we pay attention to the spirit which prevails in all the instructions of the Popes relating to the Inquisition; if we observe their manifest inclination to range themselves on the side of mildness and to suppress the marks of ignominy with which the guilty as well as their families were stigmatized, we have a right to suppose that, if the Popes had not feared to displease the kings too much, and to excite divisions which might have been fatal, their measures towards mildness would have been carried still further.

103. Therefore we have a right to protest against many writers of the present day, who show bad

faith in appealing to the feelings with respect to the Inquisition, which ought to be examined by the light of reason alone, if it is to be properly examined. The dungeons, the burnings of the Inquisition and the intolerance of some Catholic princes, furnish these enemies of the Church with one of their most effective arguments in depreciating her and rendering her an object of odium and hatred; for the generality of readers, without undertaking to examine things to the bottom, allow themselves to be influenced by their feelings and imagination and are thus led astray. Readers who have sensitive hearts are prompt to pity the unfortunate, and what is more likely to excite their indignation than the exhibition of dark dungeons, instruments of torture and burnings? Imagine what effect must be produced, amid our toleration, our gentle manners, our humane penal codes, by the sudden exhibition of the severities, the cruelties of another age; the whole exaggerated and grouped into one picture, where are shown all the melancholy scenes which occurred in different places and were spread over a long period of time. Moreover, such writers take care to remind their readers that all this was done in the name of the God of peace and love; thereby the contrast is rendered more vivid, the imagination is excited, the heart becomes indignant; and the result is, as they desire, that the clergy, magistrates, kings and Popes of those remote times appear like a troop of executioners, whose pleasure consists in tormenting and desolating the human race.

Let there be fairness and honesty in the treatment of these questions. Moreover, let it not be forgotten, as was shown above, that Protestants as well as Catholics have been intolerant of what they considered heresy; let it not be forgotten that the religious wars with which Protestants devastated the fairest parts of Europe, in a few years put to death many more people than all the tribunals of the Inquisition convicted of heresy and handed over to the civil power throughout the whole time of its existence. And who shall count the immense number of Catholics put to death by the Protestant rulers of Holland, England and Ireland, simply because of a difference in religious views? There were thousands of them. And who, if not Protestants, burned witches in America? Had there not better be an end of abuse? Happily the spirit of our age is not the spirit of five hundred years ago.

104. The Sacred Congregation of Universal Inquisition was established as a committee in the year 1542 by Pope Paul III. who wished to enlarge the scope and extend the work of the Roman tribunal of the Inquisition so that it should examine doctrines as well as try persons. Pope Sixtus V. later enlarged and confirmed it as a Congregation and decreed that it should rank as the chief of all the Roman Congregations. The Sovereign Pontiff himself is its prefect, and according as he judges fit, assigns cardinals to it who are known as General Inquisitors. There are ten cardinal-inquisitors at the present time. The oldest cardinal of the Congregation is supposed to fill the office of secretary and he is rarely other than the dean of the Sacred College. At present, the dean is secretary, though he is not the senior cardinal. To aid the cardinal-inquisitors twenty-two

consultors, six qualificators and four lesser officials are assigned to the Congregation, all chosen by the Pope himself.

105. First among all the officials is the assessor of the Holy Office who is selected from the secular prelates or honorary chamberlains of the Pope. He presides over the meeting of the consultors which takes place every Monday, and lays before the cardinal-inquisitors, who meet on Wednesday, the business to be done and the questions to be treated, together with the vote or opinion of the consultors previously obtained. When a sentence is reached by the cardinals, he lays it before the Pope. The assessor also has charge of the office of the secretary of the Congregation and superintends the work done therein.

The second official is the commissary of the Holy Office who is taken from the Dominican order and from the province of Lombardy. He performs the work of an ordinary judge and especially prepares judicial processes. He has an assistant who is also a Dominican.

The third official is the fiscal procurator. He sits with the consultors in their meeting, defends the observance of the laws and prepares instructions by which diocesan courts are directed in making out the acts of trials. There is also an advocate for accused persons, an archivist and a notary with assistants depending on him.

The consultors of the Holy Office are chosen by the Pope himself from the most learned canonists and theologians of the secular and regular clergy. The number is optional, but among them are always the general of the Dominican order, the master of the Sacred Palace who is also a Dominican, and a theologian of the order of Conventuals. Besides the consultors, there are qualificators whose duty is to examine books at the order of the Congregation and report what note of censure they think should be applied to the book or certain propositions taken from it.

All these officials and consultors are bound to absolute secrecy in regard to all acts of the Congregation under pain of excommunication to be incurred *ipso facto* for any violation of this obligation. This is but right, for when we consider that the most secret and delicate matters of Church administration come before this Congregation, it appears evident that without such a strict obligation of secrecy these matters might be divulged to the great prejudice and even ruin of innocent people.

106. The Sacred Congregation of Universal Inquisition is truly a supreme and universal tribunal in matters belonging to it, and therefore has jurisdiction over all the faithful of every order and dignity, even over patriarchs, archbishops and bishops, as well as over all other inquisitors throughout the world. Its competency, as laid down by Pope Sixtus V., extends to all causes concerning heresy, schism, apostasy from the faith, magic, sortilege, divinition and abuse of the sacraments. Hence this Congregation tries and condemns, if found guilty, Catholics who may be accused of heresy or any other of the above mentioned crimes, and also condemns any of their writings which may be erroneous. Hence also the matter of solicitation in sacramental

confession, as well as the marriage of Catholics with heretics or schismatics as regards both the dispensation and the consequent difficulties, belongs exclusively to this Congregation. Hence, too, it issues rules for the guidance of diocesan courts in proving the liberty of a person who wishes to contract matrimony. Finally to it are referred questions concerning faith and concerning secret or other societies, when by way of appeal or interpellation these matters are brought before the Sovereign Pontiff.

At times, also, the Pontiff commits to this Congregation the examination of a question, which, it is true, does not pertain to faith, but which because of the quality of the question itself or the persons whom it concerns, should be treated secretly and not with the regular public judicial process of the other Congregations.

107. The great care manifested by this Congregation in the examination of books and writings which may come before it, is evident from its method of proceeding, as laid down by Pope Benedict XIV. in 1753. The Pope says: "When any book is brought before the Congregation of the Holy Office as deserving censure, if the Congregation does not send it to the Congregation of the Index to be judged, as is usually done, but, because of the matter or the circumstances, prefers itself to judge the book then we order that this method be followed: First the book shall be given to one of the qualificators or consultors to be designated by the Sacred Congregation, and he shall read it attentively and weigh it diligently. Then he shall put his censure in writing, indicating the passages and pages in which the

detected errors are found. Then the book with the animadversions of the reviser shall be sent to each of the consultors, who shall pass sentence on it and on the censure, in their meeting held as usual on Monday in the rooms of the Sacred Office. The censure and the book together with the votes of the consultors shall then be given to the cardinals that they may definitely judge the whole matter in their meeting held on Wednesday in the monastery of the Dominicans, called St. Mary *supra Minervam*. After this, all the acts shall by the assessor of the Holy Office be brought to the Pontiff at whose will the whole trial shall end. But since by ancient usage it is received that a book by a Catholic author shall not be proscribed on the censure of only one reviewer, We desire that such a custom shall be maintained; so that if the first censor judges that the book should be forbidden, even though the consultors agree to the same opinion, nevertheless the book and the censure shall be given to another reviewer, to be chosen by the same Congregation, which second reviewer shall not be given the name of the first reviewer, in order that he may more freely give his opinion. If the second reviewer agrees with the first, then the animadversions of both are sent to the cardinals, that they may decree concerning the book. But if the second disagrees with the first and thinks the book should be left uncondemned, then a third censor is to be chosen, to whom the opinions of the former reviewers are given without their names being mentioned. This third opinion, if it harmonizes with the previous sentence of the consultors, is immediately sent to the cardinals that they may decree what is opportune. Otherwise the third opinion is to be laid before the consultors for their vote. All the opinions and the votes of the consultors are then to be referred to the cardinals, who after carefully weighing the matter, shall give judgment. If, however, the Pontiff, either because of the gravity of the subject treated in the book or because of the author's merit or other circumstances, shall order that judgment on the book shall be given before himself in the Congregation held on Thursday, then the censures and the votes of the consultors, without the cardinals having acted on them, shall be laid before the Pontiff by the assessor of the Holy Office. For then by the votes of the cardinals in the presence of the Pontiff and his definitive sentence, or by some other opportune method which may be adopted in that meeting, the matter shall be finished."

108. There are, as is insinuated above, three meetings or gatherings of the Congregation of the Holy Office; the meeting of the consultors without the cardinals, the meeting of the cardinals without the Sovereign Pontiff and finally the meeting of the cardinals with the Pontiff. The meeting of the consultors is held regularly every Monday in the palace of the Holy Office, Palazzo del S. Uffizio, near the Vatican basilica. At it are present the consultors, the assessor, the commissary and the other officials, and the business which has come up is laid before them by the assessor for discussion and decision, so that it may be in shape for the Congregation of the cardinal-inquisitors which is held each Wednesday.

The meeting of the cardinals was held formerly in the Dominican monastery near the church of St.

Mary *supra Minervam*, but now is held in the Vatican palace. At this meeting the cardinal-dean usually presides. When the cardinals are convened, the assessor enters alone, and standing, lays before the Congregation the business prepared in the meeting of the consultors, reading the letters, processes, opinions and votes of the consultors on the matter in hand. The consultors are then admitted if the cardinals so desire, and after hearing their opinions, the cardinals pronounce definitely and prepare a decree, unless the matter is so important that the Supreme Pontiff desires to hold a third Congregation before himself. When a decree is issued by the cardinals alone, it is prepared in their meeting and on the same day laid before the Sovereign Pontiff for his approval. It is worded like this: "Wednesday,——, The Sacred Congregation of the Most Eminent and Most Reverend Cardinals of the Holy Roman Church, after an examination made by the theologians deputed for the purpose, and report being made to the Holy Father, by the present decree declares——."

One peculiarity of this Congregation is that what is determined by the majority of the cardinals present, and even by two if they alone are present, has the same force as if determined by all belonging to the Congregation.

109. The third meeting of the Congregation formerly was held every Thursday in the presence of the Sovereign Pontiff, and at it he presided. But now such meetings are held only when the Pontiff desires them. They are held in the apostolic palace, and at the beginning only the cardinals with

the assessor are present before the Pope. A summary is given of the matter treated in the meeting of the previous day, and each cardinal, beginning with the junior, gives his opinion, so that the one which seems most acceptable may be confirmed by pontifical decree. Then the consultors are admitted, and their advice having been heard, what should be done in the matter is determined, and a decree issued to that effect. The decree is generally worded in this way: "Thursday,——, in the General Congregation of the Holy Roman and Universal Inquisition, held in the apostolic palace before His Holiness Pope —— and the Most Eminent the Cardinals of the Holy Roman Church, inquisitors in the whole Christian world, the Holy Father, having heard the opinion of the same, has ordered and decreed that ——".

110. The authority of the sentences and judgments of the Sacred Congregation of the Holy Office is the authority of the Holy See itself, and therefore there is no canonical appeal from it to any other tribunal. Nevertheless the interested parties may sometimes obtain from the Holy Father a rehearing of the case, if considerable new evidence is produced; and it may happen also that the previous judgment is modified at the rehearing because of this new information.

The doctrinal decrees of the Holy Office without doubt are to be treated with the greatest reverence, for they are issued by a competent tribunal and after a thorough examination of the question by men whose knowledge and probity are above exception. But nevertheless these decrees are not infallible nor irreformable. For infallibility belongs to the Pope alone, and these replies or decrees are not papal acts. Even if the Sovereign Pontiff approves them, they still retain the nature of a decision of the Sacred Congregation, and as such the Pontiff approves and orders them published. (De Angelis, Santi and others.)

The case would be different, if the Pontiff should make the decision of the Sacred Congregation his own and solemnly publish it by his apostolic authority as the teacher of the whole Christian world. For then he would be speaking *ex cathedra* and his definition of the doctrinal matter would be irreformable.

CHAPTER III.

THE CONGREGATION OF THE INDEX.

111. The Sacred Congregation of the Index may be considered an auxiliary of the Congregation of the Holy Office. For since the Congregation of the Holy Office, because of the gravity and multiplicity of the matters referred to it, found it impossible to devote the required time to the examination of books and to the separation of the bad from the good, so that danger to the faith and morals of Catholic people might be warded off, it was deemed expedient to establish a special Congregation for the purpose of examining books and making an index or catalogue of those condemned as dangerous. The Church from the very beginning of her mission, which is to procure integrity of faith and sanctity of morals by pointing out good pastures and warning the faithful against those infected with poison, has exercised the right of condemning certain books, the reading of which might prove injurious to sound faith and Christian morality.

112. Because she has been charged by Christ with the duty of preserving the deposit of faith and handing it down intact; and also with the duty of teaching this faith throughout the world, it follows necessarily that she must have the right of pointing out bad and dangerous books, and of prohibiting the

114 THE ROMAN COURT.

diffusion and perusal of them. For there is no doubt whatever of the influence of books on man's mind. They are actually food for the mind as much as bread is food for the body. An evil book will not only prevent the mind from receiving the spiritual and intellectual food of revelation, but moreover will poison and destroy whatever of such food has been received. From the first ages, therefore, bad and dangerous books were condemned; but up to the sixteenth century no index or catalogue of such books was compiled. Paul III. committed to the Congregation of Universal Inquisition the duty of prohibiting evil books, but Paul IV. in the year 1559 was the first to make and publish a catalogue of them.

113. This first catalogue was found incomplete and inconvenient. Therefore at the request of Pope Paul IV., the Council of Trent appointed eighteen of its members to complete the work and add rules for the guidance of the faithful. When this committee reported the council was about to adjourn, and thus the report was referred to the Sovereign Pontiff without any action by the council.

Pius IV. committed the work to several other learned men for further examination, and finally published the Index with ten rules, ordering it to be observed by all. Pope Clement VIII. enlarged the list of books and in 1595 ordered that it be published throughout the world.

Pope Pius V. in the year 1571 instituted the special Congregation of the Index whose peculiar and almost sole duty is to examine books that are to be either proscribed, amended or permitted. It is not the duty of the Congregation to inquire whether books against faith and morals are published anywhere, but rather to examine the books which may be brought to its notice. To this Congregation, moreover, was given the right to point out needed corrections in prohibited works, and after these corrections are made, to take them off the Index and permit them to be used generally. It has the right also to grant certain persons faculties to retain and read prohibited books, if necessity or prudence demands it.

114. The Congregation of the Index is now composed of thirty-one cardinals, the number being optional with the Pope. Nineteen of these cardinals are bishops of residential sees in various countries, and live *extra curiam*. One of the cardinals *in curia* is appointed prefect. His assistant is always the master of the Sacred Palace. The secretary, from the first organization of the Congregation to the present day, has been chosen by the Pope from the order of Dominicans. There are also thirty-two consultors and four relators, chosen from both the secular and regular clergy. A minutante and archivist has charge of the office of the Congregation, which is the Palazzo della Cancellaria Apostolica. The work of the relators is to read the books referred to them and give a written opinion, pointing out the errors that require correction or condemnation.

115. The method to be followed by the Congregation of the Index is prescribed by Pope Benedict XIV. in his constitution *Sollicita* of July 9, 1753. "Since the Congregation of the Index," the Pontiff says, "has been instituted solely for the censure of books,

it is not convened as often as the Congregation of the Holy Office; and therefore we commit to its secretary, according to former practice, the peculiar right and duty of receiving denunciation of books. He will, therefore, when anyone brings a book for condemnation, diligently inquire of him the reasons why he requests censure. Then he will carefully examine the book to see whether there is any foundation for the complaint, and select two consultors to assist in the examination, they to be approved by the Sovereign Pontiff or the cardinal-prefect or him who supplies the prefect's place. If according to the consultors the book seems deserving of censure, a relator, competent to pass judgment because of his knowledge of the subject treated, shall be chosen; and he shall report in writing his animadversions, noting the pages on which are found each of the points he deems censurable.

"But before his report is referred to the cardinals, We desire that a private meeting of the consultors be held, that judgment may be had on the weight of the animadversions of the relator. A meeting of this kind shall be called once each month, or oftener if advisable, by the secretary of the Congregation; and at it shall be present the master of the Sacred Palace, together with six others of the consultors who are each time to be chosen by the secretary according to the subject matter to be discussed. The secretary himself shall be present and write down the opinions of the consultors, which he will then send to the Congregation of the cardinals with the censure prepared by the relator.

"Finally in the general Congregation all shall be

observed which was prescribed above for the examination of books by the Congregation of the Holy Office; and as it is the duty of the assessor of the Holy Office to inform the Sovereign Pontiff of the acts of the Congregation, so it will pertain to the secretary of the Congregation of the Index, whenever it judges that a book should be condemned or corrected, to seek the assent of the Sovereign Pontiff, and present a careful relation of all the acts in the matter."

The decrees of the Sacred Congregation of the Index are worded as follows:

"The Sacred Congregation of the Most Eminent and Most Reverend Cardinals appointed and delegated by His Holiness and the Holy Apostolic See over the Index of books of evil doctrine and for the proscription, expurgation and permission of the same in the universal Christian commonwealth, held in the Vatican palace, has condemned and condemns, has proscribed and proscribes, has ordered and orders the following works to be placed on the Index of books ——————. Therefore let no one of whatever grade or condition in any place or in any language for the future either publish, or if published, read or keep the aforementioned condemned works; but let everyone be bound to deliver them to the ordinaries of places or the inquisitors of heretical pravity, under the penalties laid down in the Index of prohibited books. Which being referred to His Holiness Pope ——by me, the subscribed secretary, His Holiness approved the decree and ordered it published. In testimony whereof————. Given at Rome——."

116. Pope Benedict XIV. in the same constitution

instructs both the Congregation of the Index and the Holy Office, that whenever a book of a reputable and well-known Catholic author is found censurable, the censure should contain the words "prohibited until the book is corrected." Further, the decree should not be issued immediately, and while its publication is suspended the matter should be communicated to the author or to some one acting for him. If after a reasonable time the book is not corrected, the decree is to be published. On the other hand if the work is properly corrected, the decree is to be suppressed.

Referring to the complaint that judgment is passed on books without giving their authors a chance to be heard, the Pontiff says, that, although the book and not the author is tried and therefore the author is affected only indirectly, still he wishes the Congregation to continue doing generally in the future what with great equity had sometimes been done in the past, that is, when there is question of a reputable Catholic author whose book with certain corrections may be published, then the author who wishes to defend his cause should be heard before the Congregation, or one of the consultors should be appointed to protect and defend his work.

The Pontiff then imposes upon all the relators, consultors and cardinals of the Congregation of the Index the same strict obligation of secrecy as is imposed on the Congregation of the Inquisition. But he gives the secretary permission to communicate to authors or their agents the animadversions made on their books when censured; provided that they keep the same law of secrecy and provided the names of the denouncer and the one reporting the censure are not divulged.

It may be added that a number of the bishops of Germany requested the Vatican Council to enact that, "no censure of new books should be promulgated, unless the ordinary of the author has first been heard; because it frequently happens that without the publication of the censure, a retraction of the error can be brought about if the author is of good will."

117. In the same constitution, *Sollicita*, the learned Pontiff lays down certain rules which the relators and consultors should bear in mind when asked to give an opinion concerning books denounced to the Congregation. "They should remember," he says, "that they are not supposed to procure the proscription of books by any and every means; but they are only to give the Sacred Congregation the reasons why they think the books should be proscribed or left without censure.

"If the relator to whom a certain book has been given for examination finds that he is not capable of forming a judgment on it, because perhaps he is not sufficiently versed in the subject treated, then he should tell the secretary who will designate another relator.

"A relator should conclude that a book is to be proscribed, not because it opposes the opinions of the school to which he himself adheres; but only because it errs in a doctrine which Catholic doctors commonly teach must necessarily be held. For there are opinions which may appear quite certain to one school, institute or nation, but which may nevertheless be licitly abandoned and contested, for the reason that the Apostolic See has left them to the disputations of the schools.

"Likewise a relator should determine his judgment from a diligent examination of the whole work, but not from some propositions taken here and there from the book and considered separate from the context. For it sometimes happens that an author may state in one passage an ambiguous doctrine and then in another part of his book professedly defend the sound doctrine."

Again he notes that in some books erroneous doctrines and systems are related historically and the authors neither refute nor profess to adhere to them. "They think they are not obnoxious to censure for this because they only relate the opinions of others. But such books may be very pernicious, and if the revisers think they are so, they may rightly conclude in their opinion that the books should be proscribed or revised. Likewise they may rightly conclude that a book should be condemned or revised, if it defames, injures or abuses opponents.

"Finally, if the author of a book gives out his own opinions as dogmas and not only denounces but boldly censures with theological notes the opposite opinion, which nevertheless is sustained by some Catholic doctors with the knowledge of the Apostolic See, then the revisers may rightly judge that such license should be stopped; for from such works dissensions and disturbances may easily be excited in the Church."

118. The Index, as published by apostolic author-

ity, consists of two parts: The former contains the laws or decrees by which certain species of books are prohibited, and by which various regulations concerning the publication and examination of books are prescribed; the latter is the catalogue of those books which have been prohibited by name. The ten rules of the Index, prepared by the Council of Trent and published by Pope Paul IV. are the following:

Rule I. "All the books which before the year 1500 were condemned by the Sovereign Pontiffs or by ecumenical councils and which are not in this Index, are to be considered condemned as they formerly were." This rule does not include the ancient classics, nor the works of heretics of the first ages, such as Tertulian, Eusebius, Origin.

Rule II. "All the books of heresiarchs, both of those who after the aforementioned year invented or started heresies, and of those who are or were heads or leaders of heretics, such as Luther, Zwinglius, Calvin, Balthazar, Pacimontanus, Schwenckfeld, and those like them by whatever name, title or argument they are known, are entirely prohibited." This prohibition even in regard to their books which do not treat of religion is made "in hatred of the author," as it is called; that the faithful may have nothing whatever to do with such persons and run no chance of being infected. "Also the books of other heretics which treat of religion professedly are entirely condemned." Anonymous books which contain false doctrine are supposed to be written by heretics and are therefore forbidden.

"But their other books which do not treat of religion, when examined and approved by Catholic theologians by order of the bishops and inquisitors, are permitted." "Books written in a Catholic spirit, both by those who afterwards fell into heresy and by those who after their fall have returned to the Church, when approved by the theological faculty of some Catholic university or by the General Inquisition, may be permitted."

Rule III. "Translations even of ecclesiastical writers which have hitherto been published by condemned authors, if they contain nothing against sound doctrine, are permitted. Translations of the books of the Old Testament should be allowed only to learned and pious men in the judgment of the bishop, provided, however, that they use these translations as explanations of the Vulgate edition to understand the Sacred Scriptures, but not as the sacred text. Translations of the New Testament, made by authors of the first class of this Index, (heresiarchs such as are mentioned in rule II. above) shall be permitted to no one, because very little good and much danger usually follows the reading of such translations. If any annotations are attached to such translations as are permitted, or to the Vulgate, after the suspected passages have been expunged by the theological faculty of some Catholic university or by the General Inquisition, such annotations may be allowed to those who are allowed the translations. On these conditions the whole volume of the Bible, commonly called the Vatabli Bible, or parts of it, may be conceded to pious and learned men. From the Bible of Isidore Clarius Brixianus the preface and prolegomena shall be cut out; but the text of it no one should consider to be the text of the Vulgate edition."

119. The Church thus endeavored to protect the integrity of the Bible against the continual falsifications of heretics. The Vulgate was the authorized edition which anyone might have and whose use was recommended to all the faithful. Danger lurked in the numerous unauthorized and falsified translations which especially in the sixteenth century were sent into the world. As late as January 7, 1836, the Sacred Congregation of the Index, by decree, recalled to the minds of all what had been previously decreed, viz., that vernacular translations of the Bible are not to be allowed unless they are approved by the Apostolic See or edited with explanatory notes.

Before the time of Luther's innovations the Catholic Church did not forbid the Scriptures in the vulgar tongue to the laity, except in France in the 12th and 13th centuries, because of the Albigensian heretics, who drew from them most abominable and seditious doctrines. It was the unheard-of system of private interpretation, brought in by the so-called reformers in disparagement of that of the Church, that caused her to put in general some restrictions to private reading. Before Luther was heard of, no fewer than fifty-six editions of the Scriptures had appeared on the continent of Europe, not to mention those published in England. Of these editions twenty-one were published in German; one in Spanish; four in French; twenty-one in Italian; five in Flemish and four in Bohemian. The Vulgate was the Latin popular edition. In defense of the faith and of the Scriptures themselves, the Council of Trent, because of sad experience, as it says, adopted the fourth rule of the Index.

Rule IV. "Since by experience it is manifest, if the Holy Bible is permitted in the vulgar language everywhere without distinction, that more harm is done, because of the temerity of men, than good; in this respect let it be left to the judgment of the bishop or the inquisitors that with the advice of the parish priest or the confessor they may concede the reading in the vulgar language of the Bible translated by Catholic authors, to those who they know will receive not injury but an increase of faith and piety; which faculty let them have in writing. But he who without such faculty shall presume to read or have such a Bible, shall not be absolved unless it is first handed over to the ordinary." Pope Benedict XIV. on June 15, 1757, through the Congregation of the Index decreed that: "If such translations of the Bible in the vulgar tongue have been approved by the Apostolic See or edited with notes taken from the Holy Fathers of the Church or from learned and Catholic men, they are allowed." Thus also the decree of the Congregation of the Index on January 7, 1836, says: "The vernacular translations of the Bible are not to be permitted, unless they have been approved by the Apostolic See or edited with notes. From the decree of Benedict XIV. it seems that no permission, not even the bishop's, is now required to read the Bible translated into any vulgar tongue, provided it be approved by the Apostolic See or be edited with notes. In fact common usage has rendered this permission so unnecessary, that most English-speaking people will be surprised to learn there ever existed a necessity for permission to read the Bible in the vulgar tongues. None was ever needed, as was said above, to use the Vulgate edition.

The reigning Pontiff, Pope Leo XIII., in November, 1893, issued an encyclical, *Providentissimus Deus*, whose purpose he clearly states: "We have for a long time cherished the desire to give an impulse to the noble science of Holy Scripture, and to impart to biblical studies a direction suitable to the needs of the present day. We desire that this great source of Catholic revelation should be made abundantly accessible to the flock of Jesus Christ, and that especially those in Holy Orders should display greater diligence in reading, meditating and explaining it." "Booksellers," the rule continues, "who, not having the aforementioned faculty, shall sell or give in any other way, Bibles written in the vulgar language, shall forfeit the price of the books to pious uses to be determined by the bishop; otherwise they shall be subject to punishment for the measure of their offense according to the judgment of the bishop. Regulars shall not read or buy such Bibles without the permission of their superiors."

120. Rule V. "Those books which are published by the work of heretical authors and which contain little or nothing of their own, such as lexicons, concordances, apothems, similies, indexes and such, if they contain anything which should be omitted, may be permitted when such parts have been cut out by the advice of the bishop and the inquisitor together with Catholic theologians." However, if such books

have been placed on the Index "until they are corrected," only the Congregation of the Index, and not the bishop can determine what corrections are necessary or satisfactory. The reason is, that the higher court always retains jurisdiction when once it has acted in a matter. This rule V., it seems, has never been observed in English-speaking countries, nor can it be, unless with extreme loss and inconvenience.

121. Rule VI. "Books in the vulgar tongue which treat of the controversies between the Catholics and heretics of our time, should not be permitted indiscriminately; but in regard to them what is ordered regarding the Bible written in the vulgar tongue should be observed." This rule, it seems, should be restricted to the "controversies of our time," that is, of the sixteenth century when the rule was made. To-day it seems impossible to observe it, at least with us. In fact, the practice of all ages since that immediately following the Council of Trent, restricts the rule to that century. "Books which are written on the subject of rightly living, meditating, confessing and similar subjects, if they contain sound doctrine, are not prohibited, nor are popular sermons in the vulgar language. If heretofore in any kingdom or province some books have been prohibited because they contain some things which it is not expedient should be read by all, if their authors are Catholics, they can be permitted by the bishop and inquisitor after they have been corrected."

122. Rule VII. "Books which professedly treat, narrate or teach lascivious or obscene matters, since regard should be had not only for faith but also for morals which are easily corrupted by the reading of

such books, are absolutely prohibited, and those who keep them should be severely punished by the bishops. But the ancient ones, written by the pagans, because of the elegance and propriety of their composition, are permitted. Children, however, should not be allowed to read them."

Rule VIII. "Books whose principal argument is good, but in which some things are inserted incidentally concerning heresy, impiety, divination or superstition, when expurgated by Catholic theologians on authority of the General Inquisition, may be allowed. Let there be the same judgment concerning prefaces, summaries or annotations which have been affixed by condemned authors to books which are not prohibited, and hereafter let them not be issued except they are corrected."

123. Rule IX. "All books and writings on geomancy, hydromancy, aeromancy, pyromancy, onomancy, chiromancy, necromancy, or which contain sortilege, venefice, auguries, auspices or incantations of magic art, are entirely prohibited. Bishops should diligently see that books, treatises or indexes on judiciary astrology are neither read nor kept, which dare to affirm that something will occur although it depends on contingencies, on successes, or chance, or on those actions which depend on the human will. But judgments and observations of nature which are written for the purpose of assisting navigation, agriculture or medicine, are permitted."

124. Rule X. "In the publishing of books and other writings let what was ordered in the Council of Lateran under Leo X. be observed. Wherefore if any book is to be published in the cherished city of

Rome, let it first be examined by the vicar of the Sovereign Pontiff and the master of the Sacred Palace or by persons to be deputed by His Holiness. But in other places such approval and examination will pertain to the bishop or to some one who has a knowledge of the book or writing which is to be published and who is deputed by the bishop; it will pertain also to the inquisitor of heretical pravity of that city or diocese in which the publishing is to be done. Moreover let it be approved in their handwriting gratuitously and without delay under the penalties and censures contained in the same decree, this law and condition being added, that an authentic copy of the book to be published shall be left with the examiner signed by the hand of the author."

The penalties mentioned above were excommunication, loss of the books and fines. But this excommunication was limited by Pius IX. in his constitution, *Apostolicæ Sedis*, of the year 1869, so that only those are anathematized who without the approbation of the ordinary print or cause to be printed books treating of sacred things. This censure is in force throughout the world. It should be noticed also that the examination and approbation of a book to be published, pertain to the ordinary, not of the author, but of the place of publication. Moreover both the examination and approval are to be given without any charge whatever and without unnecessary delay.

Approbation cannot be refused by the bishop for the reason that the book contains opinions different from those he himself holds; but only because the book is found to contain what is opposed to sound doctrine or good morals; or because, considering peculiar circumstances, it is judged that great damage to the Church will be the effect of the publication. This follows from the constitution, *Sollicita*, of Benedict XIV. An appeal will lie against a bishop who unjustly refuses the necessary approbation of a book, for against any unjust grievance an appeal may be taken to higher authority. The approbation, however, which the law requires, is not a positive, but only a negative one, couched in the words, "It may be printed," "There is no objection to printing." A positive approbation would imply that the bishop also assumes responsibility for the opinions of the author, which is neither required nor wise.

The rule continues: "Those who publish manuscripts, unless they have been previously examined and approved, the deputed Fathers think should be subject to the same penalties as those who print; and they who keep or read the manuscripts, unless they make known the authors, shall be considered the authors. The approval of such books shall be given in writing and shall authentically appear in the beginning of the book either written or printed; the approval and examination and all else shall be done gratis."

125. "Moreover, in each city and diocese the houses or places where printing is done and the bookstores should be visited quite often by the persons deputed for that by the bishop or his vicar; and also by the inquisitor of heretical pravity, in order that nothing which is prohibited may be printed or sold or kept. All librarians and booksellers shall keep

in their libraries an index of the books for sale with the signature of the aforementioned persons, nor shall they keep or sell or give any other books without the license of the same persons under pain of loss of the books and other punishment at the option of the bishops or inquisitors. Those who buy or read or print such books shall be punished according to the will of the same persons. If people bring any books into any city they are obliged to report to the same deputed persons; or if a public place is set apart for such sales, the keepers of such public market shall report to those persons that books have been brought in. Further let no one dare give or in any other way dispose of or lend anyone a book which he has brought into a city, unless he has first shown the book and obtained license from these deputed persons, or unless it is known generally that the book is permitted. Let the same be observed by heirs and executors of last wills, that they may bring to the persons deputed the books or a catalogue of them left by deceased persons, and obtain a license before they use them or transfer them in any way to other persons. In all and each of these matters let a punishment be established, either the loss of the books, or some other, according to the judgment of the bishops or inquisitors, in proportion to the contumacy or the fault."

The part of rule X. of the Index which begins with the word "Moreover," and all of it contained in this our number 125, cannot be observed in English-speaking countries or scarcely anywhere else at the present time. It supposes the union of Church and State which existed when the rule was compiled.

Hence practically it is in abeyance, even though theoretically all the rules of the Index should be considered binding on all the faithful.

126. "Concerning the books which the deputed Fathers have examined or corrected or given to be corrected, or have allowed to be reprinted on certain conditions, whatever they have enacted, let both booksellers and others observe. However, bishops and general inquisitors, according to the faculties they have, may prohibit also those books which by these laws seem to be permitted, if they judge this to be expedient in their kingdoms, provinces or dioceses. The secretary of the deputed Fathers shall, according to the order of His Holiness, send to the notary of the Sacred Universal Inquisition the names both of the books which have been corrected by the deputed Fathers, and of those to whom they have assigned this work."

"Finally to all the faithful a precept is issued that no one dare read or keep any books, contrary to the prescription of these rules or the prohibition of this Index. And if anyone shall read or keep the books of heretics, or the writings of any author which are condemned and prohibited because of heresy or because of the suspicion of false dogma, immediately he shall incur the sentence of excommunication. But he who shall read or keep books prohibited by another title, besides the guilt of mortal sin which he incurs, shall be severely punished according to the judgment of the bishop."

127. The excommunication mentioned above has been modified by Pope Pius IX. in his constitution, *Apostolicæ Sedis*, so that now excommunication

specially reserved to the Pope is incurred *ipso facto* only by "all those who knowingly read, without the authority of the Apostolic See, the books of apostates and heretics, which defend heresy; or the books of any author which have been by name prohibited by apostolic letters; and also those who print, keep or in any way defend these same books." On which it may be remarked, that to be subject to this censure one must *knowingly* read books—which term does not include papers or manuscripts—and such books must not only contain some heresy, but be written to defend heresy. Reading books written by infidels will not subject one to this excommunication, even though the books contain heresy. Further, the books prohibited or placed on the Index by decrees of the Congregation of the Index or of the Holy Office are not the ones meant in the censure; but only those which are prohibited by apostolic letters, such as briefs or enclyclicals.

128. Besides the books prohibited by the ten rules of the Index and those prohibited by name in apostolic letters, certain classes of books and writings are forbidden, among which may be mentioned: "Books which are used in heretical worship; all books of indulgences which are published without the approval of the Sacred Congregation on Indulgences; all ecclesiastical blessings unless they have been approved by the Sacred Congregation of Rites. Further, no litanies except the most ancient and common ones which are found in breviaries, missals, pontificals and rituals and except the litany of the Blessed Virgin Mary which is sung in the house of Loretto, shall be published without the revision

and approbation of the ordinary, nor shall they be publicly recited in churches, public oratories or processions, without the license and approbation of the Sacred Congregation of Rites; however, in the year 1862 the public recitation of the litany of the Holy Name of Jesus was authorized for certain dioceses, provided it be recited in Latin.

129. In the Vatican Council of 1870 many petitions were presented by bishops of France, Germany and Italy praying that the rules of the Index might be amended. They asked, "that the rules of the Index, which partly in mixed regions could never be observed at all, and partly on account of the entirely changed state of human society, especially in literary affairs, at the present time can be observed scarcely anywhere, and therefore give rise to many anxieties of conscience and doubts of confessors, may be submitted to revision and republication."

No action, however, was taken in the matter before the interruption of the council, and in the meantime it must be held that the rules of the Index and the decrees of the Sacred Congregation are both directive and obligatory in every place on all the faithful, so that all are obliged to obey them, unless a moral impossibility prevents, or the tolerance of the Holy See, because of the times, allows the rigor of the law to be somewhat relaxed.

No Catholic can doubt the right of the Sovereign Pontiff to proscribe and interdict dangerous books, and, as a matter of fact, various Roman Pontiffs have from time to time declared the laws of the Index binding on all the faithful. Thus Benedict XIV. in his constitution, *Quæ ad Catholicæ*, of the year 1757, decreed that, "these rules should be inviolably observed everywhere by all and everyone, notwithstanding usage, writings and customs, even immemorable, or anything else to the contrary." Again in his encyclical letter of March 8, 1844, Pope Gregory XVI. declares that, "the general rules and decrees which are prefixed to the Index of prohibited books must be observed, and therefore the faithful must avoid not only those books which by name are placed on the Index, but also those which are mentioned in the aforesaid general prescriptions." Finally in the last edition of the Index published in Rome in 1877 by order of Pope Pius IX., and under care of the secretary of the Congregation, the following was inserted: "Both the rules of the Index, edited by order of the Holy Council of Trent, and the other subsequent additions, remain firm and in full force, only those points excepted which do not agree with the articles of the constitution, *Apostolicæ Sedis.*" These modifications were pointed out above, and regard the censures for reading or printing certain books.

130. Thus it will be seen that the rules of the Index and the decrees of the Sacred Congregation are in themselves of obligation everywhere throughout the Church. If some of them are not everywhere observed, it is owing to the times in which we live and the circumstances whereby we are surrounded, which render such observance morally impossible. Thus in English-speaking countries rules five, six and eight seem to be in abeyance as positive law. Nor is it to be supposed that a few are obliged with great inconvenience to observe a posi-

tive law or parts of it, when the vast majority neglect or claim exemption from its obligation.

But since books are prohibited by the Index chiefly because they are pernicious and the immediate occasion of perversion or of sin, and since by natural law everyone is obliged to avoid such a danger, it follows that, even though all the rules of the Index are not observed, nevertheless the reading of books placed on the Index is prohibited under pain of mortal sin at least in general. Thus, not even with the express permission of the Apostolic See can a book be read which one knows will be the occasion of one's perversion. On the same principle newspapers may be even more dangerous and pernicious to faith and morals than books; and therefore however silent positive law may be regarding them, the natural law forbids the printing and reading of immoral and infidel papers.

131. The Congregation of the Index was instituted for the purpose of aiding the enforcement of the natural law by warding off danger from the faithful, which might come through evil or dangerous books. Books may be dangerous to some and not to others. The positive law of the Index binds all, even priests, bishops and the cardinals themselves who are members of the Congregation. But since what may be dangerous in general, may not be dangerous to some particular persons, and since it may be necessary or advisable for some of these persons to read prohibited books, license or faculty for that purpose may be obtained from the Sovereign Pontiff or the Congregation of the Index. Bishops cannot grant such permission unless they have delegated

jurisdiction for the purpose; because the law of the Index is a pontifical law, from which dispensation can be granted by no one inferior to the Sovereign Pontiffs who prescribe its observance. This is expressly decreed by Urban VIII. in his constitution *Apostolatus Officium*, and by Julius III. in his constitution *Cum meditatio Cordis*.

132. While the Apostolic See claims and exercises the right of proscribing certain books, still it does not follow that no one else may point out dangerous books. The Apostolic See does this with plenary authority; others may do the same by way of advice or through delegated authority, if necessity or prudence dictates such action. "For," as Zaccaria says in his work, *Storia Polemica delle prohibitioni de' libri*, "as soon as a work appears in public every learned man has the right to express his opinion concerning it. He may censure it, but his censure is a private one."

Public censure of a book supposes jurisdiction in the external forum of the Church. Hence parish priests, who have jurisdiction only in the internal forum, have no authority to publicly prohibit any book, though they may announce the prohibitions made by proper authority. Neither have univerversities or their doctors; for although the celebrated Gerson, chancellor of the Sarbonne, claimed that doctors and licentiates have such power, Zaccaria wisely says: "John Gerson, in his treatise, *On the Examination of Doctrines*, extols too highly the power of licentiates and doctors in theology, when he contends that by the Apostolic See it has been granted them that in every place they may read, dispute, teach and *prohibit bad books*; although he confesses that this power of theirs is subject to the immediate bishops and for a just cause may be impeded by them. For the faculty which the said laureates receive from the chancellor, at most makes them apt so that they may be chosen and deputed by the pastors of the Church, that is, the bishops, as examiners and consultors in regard to books and propositions; but by their degree they are not made pastors with whom alone resides the authoritative and authentic power of condemning books."

133. For the same reason prelates of religious orders, if they are not bishops, have no authority to prohibit books as judges of faith; although their prohibitions regarding books are truly obligatory in conscience on their subjects by virtue of religious obedience.

But bishops, because they have been placed by the Holy Ghost to rule the Church of God, have power to prohibit books, papers and other writings, each in his own diocese. "Still it is nearly always expedient not to use this power," as Zaccaria tries to show. The bishop has ordinary jurisdiction in his diocese; he is the judge of faith, not indeed infallible, but as it were in the first instance, and on him, as a true and properly called pastor, it is incumbent to ward off everything hurtful from the sheep committed to him. Hence from this it follows that he has the power of prohibiting the reading and printing of noxious books.

"That it is nearly always expedient not to use this power," Zaccaria tries to show by saying: "The prohibitions of books pronounced by particular bishops bring along a twofold inconvenience; the one is, that such prohibitions have no weight outside their own dioceses; the other, that even in their own dioceses they have not full and absolute force. For, since bishops, although judges of faith, are nevertheless fallible, such prohibitions pronounced by them are easily liable to contradictions and lawsuits. This especially happens when bishops prohibit books because of propositions related to errors already condemned, but which propositions are still tolerated in the whole Church and seem capable of being defended somewhat licitly."

134. But on the other hand, the tenth rule of the Index explicitly gives bishops the faculty of prohibiting books in their dioceses, if they judge it expedient; and it further expresses reliance on the bishops that they will see to the observance of the prescriptions of the Index by punishing those who violate them. In the present century also, on March 26, 1825, Pope Leo XII. issued an instruction, which is placed after the rules of the Index, asking all patriarchs, archbishops and bishops, "that, because it is quite impossible to place on the Index all the noxious books which are incessantly issued, they should endeavor to take them out of the hands of the faithful by their own authority, and that the faithful themselves should be taught by them what kind of food they should deem salutary for themselves and what kind noxious and deadly."

This latter clause indeed seems necessary in the present circumstances; for, with absolute liberty of the press, and with mixed communities such as inhabit nearly all English-speaking countries, with, moreover, the universal habit and desire of people to spend much time in reading, it seems impossible to do much better than thoroughly instruct the faithful in regard to the kind of mental food they should seek, and the kind they should avoid. For the immense number of books of every nature renders an authoritative judgment on them impossible.

135. The decrees issued by the Sacred Congregation of the Index are mostly disciplinary. They prohibit the reading or printing or keeping of certain books, because either they are bad in themselves or on account of circumstances are considered dangerous. But while proscribing books, the Congregation does not expressly define that such or such a proposition is to be held or rejected.

Moreover the prohibitions of books made by the Congregation of the Index are not infallible, so that it can happen that a book is prohibited which is neither bad nor hurtful and therefore should not be prohibited. Such a case, however, is rare, but the possibility of it occurring does not remove the obligation of obedience on the part of the faithful; for the general good demands, and the natural law exacts, that the prohibitions of legitimate authority should be obligatory even when by error something is prohibited as bad or noxious which really is not such. Concerning this case St. Ligouri says: "We confess indeed that in the condemnation of books, errors and frauds may intervene, as in all other human judgments, but what then? Is therefore legitimate authority to be disobeyed? This one conclusion only can thence be drawn, namely, that honest and experienced censors should be selected."

CHAPTER IV.

THE CONGREGATION ON STUDIES.

136. Since the Church has the right of exercising vigilance over the literary and scientific instruction of the faithful, especially in order that youth may not incautiously be imbued with errors against faith and morals, and since chiefly in sacred matters she should have a great care that truth and purity of faith be not depraved; rightly has she claimed the office and duty of directing and regulating the province of studies, and wisely has she instituted a special Congregation for this purpose.

Because the Congregation on Studies tends to preserve the faith and guard the faithful against religious error, it may be grouped with the Congregations of the Inquisition and the Index, and be treated before the Congregations which have been established for the guidance of Catholic worship and the preservation of ecclesiastical discipline.

137. The Church has not received a divine commission to teach science and literature; but she has received a broad and unlimited commission from Jesus Christ to preach the Gospel to every creature and to teach men to observe whatsoever he has com-

manded. While, therefore, she should keep strictly within her commission, nevertheless she has not only the right but the duty to use the most advantageous means for the spreading of the Gospel and the inculcation of divine faith in individual souls. Knowledge is a preparation for faith, and correct information removes many obstacles which prevent people from believing. Hence we find that when studies were dormant, if not dead, throughout Europe after the inroads of the barbarians, the Church appointed a teacher in all cathedral churches, and founded and nourished schools both in chapters and in monasteries.

138. Out of these schools grew other schools, each renowned for its specialty in the sciences and all noted for a spirit of practical liberty and independence. The cathedral and monastic schools were under the immediate and absolute control of the bishop or of the abbot, but the later specialized schools of law, of medicine, of philosophy and of theology soon became self-governed corporations. Thus by the process of evolution, the early monastic and cathedral schools developed into celebrated universities. Salerno, noted for medicine, Bologna, for law, Paris, for philosophy and theology, as well as Oxford, had this origin.

The Church did not found these early universities, but she blessed and approved them. Democratic in their tendency, liberal in their spirit, it required the strength of papal recognition to give them and their degrees universal endorsement, not only in the communes and free cities, but also at the courts of kings. The earliest documents coming from the Holy See in recognition of these universities suppose them to have been long in existence, and are not charters of foundation.

139. While, however, the Church did not found directly these early universities, still in many respects they retained the ecclesiastical character of the schools from which they were evolved. For the rector and chief officers were clerics; the costume of the masters and students was clerical; degrees were granted by apostolic authority after a profession of faith by the candidate; the doctor's graduation took place in the church and was followed usually by a Mass of thanksgiving and the solemn singing of the *Te Deum*

Again, when the Holy See approved these universities and granted them special privileges and exemptions, it obtained thereby, and exercised immediate jurisdiction over them, through a chancellor specially appointed to grant degrees and to govern conjointly with the various faculties. The older universities, because of their numerous and peculiar privileges, had also special conservators of pontifical privileges, whose chief duty was to defend in the name of the university these privileges and exemptions granted by the Holy See, whenever any encroachment was threatened by the civil or the local ecclesiastical authority.

Moreover, universities were often consulted by bishops and Popes, and as corporate bodies they were allowed to sit and vote in ecumenical as well as in provincial councils. They had also the right of censuring (but not of prohibiting) books, especially of their own members, and some had the right of inquisition against heresy.

140. The later universities were not evolutions or spontaneous growths like Oxford, Paris, Salerno and Bologna, but they were direct foundations. As they arose, they always sought the approbation of the Apostolic See, and from it received their constitutions and a chancellor. The Pope was for them all the supreme arbiter in important matters as well as a referee in questions of lesser moment. A special tie thus bound them to the Holy See. Before the Reformation there were in Europe sixty-six universities, sixteen of which belonged to Germany, all due, if not to the direct foundation, at least to the approval and encouragement of the Roman Pontiffs.

Protestantism took away from the Holy See the control of the universities in all countries which forsook the unity of faith; but after recovering from the shock of the Reformation and the ravages of the bloody wars which it entailed, the Church set about the re-establishment of her cherished institutions and powerful auxiliaries. Not to speak of the numerous theological seminaries established in and out of Rome in consequence of the Council of Trent, there were thirty universities founded by the Church in various parts of Europe between the years 1552 and 1834; and since this latter date there must be added to the number, the universities of Lille, Paris, Lyon, Angers, Friborg, Ottawa, Laval, Washington.

141. The Congregation for Studies was instituted by Pope Sixtus V. in the year 1587 that there might be a competent tribunal for the settlement of all questions which might be referred to the Apostolic

See by these universities regarding their rights, privileges, exemptions; and that through it at the same time new institutions of learning might be founded throughout the Christian world which might greatly assist in the work of stemming the tide of heresy and infidelity and of spreading the true doctrine of Christ. The Congregation is composed of twenty-six cardinals, one of whom is its prefect, and it has a secretary chosen from the Roman prelates.

Eleven consultors and six officials are attached to it. These officials are not clerics. Its office at the present time is number 8 Via S. Apollinare.

The power of this Congregation was very great, especially in the pontifical states, as we learn from the constitution of Leo XII. *Quod divina sapientia*; and on it all universities depended. But with the changed conditions of our times, the chief work of the Congregation is to examine and approve the establishment of new Catholic universities in various regions, and formulate constitutions and rules for them in regard to the establishment of chairs and the conferring of academic degrees. Questions, also, which may arise respecting the privileges of Catholic universities already existing are referred to this Congregation for examination and settlement.

Thus if a complaint were made that a Catholic university was conferring degrees on ignorant or unworthy men, such complaint would be referred to the Congregation on Studies. By a Catholic university is meant one which confers degrees by apostolic authority. Universities which are Catholic in name, but confer degrees only by state or civil authority, are not amenable to this Congregation and may give their honorary degrees, as they sometimes do, to incompetent men without any other punishment than that which arises from the well-directed disgust of the educated classes. Degrees conferred by any other than apostolic authority are not recognized by the Church, and laureates of that kind are not entitled to any canonical privileges.

CHAPTER V.

THE CONGREGATION OF RITES.

142. Worship is the expression of faith; and as faith should be exact and sure, so should the external acts by which it is professed be strictly in accord with what we are obliged to believe. Hence the Church has always been careful of her rites and ceremonies, and jealously has warded off all attempts by private persons to attach their peculiar ideas to her public worship. Still with all her care, the Council of Trent found it advisable to recommend to the Sovereign Pontiff a reformation of ecclesiastical ceremonies and sacred rites. Acceding to this request, Pope Sixtus V. in the oft-quoted constitution, *Immensa*, of January 22, 1587, instituted a special Congregation of cardinals which was called the Sacred Congregation of Rites.

143. The Pontiff himself expresses the office and work intended for this Congregation when he says: "We have chosen some cardinals, whose care it shall be to see that the ancient sacred rites are diligently observed by all persons everywhere, in all churches of the city and the world, even in our pontifical chapel, in Masses, divine offices, the administration of the sacraments and other things pertaining to divine worship; to see that ceremonies are restored if they have been neglected, that they are reformed

if they have been depraved; further, they are to reform and amend, if need be, books on sacred rites and ceremonies, especially the pontifical, ritual and ceremonial; they are to examine the divine offices of saints, and, We being first consulted, they may grant them. Likewise they are to exercise diligent care in regard to the canonization of saints and the celebration of feast days, that all may be done rightly and religiously and according to the tradition of the Fathers; they are also to take thought and sedulously provide that kings and princes and their representatives and other persons, also ecclesiastics, coming to the city and the Roman Court, shall be received honorably in the manner of our predecessors, for the sake of the dignity and benignity of the Apostolic See. Moreover they shall consider, summarily terminate and settle all controversies concerning precedence in processions and elsewhere, as well as all other difficulties of this kind incident to rites and ceremonies." The work therefore of this Congregation is twofold, first in regard to causes of beatification and canonization; then in regard to all other things which concern rites, ceremonies and divine worship. But, although it participates in discussing causes of beatification and canonization, still its office is not to decree beatification or canonization. This decree the Sovereign Pontiff himself issues in Consistory, having first heard the opinion of all the cardinals and bishops present in Rome.

144. As the work of the Congregation of Rites is twofold, so is the Congregation itself twofold; the one called the ordinary for sacred rites and for deciding controversies of precedence; the other called the

extraordinary for the canonization or beatification of saints. To both the same cardinals are assigned by the Sovereign Pontiff; but the prelates and inferior officials are not all the same. The number of cardinals belonging to the Congregation is not definite, but depends on the reigning Pontiff. At present thirty-five cardinals are assigned to it, sixteen of them being bishops of residential sees. One of the resident cardinals is chosen prefect by the Holy Father, and the secretary is taken from the prelates of the Court, as is also an ecclesiastic, who fills the office of fiscal promoter and is called the promoter of the faith. He has an assistant who is called the assessor, or sub-promoter of the faith. There is also a chancellor, not a cleric, and a hymnographer, whose duty it is to arrange and correct the offices of saints and other such matters. Moreover there are thirty-one consultors appointed for this Congregation, among whom certain ones are ex-officio consultors and are therefore called prelate officials. They are the sacristan of the Pope, the master of the apostolic palace, the three senior auditors of the Rota, the pontifical auditor, the assessor of the Holy Office, and one of the participating protonotaries apostolic. The other consultors are chosen from both the secular and the regular clergy; those from the regular clergy being taken, one from the Dominicans, one from the Minor Observants, one from the Society of Jesus, one from the Minor Conventuals, one from the congregation of Regular Barnabite Clerics, one from the Redemptorists, and one from the order of Servants of the Blessed Virgin Mary. The first and second master of apostolic

OFFICIALS OF CONGREGATION.   149

ceremonies also assist, and sometimes when there is question of sacred rites their vote is requested.

145. The method of proceeding in the ordinary Congregation is different from that of the extraordinary. In the ordinary Congregation the causes are prepared in writing, *in folio* as it is called, and some days before the meeting printed copies of the cause are distributed to the cardinals. The Congregation being gathered in the apostolic palace, the cardinal who was appointed to propose the cause, and who is called the proponent, states the case. Only the cardinals have a vote, but the others reply to questions. When a decision or resolution has been reached the secretary refers the matter to the Sovereign Pontiff, and if he approves it, a decree in authentic form is drawn up, subscribed by the cardinal-prefect and the secretary and fortified by the seal of the Congregation.

146. In this ordinary Congregation two kinds of business are transacted; the one in a gracious and pacific way, the other by way of contest between litigants. By the pacific method the Congregation watches that the ancient sacred rites are observed by all persons everywhere in all churches of the city and the world, even in the pontifical chapel, in Masses, divine offices, the administration of the sacraments and other things pertaining to divine worship; ceremonies are approved or reformed, books treating on them are amended if need be, and the proper observance of feast days is regulated. Moreover questions and doubts concerning any of the aforesaid matters or concerning the meaning of the rubrics are resolved by the ordinary Congregation

either of its own motion or in answer to a petition. It also approves offices and Masses proper to saints and arranges the changes of offices from a lower to a higher rite and transfers of feasts from one day to another., Finally to this Congregation belongs the duty of examining and approving the business of choosing some saint as the heavenly protector of countries, cities and towns when application is made to the Holy See for the purpose.

It happens at times that the Sovereign Pontiff orders some matter to be examined not by all but only by some of the cardinals of the Congregation; and this is to be done without any of the consultors or with only some of them. Such a Congregation or commission is called a particular one. At it the secretary and promoter of the faith are always present.

147. By the contentious method of procedure the Sacred Congregation hears and determines questions between parties contending in the matter of precedence and pre-eminence in processions and other sacred functions, or in honorary acts and ecclesiastical gatherings, whether these questions arise between seculars and regulars or between secular and regular chapters or finally between the dignitaries and the members of the same chapter. Thus also it determines the respective rights of parish priests and lay confraternities and decides questions regarding the establishment of new confraternities.

In treating and deciding all these questions the Congregation uses the summary or extra-judicial process, after first receiving and hearing extra-judicial information from the ordinaries or the regular superiors of the contestants as the nature of the cause demands. All these causes are decided without any charge or cost whatever, at least such is the law. The office of the Congregation of Rites is in the Palazzo della Concellaria Apostolica.

148. The extraordinary Congregation is not held except in regard to causes of beatification and canonization, to deliberate either on the virtues, the miracles or the martyrdom of a servant of God, or in regard to the question whether proceedings can safely be taken for beatification or canonization. When such a cause is to be examined, the cardinal who proposes or has charge of it, is called the proponent or relator. The Sovereign Pontiff himself, according to Benedict XIV., *De Beatificatione*, is the one who commits the cause for report to one or another cardinal as he judges best. This is in accordance with a decree issued on February 25, 1665, in these words: "Our Most Holy Father, Pope Alexander VII., in a gracious audience held by His Holiness, signified to me as secretary, that it is the mind of His Holiness that hereafter in each cause of beatification and canonization of the blessed or the servants of God, he himself will depute and choose for relator some cardinal whom he thinks proper, and he orders that it be so done and observed for the future."

In another decree, under date of May 11, 1733, Clement XII. orders, "that when the causes of any beatified or servant of God, who when alive belonged to some order or religious congregation, are treated, the consultors who are of that order or congregation shall not be present at any Congregations, either ante-preparatory and preparatory or the general one before His Holiness; excepting always persons in episcopal dignity and the master of the apostolic palace.

149. The ante-preparatory extraordinary Congregation is convened in the house of the cardinal-relator when he judges it opportune; and at it are present the consultors of the Sacred Congregation and the masters of ceremonies. The consultors vote in this meeting, but the cardinal himself does not. In it one cause of beatification or canonization is discussed, either on the question of virtues or of martyrdom, or on the question of miracles performed. There is no mention of this ante-preparatory meeting in the decrees of Urban VIII. or of Innocent XI., because it was instituted after their time, in order that the mind of the cardinal-relator might be informed and that he, hearing the opinions of the consultors, might have the merits and difficulties of the cause thoroughly mastered.

The preparatory Congregation, of which mention is made in the general decrees of Urban VIII. is convened at the option of the cardinal-relator in the apostolic palace in which the Pope resides; and at it are present all the cardinals assigned to the Congregation of Sacred Rites, the consultors and masters of ceremonies. A vote is given only by the consultors and not by the cardinals. For as the ante-preparatory meeting is held that the mind of the cardinal-relator may be informed, so the preparatory Congregation is held to inform the minds of all the cardinals who are later obliged to announce their opinion and give their vote in the general Congregation,

Afterwards the general Congregation is held before the Sovereign Pontiff; and in it a vote is first given by the consultors, then by the cardinals, either on the virtues, the miracles, the martyrdom of the servant of God, or on the final question whether in this or that cause they can safely proceed with the beatification or canonization. Such a general Congregation is held at most only twice a year and in each, as a rule, only one cause is discussed.

150. Extreme care is taken in the matter of beatification and canonization, and the Congregation may be said to assume the form of a contentious tribunal. For it prepares a process, which is called apostolic, and examines witnesses before delegated judges and a notary who narrates all the proceedings and testimony. Furthermore the promoter of the faith is present and performs the duty of fiscal procurator, preparing interrogatories and watching that the whole process be rightly completed. The aid and advice of experienced men is also obtained, who under oath give an opinion whether the works which are advanced by the postulator as miracles are really supernatural and cannot in any way be produced by the powers of nature. Then the promoter of the faith officially proposes difficulties and arguments either of law or of fact; and if these difficulties and arguments are not satisfactorily answered the process is suspended. If, however, the process seems properly completed, then it is turned over to the cardinal-relator who at his option calls the first or antepreparatory meeting.

151. The consultors of the Congregation of Rites cannot assume to act as postulators in any cause of

beatification or canonization. Their work and duty is to carefully read all informations, summaries, writings of fact and law, animadversions of the promotor of the faith, as well as the replies thereto and replications. They are obliged to hear the verbal informations of the procurators, advocates and postulators. They are also obliged on appointed days to attend the Congregations, and in them give their votes. When voting in the ante-preparatory and preparatory Congregations they remain seated; but when voting in the general Congregation before the Sovereign Pontiff they stand. Their vote is consultive, not definitive. After all the consultors have given their votes they leave the hall of the Congregation, only the cardinals of the Congregation, the secretary, the promoter of the faith and the masters of ceremonies remaining with the Pontiff.

152. All who participate in the extraordinary Congregation are obliged to strict secrecy in regard to everything that occurs in or is brought before the Congregation, not only in the general, but also in the preparatory and ante-preparatory meetings. This obligation is so strict that breaking it entails excommunication *ipso facto*, from which no one but the Pope, not even the major penitentiary, can absolve except in danger of death. Everyone who participates in the meetings of the Congregation is under this obligation, so that the cardinals, the consultors, the secretary, the promoter of the faith, the three aforementioned auditors of the Rota and the masters of ceremonies cannot speak except among themselves of any of the matters which regard beatification or canonization.

Each cardinal, however, is allowed the assistance of two of his familiars for reading and studying the causes; and likewise each auditor of the Rota can have the help of one assistant in his work which pertains to causes of beatification and canonization; but all these assistants are bound by the same obligation of secrecy as the members of the Congregation. The consultors, except by special concession of the Pontiff, are not allowed an assistant, but are bound to read and study the causes by themselves. In the same way no member of the Congregation is allowed to receive any communication regarding the causes before it, and if any should come to him he must turn it over to the secretary.

153. The form of oath taken by the cardinals and other members of the Congregation of Rites is as follows: "We, the subscribed cardinals of the Holy Roman Church, of the Congregation of Sacred Rites, touching the Holy Gospels placed before us, swear and promise to faithfully exercise our office in those matters which are proposed in the Congregations to be held before His Holiness, and not to reveal or converse, except with other cardinals of the said Congregation, with the three senior auditors of the Rota, with the consultors and officials of the aforesaid Congregation, and with two familiars to be deputed by each one of us, on those things which shall occur or be treated, not only in causes pertaining to the said Congregation but also in others not pertaining to it, in the said Congregation before His Holiness, on the occasion of a discussion concerning the affairs of magnates, of religious orders or other grave matters occurring, under pain of perjury and

excommunication *ipso facto*, from which we can be absolved by no one except the Sovereign Pontiff, not even by the major penitentiary, unless in the article of death; and under the same pain of perjury and excommunication mentioned above, we likewise swear and promise that if by letter or by word of mouth or through the agency of any person, commendations shall be made to us by anyone, no matter of what dignity or prominence, in regard to causes which are to be treated in the same Congregations, we shall not knowingly open the letters, but closed and sealed we shall order them to be given to the secretary of the said Congregation; but if it should happen that we, not knowing the contents of said letters, should open and read them, if they contain only such commendations we shall likewise transmit them to the same secretary; but if the letters treat other matters, we shall order those parts to be transcribed which contain the said commendations, giving the date, place and signature of him who sent the commendation, which transcript we shall send to the aforementioned secretary; further, to such letters we shall not reply except by order of the said Congregation; and at least in the act of voting we shall mention by whom the cause may have been commended to us. And thus we, the aforementioned cardinals (consultors *et alii*) promise and swear. So may God and these Holy Gospels help us."

154. Great care is taken in regard to the whole process of canonization. The Holy See does not begin the cause of beatification of the servants of God unless fame of their sanctity precedes, and is

proved by juridical process. "By fame of sanctity," says Benedict XIV., "is meant a common opinion concerning the integrity of life and the virtues practiced by the servant of God, not in an ordinary way but by continual acts above the manner of life of other good people; further it includes a report of miracles obtained from God through his intercession; so that, devotion being conceived for him at least in one place, he is invoked by many and is considered worthy to be placed by the Apostolic See in the catalogue of the Blessed or the Saints."

When the fame of sanctity and miracles is sufficiently proved, the Holy See orders that the decree of non-worship be carefully observed. This means that no act of public worship or anything that may mislead the people can be tolerated until the proper decree declaring the servant of God beatified or a saint has been issued. Then an examination of the doctrine of the servant of God is begun. All writings left by him are examined to ascertain whether anything against Christian prudence or the teaching of the Church appears in them; but this examination, if nothing is found objectionable, gives only a negative approval of his writings, to the effect, namely, that nothing in them interferes with proceeding to his beatification.

All this being done, the introduction of the cause is allowed by the signing of the commission, or in other words, the Sovereign Pontiff having admitted and signed the supplication offered him by the postulators of the cause, imparts to the Sacred Congregation of Rites the faculty of proceeding in the cause of beatification. By this introduction of the cause the servant of God receives the title of "Venerable."

155. The commission having been signed, a new process is begun by authority of the Congregation of Rites, and the taking of testimony for it is usually delegated to three bishops of the vicinity interested. First, inquiry is made juridically in regard to the fame of sanctity and non-worship. Then follows an examination of virtues, whether the servant of God practiced the theological and moral virtues in an heroic degree, for this is the foundation of sanctity. After this there is an examination of miracles, whether they are of such a nature and wrought in such circumstances that they can be ascribed to no other cause than true sanctity confirmed of God by these signs. Several miracles are required for beatification, though the exact number is not specified.

The ante-preparatory and preparatory meetings of the Congregation of Rites having been held on these matters, as stated above, the extraordinary general Congregation in the presence of the Sovereign Pontiff deliberates whether beatification can safely be declared. If the conclusion is favorable, the Pontiff appoints a day for celebrating the solemnity of beatification, which according to a decree of Alexander VII. is to take place first in the Vatican basilica. Thereafter in certain specified places public worship with restrictions is accorded the beatified.

Beatification is therefore a decree which permits that a servant of God may be honored by public worship in a certain province. The solemnity of beatification consists in the reading of this decree, in uncovering the images of the servant of God and in reciting a collect, incensing the image of the beatified and celebrating Mass. However the faculty of holding public worship which is given by this decree is limited not only as to place but also as to the manner of this worship, for the beatified are not honored like the saints. Unless an express indult is obtained, the names of those beatified are not inserted in the common martyrology nor in the litany of the saints; neither can the beatified be chosen as patrons, nor are their feasts celebrated with an octave. The relics of the beatified are not carried in processions nor placed on altars. Their images cannot be made with a diadem or circle, but only with rays. All of which must be strictly observed, according to a decree of Alexander VII.

156. After the beatification, if new miracles occur, the postulators of the cause may request a signature for re-assumption, so that the process for canonization may be begun. At least two miracles having been proved, the Congregation of Rites holds various meetings, the general one before the Sovereign Pontiff being for deliberation of the question whether the decree of canonization can be issued safely. Then the Pontiff holds several Consistories on the subject, the one secret at which all the cardinals of the Court are present, the other a semi-public one in which, besides the cardinals, all the patriarchs, archbishops and bishops present in Rome participate and vote. Then in a subsequent more solemn Consistory the day for canonization is appointed.

On the appointed day the Sovereign Pontiff proceeds to the Vatican basilica with much ceremony; and there, after new postulations and many prayers, having invoked the aid of the Holy Ghost, by the authority of the Almighty God, and of the Apostles Peter and Paul, he decrees and defines that N. N. is a saint and is to be inscribed in the catalogue of saints and to be honored as such by the universal Church. A pontifical constitution to this effect is issued later and addressed to the whole Church. This constitution also declares the title, such as martyr, confessor, virgin, by which the saint is to be honored.

The expenses of the beatification or canonization of a saint, which are necessarily very great, are supposed to be defrayed by the postulators of the cause.

157. Canonization is therefore a definitive sentence by which it is decreed that a certain one is to be inscribed on the catalogue of saints and to be publicly honored as such in the universal Church. This sentence is infallible and irreformable, for it is issued by the Sovereign Pontiff to the whole Church; and if in such a definitive sentence the Pontiff could err, the whole Church would be brought into error in its public worship, which supposition is entirely against Catholic faith.

The sentence of beatification is not considered infallible, for it is not addressed to the whole Church; though it cannot be impugned without temerity and the sin of presumption. In fact, abstracting entirely the supernatural assistance of the Holy Ghost, the whole cause of beatification and canonization is treated with such extreme prudence and care that the judgment pronounced must be morally certain.

158. The decrees of the Sacred Congregation of

Rites have been gathered into a collection by Gardellini, and according to the order of Pius VII. any decree found in this collection is to be considered authentic. Ordinarily a decree of a Congregation in order to have the force of law, must be produced in authentic form, that is, subscribed by the cardinal-prefect and fortified by the accustomed seal. But in regard to the decrees of the Congregation of Rites, that they may have the force of law, it is only necessary that they be found in the collection of Gardellini.⁴

The Sacred Congregation has received the power of interpreting the rubrics and the other laws which have reference to sacred rites. And not only may it interpret these laws, but it has also a legislative power, for by the constitution of Sixtus V. it is empowered to restore or reform ceremonies and to amend and correct books treating of ceremonies and sacred rites. Archbishops, bishops and prelates cannot be judges to decide doubts concerning the rubrics and ceremonies; nor may canons or other priests infringe or omit rubrics, even if such is the express will of the bishop. (S. R. Cong. Jan. 10, 1852.) On the contrary, the ordinary is strictly obliged to see that the rubrics and decrees of the Sacred Congregation of Rites are faithfully observed. (S. R. Cong. Sept. 7, 1822.)

159. The decrees of the Congregation of Rites are either particular or general. A particular decree is one issued regarding the peculiar law or privilege of a certain place or particular persons. It has binding force only for the particular persons to whom it refers. General decrees are of two kinds. Some

are formally general, others equivalently general. Those decrees are formally general which have the words "a general decree," "for the city and the world," prefixed to them, or which enact something to be observed "in all the churches of the world." Without doubt all such decrees have binding force throughout the world, for they are issued by the authority of the Sovereign Pontiff and are formally promulgated.

Those decrees are equivalently general which are issued in general terms, as a response to a doubt expressed in general terms, but which was proposed by a particular diocese or monastery, or because of particular cases. For instance: *In Melitensi*, *Feb. 13, 1839*, the prefect of ceremonies of that cathedral asked: "Whether a priest, when he blesses the people with the sacred pyx, should cover it entirely with the extremities of the humeral veil, as the Roman ritual orders in carrying the Viaticum." The Sacred Congregation replied, "He should do so." Such a decree is issued to solve a doubt which pertains to general law, and therefore it is of universal obligation, even though it is not formally promulgated, for it simply declares the sense of the general law already promulgated and of obligation.

If, however, such a decree should extend the law, it would not induce a general obligation unless promulgated, because it is a new law. The practice of the Sacred Congregation, which is the best possible argument, holds that an equivalently general decree which declares the law, is of universal obligation throughout the Church even though it is not formally promulgated.

CHAPTER VI.

THE CONGREGATION ON CEREMONIES.

160. The Congregation on Ceremonies was instituted by Pope Sixtus V. and is considered a participation or derivation of the Sacred Congregation of Rites. It is composed at present of sixteen cardinals, and the dean of the Sacred College is its prefect.

One of the masters of ceremonies of the apostolic palace is assigned to perform the duties of secretary, and the other masters of ceremonies fulfil the duties of consultors. The office of the Congregation is at Number 5, via Principe Umberto.

161. The Congregation exercises a watchful care over the rites and ceremonies both sacred and civil which are observed in the Court of the Roman Pontiff, and over the respective rights of the persons concerned in these ceremonies. Hence it watches that the laws of the sacred liturgy are observed and rightly executed in public papal functions. It also resolves questions regarding pre-eminence among the cardinals, among prelates and among other persons who have the right of assisting at sacred papal functions. Further, the Congregation on Ceremonies lays down the rules that are to be observed in the solemn presentation or approach of princes and their legates to the Roman Pontiff. And for this reason when such a presentation occurs, the secretary of the Ceremo-

nial Congregation is always present in the apostolic palace and has a care that everything be done properly.

162. The secretary also communicates to new cardinals opportune instructions in regard to the solemn acts which are proper to the cardinalitial dignity, and in regard to the formulas to be used in letters which they write to other cardinals and to princes. Likewise the secretary gives instructions to the ablegates and the noblemen who are of the bodyguard of the Supreme Pontiff, and are chosen to carry the insignia of the cardinalate to newly-created cardinals residing away from Rome; and he explains precisely the rites and ceremonies which are to be observed both by them and by the cardinals on the occasion of presenting these insignia.

CHAPTER VII.

THE CONGREGATION FOR INDULGENCES AND RELICS.

163. Pope Clement IX. instituted the Sacred Congregation on Indulgences and Relics by his constitution, *In ipsis*, of July 6, 1669. Previous to this, on August 4, 1667, he had begun the establishment of the Congregation and it existed as a temporary organization until the constitution of 1669 made it permanent. It is at present composed of thirty-two cardinals. Prelates and other ecclesiastics distinguished for religion, piety, knowledge and experience are attached to it, all of whom are appointed to their positions by the Sovereign Pontiff. One of the cardinals residing *in curia* is its prefect, and the secretary is a Roman prelate. The secretary has a substitute, and seventeeen consultors, all prelates, are attached to the Congregation. Its office is in the Palazzo della Cancellaria Apostolica.

The Congregation was established to do away with any chance of abuses in the matter of indulgences and sacred relics. Its object is well expressed in the constitution by which it was established, and by which it received the permanent faculty of settling every difficulty and doubt which may arise regarding the relics of saints and indulgences, if such difficulty does not pertain to a dogma of faith. The Roman Pontiff, however, is to be consulted in the more important and difficult matters which may arise.

164. Further, the Congregation has the right and duty of correcting, without the form of trial, any abuses which may arise or be found in the matter of indulgences and relics; of forbidding the publication of false, apocryphal and indiscreet indulgences, or, if already published, of reviewing and examining them, and, after submitting the matter to the Sovereign Pontiff, of rejecting them by his authority. The Congregation is also to examine and authorize newly-found relics, but is instructed to see that moderation is used in conceding indulgences and giving relics of the saints, so that all may be done piously, holily and without corruption of any kind.

165. It should be noted that this Congregation has no faculty in regard to causes which pertain to dogma, even though the matter specially concerns indulgences and relics. If, for instance, a person denied the power of the Church to grant indulgences, such a proposition and its defender would be amenable to the Congregation of the Holy Office, not to the Congregation on Indulgences and Relics. The Congregation on Indulgences must refer to the proper judges all causes which require a judicial process.

Again it should be noted that general concessions of indulgences, obtained from the Sovereign Pontiff, are null and void unless a copy of the concession is brought to the secretary of the Congregation. This was decreed by Pope Benedict XIV. on January 28, 1756, to do away with the confusion and abuses apt to rise out of the contrary practice. Pope Pius IX. confirmed this decree by another under date of April 14, 1856. Hence for the validity of indulgences granted in a general concession, a copy must be shown to the secretary of the Congregation on Indulgences. This, however, is not necessary in case of a particular concession, such as is made to one or more people personally.

166. Indulgences granted by the Holy Father at present are expedited through the secretary of Briefs, through the secretary of Memorials and through the Congregation of Indulgences. Under Pius IX., for a time at least, the granting of indulgences pertained to the secretary of Briefs as if by exclusive right. Under Pope Leo XIII. an authentic publication of all the decrees of the Sacred Congregation on Indulgences and Relics was ordered and made from the year 1668 to the year 1882. The decrees were copied by the officials of the secretary's office and after a thorough examination and comparison were printed by Fr. Pustet whose work was declared authentic.

167. Rescripts or concessions of indulgences, besides being shown under pain of nullity to the secretary of the Congregation on Indulgences, if they are general concessions, should also be shown to the ordinary of the diocese where they are to be published. This is the requirement of the Council of Trent, Session XXI. Chapter IX., De Ref., but it does not seem absolutely necessary for the validity of the concession or publication of the indulgences. Private concessions need not be shown to the ordinary. No charges of any kind are supposed to be

made by the Congregation on Indulgences and Relics.

The method of procedure in the Congregation is entirely informal. When a cause is brought before the Congregation it is referred to one of the consultors who studies it attentively and reports his opinion. This opinion is then submitted to the cardinals of the Congregation who decide the matter by vote. In important matters the cardinal-prefect consults the Holy Father and requests his approval of the decision of the Congregation. A decree is then issued, signed by the prefect and secretary and sealed with the seal of the Congregation.

168. The Congregation of Indulgences does not grant any indulgence; this is done by the Sovereign Pontiff. The special work of the Congregation is to see that indulgences are not abused; and indeed such is the misunderstanding in regard to what an indulgence really is that it may be well to give the Catholic teaching on the matter: "Theology" in the words of the Fathers of Trent, "distinguishes in sin, the guilt and the punishment. The guilt is the offense done to God; the punishment is the chastisement deserved by the offense, whether temporal or eternal. The Church having received with the keys the power of binding and loosing, exercises that power in regard to sins committed after baptism, both in the sacrament of penance and in the granting of indulgences. In the sacrament of penance the Church remits the sin as to the guilt and the eternal punishment, but not always the whole of the temporal punishment. By an indulgence the Church releases wholly or in part from the temporal punishment which is to be undergone for sin, in this

world by works of satisfaction, in the other by the pains of purgatory. The indulgence, then, remits the punishment, not the guilt. The treasure of indulgences, which can be dispensed only by the Popes and bishops, is supplied from the superabundant satisfaction of Jesus Christ; a single drop of the sacred blood of the God-man being a thousand times sufficient to redeem thousands of worlds. To these exhaustless springs of merit are added—as agreeable to God and meritorious, because of their union with the satisfaction of the Saviour, and as applied in virtue of the communion of saints—the abounding merits of Mary, the Mother of Sorrows, who never had a fault to expiate, together with those of numberless saints who have suffered for justice' sake and practiced long-continued penances to atone for slight imperfections." Such, then, is the Catholic doctrine on indulgences.

CHAPTER VIII.

THE CONGREGATION FOR THE FABRIC OF ST. PETER'S.

169. The building of the present St. Peter's church in Rome was undertaken by the warlike Pope, Julius II., in the year 1506. The old basilica was fast decaying and so also was the morality of that period. The erection of the new St. Peter's proved the occasion of convulsing the Christian world and clearing the Church of much that kept her heavy and unfit for great spiritual development.

Pope Julius II. needed funds for his immense undertaking, and therefore he issued an appeal to the Christian world, granting indulgences and other spiritual benefits to those who by their alms would assist the pious work. Leo X. succeeded to the papal throne and likewise to the re-building of St. Peter's. He was munificent and splendid, and with corresponding recklessness had indulgences published in Germany, the proceeds of which were to be applied to this great undertaking. The civil and ecclesiastical authorities had but recently enacted measures restricting the grants of indulgences and therefore this publication of them gave no little offense.

Pope Martin V. had in 1418 made a corcordat with the Germans by which it was hoped to remedy the terrible evils and correct the flagrant abuses which afflicted the Church. The tenth article of it was concerning indulgences, and by it the Pope agreed "to avoid for the future too great an effusion of indulgences lest they become despised, and to recall and annul all the indulgences granted since the death of Gregory XI." (Hardt, Concil. Const. Vol. I.) Later, in the year 1500, the electoral princes entered a protest against the publication of indulgences, for the corcordat was ignored, and enacted in 1510 that sums of money arising from this source should not be sent out of the country. The emperor, Maximilian, was at special pains to see that the latter provision was faithfully executed.

John, Bishop of Meissen, had also issued a prohibition cautioning everyone in his diocese against receiving the preachers of indulgences; and a similar prohibition had been published in the diocese of Constance. Luther was therefore not the first to protest against the flagrant abuses incident to unwise concessions of indulgences; but had he been, no blame could have been attached to him, for he would have been only exercising a right which he had in virtue of his offices of preacher, confessor and doctor of theology. No fault could have been found with him for having denounced whatever was really extravagant and excessive in the preaching of indulgences and for having called for some authoritative settlement of the question of which he afterwards confessed "he knew no more at that time than those who came to inquire of him." (Alzog, Vol. III., page 11.)

170. If Luther had confined himself to reforming

abuses and denouncing what everyone knew was corrupt and should be remedied, he would simply have been doing what many saintly men in his own time were undertaking, and what every sincere Christian preacher or doctor is fully entitled to do in our day. If, for instance, (returning to the subject of this treatise,) corruption should be shown to exist among the Roman Congregations of to-day, (which cannot be shown) and if the officials employed therein should be proved venal, what is to prevent anyone from exposing them?

What ailed Luther was not a Christian desire for reform in the Church, but a heartfelt soreness caused by jealousy that another order and not his own was chosen to preach the newly-granted indulgence. Instead of reforming, he endeavored to overthrow the Church. Instead of showing up the immorality of certain individuals, he denied the dogmas of faith which the Church held as truly and firmly in his day as in the time of the apostles.

The upheaval in Germany was great; and indulgences inopportunely granted with a view that the faithful would contribute towards the re-building of St. Peter's in Rome, were the occasion of all northern Europe separating from the unity of faith.

171. Pope Leo X. conferred on those in charge of St. Peter's the right to accept and execute legacies as well as to receive alms, and Pope Clement VII. later instituted a college of seventy men who were to administer the funds and superintend the rebuilding of the basilica. But in order that its affairs might be managed in a safer and nobler way, Clement VIII., in the year 1593, erected a special

Congregation for the Fabric of St. Peter's, after the manner of the other Congregations instituted by Pope Sixtus V. Originally this Congregation was composed of some cardinals of the Holy Roman Church, who had as assistants the auditor of the apostolic chancery, the treasurer general, the prefect of the pontifical household, one of the auditors of the Rota, one of the Pope's chamberlains, and the manager of the fabric, who performed the duties of secretary to the Congregation.

172. The scope and office of this Congregation according to its original institution is manifold. For it is charged to see that donations for pious causes made either by the living or by last will are properly executed, and it has the right to apply to the fabric of St. Peter's all proceeds therefrom which should be applied to some good work. To the same fabric it can apply all donations which are uncertain or which are found made for an uncertain work. It can also apply to the fabric of St. Peter's legacies which are made for some specified purpose, but which cannot be used for such a purpose because they are insufficient for the designated object. Again it can apply to St. Peter's all goods left or attributed to persons, churches or pious places which according to their institute are incapable of acquiring and possessing property. Thus bequests left to the Capuchins, the Minor Observants and those under similar rule would be applied to the fabric of St. Peter's.

Finally this Congregation can review and decide causes concerning contracts which alienate goods belonging to any pious place, and it can devote to the fabric of St. Peter's the ill-gotten proceeds from such contracts whenever they have been made without apostolic sanction.

173. That the Congregation might fulfil its duties properly, it was accustomed to appoint commissioners in various provinces, who had a proper and coercive tribunal for deciding questions in the first instance, an appeal from which lay to the Congregation itself in Rome. Further, in order that they might properly fulfil their duty in regard to pious legacies, the notaries and keepers of records, by general edict of August 16, 1788, were obliged to show these commissioners all records regarding donations to pious causes made either by the living or by last will.

Moreover, for the papal states a special tribunal was founded at Rome known as the tribunal of the Fabric of St. Peter's, which by regular contentious process decided causes in relation to the administration of St. Peter's. This tribunal had jurisdiction even over criminal offenses which were committed in St. Peter's itself or in the immediate vicinity.

174. With the lapse of time, however, changes occurred, for in the year 1863, the aforementioned tribunal was abolished, and at the same time the work and office of the commissioners ceased. The Congregation itself remained, and still remains in existence, though it is now composed only of eight cardinals and a secretary who at the same time fulfils the duties of manager of the fabric of St. Peter's. The prefect of this Congregation is the cardinal archpriest of the Basilica of St. Peter's, though for-

merly, according to DeLuca, the senior cardinal of the Congregation was its prefect.

175. The ordinary office or duty of this Congregation at the present day is to exercise in a gracious way its faculties in respect to pious legacies and the obligation of Masses. Business of this kind done by the Congregation is twofold. It grants to the faithful who may be oppressed by obligations coming from pious legacies, a compromise for just reasons in regard to past omissions, and absolves them from the obligation after they have given a specified sum of money to the fabric of St. Peter's; and likewise for just reasons it also reduces their obligations for the future. Further, it gives bishops who request them, faculties for a certain time by which they are empowered to reduce similar obligations.

The Congregation also transfers the obligations of Masses from one church or altar to another, and extends the time for saying manual Masses longer than the usual two months allowed by law. The other special work of the Congregation is that it allows and approves the redeeming of pious obligations induced by legacies. Those asking such a favor must pay to the ordinary of the diocese where the case arises a certain sum of money as a principal, which he must then invest and hold in trust that from the interest on this principal the yearly obligation imposed by the legacies may be properly satisfied.

CHAPTER IX.

THE CONGREGATION OF THE COUNCIL; THE SUB-
ORDINATE CONGREGATIONS FOR VISITS AD
LIMINA, FOR REVIEWING PROVINCIAL SYNODS,
FOR ECCLESIASTICAL IMMUNITY, FOR THE RESI-
DENCE OF BISHOPS.

176. After the Congregations which specially treat matters of faith and those which attend to questions of worship in the Church, the several Congregations whose specified object is the enforcement of proper discipline invite attention. The Council of Trent issued many decrees concerning reformation and discipline but left to the Sovereign Pontiff the care of enforcing and interpreting its enactments. Pope Pius IV. in the year 1564 confirmed the acts of the council and at the same time absolutely prohibited the publication of any commentary, glossary, annotation or interpretation of its decrees. During the same year he established a Congregation of six cardinals whose express duty was to see to the observance of the decrees of the council concerning reformation. This Congregation had no authority to interpret the council, for this matter the Pope specially reserved to himself.

But Pius V. enlarged its powers and ordained that in all cases in which there was no doubt of the meaning of the decrees, the Congregation could pass a definitive sentence; but in all other cases it should recur to the Supreme Pontiff. Later Pope Sixtus V. confirmed the establishment of the Congregation and gave it general powers to interpret the decrees of the Council of Trent on reformation, with the one condition that the head of the Church must first be consulted in the matter. The Congregation itself now passes sentence and the Sovereign Pontiff confirms it. Hence its name was broadened so as to include its additional work, and it is called the Congregation of Cardinals who interpret the Council of Trent. Their faculties extend to all the Tridentine decrees on reformation or discipline, but not to the decrees on faith or dogma. The interpretation of these is reserved to the Pope himself, and questions concerning them are usually referred to the Holy Office for examination. Since, however, the reformatory decrees of Trent touch nearly every point of ecclesiastical jurisprudence, the committee or Congregation for interpreting them has the power to explain authoritatively all canon law. Moreover, in matters of discipline it has not only judicial but legislative authority over the entire Church, being empowered to make such laws as are deemed opportune.

177. The Sacred Congregation of the Council has therefore a threefold power. It can interpret the Council of Trent, it can decide controversies, except such as pertain to dogma; and it can make regulations concerning discipline. These things it can do and its rescripts it can issue in the name of the Pontiff, according to a faculty given to this effect by Gregory XIV. The right to interpret the disciplin-

ary decrees of the Council of Trent belongs to this Congregation exclusively; but the faculties regarding other matters it holds in common with other Congregations. Thus to the Congregation of the Council or to the tribunal of the Rota, matrimonial causes which are appealed to the Holy See may be referred. Again, causes concerning nullity of a religious profession which are appealed to the Holy See may be referred to this Congregation or to the Congregation on Bishops and Regulars.

Because of a similar dependence on the Council of Trent, causes concerning the residence of bishops and other beneficiaries may be treated before this Congregation, and for a just reason leave of absence to such incumbents without loss of revenues may also be granted by it. This Congregation can also grant the faculty for reducing the obligation of founded Masses because of a diminution of revenues.

178. Matrimonial causes, especially in regard to the bond and in regard to dispensations from an unconsummated marriage, are adjudicated by this Congregation. And for this reason among its officials there is one called the defender or advocate of marriage, whose duty is to produce reasons in defense of the marriage which is being contested. Irregularities of clerics are also examined by this committee and at its instance dispensation is granted by the Sovereign Pontiff. Questions, also, which relate to the excardination of clerics and their incorporation into other dioceses than those for which they were ordained, are heard and decided by the Congregation of the Council.

Moreover in regard to benefices this Congregation

has competent jurisdiction, particularly when the matters are in any way connected with the decrees of Trent. Thus questions arising out of the union or attempted union of benefices or parishes with a cathedral or seminary would be referred to this Congregation for examination and decision. The same would be done in the case of several contestants for an appointment to ecclesiastical office, or in case of a complaint that unworthy persons are appointed, or that the proper method of appointment has not been followed. Finally all questions which relate to the alienation of church property come under the jurisdiction of the Congregation of the Council.

179. The Sacred Congregation of the Council is now composed of twenty-eight cardinals, one of whom is appointed prefect by His Holiness. The number of cardinals is not fixed and they are selected also from those who reside away from Court. The prefect superintends the work of the committee and its officials, and signs letters and decrees which are then countersigned by the secretary.

The office of secretary to this Congregation is considered a most important one and to it a titular archbishop is usually appointed. One reason for this appointment of a bishop as secretary, is because he has frequently to write to bishops, and should be their equal. This position is considered a cardinalitial one, and its incumbent after serving a certain time, is almost sure of being promoted to the dignity of the cardinalate. The Congregation has an auditor whose position is also of great prominence, for he assists the secretary and supplies his place in many things. The auditor generally prepares or summarizes the causes which are to be printed and in the name of the secretary distributed to the cardinals of the Congregation. Likewise he attends to the other writings which pertain to the secretary's office, and either by himself or with the assistance of the subsecretary and inferior officials keeps a record of all matters belonging to the committee and of the documents which have been referred to bishops for their opinions. The officials are an archivist, two minutanti, a protocolist, and four scrittori or writers.

180. A Latin secretary is usually appointed for the special work of writing letters to bishops in the Latin language. Pope Benedict XIV. mentions this official in these words: "He whose work in this Congregation in replying in Latin to the letters of bishops." This office at present is filled by one of the other officials.

Attached to this Congregation at the present time are a number of prelates of the Roman Court. For when Pope Leo XIII. ascended the throne, he immediately turned his eyes to the prelates of the Court and began seeking a way in which their services could be utilized for the benefit of the whole Church, and they could at the same time improve their knowledge of canon law and obtain experience in treating ecclesiastical affairs or in solving difficult questions. Therefore, by command of His Holiness, the Secretary of State issued an order by which quite a number of these prelates were attached to the Sacred Congregations of the Council, of Bishops and Regulars and of the Propaganda; and to them was assigned the work of examining and discussing causes in the presence of the cardinal-prefect and the secretary of their respective Congregations, and of giving a consultive vote before the causes are proposed for hearing and decision in the general meeting of the cardinals.

181. There is also a school for young canonists attached to the Congregation of the Council, wherein they may be initiated into the intricacies of church law and become accustomed to the method of treating cases. In a measure they take the place and do the work of consultors. The secretary admits a certain number of young priests or clerics to this school, which is called the studium or study, and over which the auditor presides. For this reason he is sometimes called the "head of the study." The students thus admitted gather at certain hours in the secretary's office, which is now in the Palazzo della Cancellaria Apostolica, and there the auditor communicates to them the various difficult causes which are to be treated in the Congregation. A certain cause is assigned them for study, and one of the students is charged with the work of preparing an opinion on it, and suggesting a decision. Then on the appointed day he reads the dissertation he has prepared in the presence of the auditor and the other students, and they also give their ideas, quoting law, authorities and reasons for their conclusions. It usually happens that the causes are so thoroughly discussed in this study, that the conclusion reached by the students, though it has no weight at all and is not even mentioned in the Congregation, is nevertheless the one which is later found to be the decision of the cardinals. Many of these students are afterwards chosen for various positions in the Sacred

182   THE ROMAN COURT.

Congregations, or to act as vicars-general to bishops in those dioceses, where the law is followed which provides that the bishop's vicar-general shall be chosen from outside his diocese. ·

Clerics of various nations may obtain admission to this study, where they neither pay nor are paid, and indeed it is a most beneficial resort for anyone who expects to devote his attention to the practice of canon law. There are no Americans in it at the present time. Why?

182. Much of the business which is referred to the Congregation of the Council does not need the consideration of the cardinals, either because it has often been decided or because it can easily be settled by a rescript of the cardinal-prefect. When therefore the secretary thinks the business is of that kind he does not place it before the cardinals in general committee, but attends to it himself together with the cardinal-prefect, after an audience with the Holy Father if the matter demands it. The letters or decrees by which he replies to applications or consultations on business of this kind are signed by both the prefect and the secretary and sealed with the seal of the Congregation.

183. Again there are other affairs which require some examination, but which are easily made clear by a short exposition and discussion. Such for instance are many doubts concerning unimportant things, and such too are nearly all causes of favor. These matters, therefore, the secretary explains in the Congregation of the Cardinals in a short form, or as it is called, by a summary of the requests, and concludes his statement with these or similar words:

"Wherefore may your Eminences deign to decide the following doubts 1°—, 2°—." The matter being thoroughly considered, the cardinals give their decision by voting yes or no to each doubt proposed.

It sometimes happens that a cause which is proposed by the secretary in a summary way, after discussion appears more serious and requires further information and discussion. In such a case the cardinals order the matter prepared in print, *in folio*, and postpone it to another meeting. But even though the cause is treated in this summary way, previous information if necessary, is requested by the secretary from the ordinaries or from other qualified persons residing in the place where the cause originated. At times also secret information is obtained in order that witnesses may not be molested or injured. The votum or opinion of the bishop who is thus consulted has great weight with the Congregation.

184. Contentious causes and also those which imply difficult doubts are not treated by way of a summary but are put in folio, that is, an exposition of them is printed and copies are distributed to the cardinals some time previous to the meeting in which the cause is to be discussed. But in contentious causes there are two ways of proceeding; either *servato juris ordine* or *ex officio*. When either or both parties wish to proceed according to the regular method of law, they declare this through their regularly appointed procurators. This declaration is usually made by the words, *nihil transeat*, let nothing be omitted; and then the Congregation as a court follows strictly the judicial form of proceed-

ing. The expenses of this method are very great, and must be paid by the contestants or by the loser if the court so decides. Hence the parties usually prefer not to proceed in this way, but *ex officio*, in an informal manner. In such a case an exposition of the whole cause is drawn up by the secretary or his auditor with the documents and arguments of each side attached; and at the end of the exposition, the matter itself which is in contest is placed in the form of a doubt. This writing is then printed at the expense of the pontifical government and distributed to the cardinals. In the meantime the interested parties or their procurators visit the cardinals to give them information, "*ad informandum*" on the merits of the case, and beg a favorable decision. At a meeting held shortly afterwards, the cardinals after deliberation, decide by a majority vote and reply either affimatively or negatively to the proposed doubts or questions, which are so drawn as to epitomize the whole case. The secretary then notifies the parties concerning the decision.

185. This method of proceeding *ex officio*, and with printed documents is followed both in contentious causes and in the more difficult causes which are not contentious but which imply much examination and discussion. Such, for instance, are some of the doubts proposed in regard to passages of the Council of Trent, a decision on which might affect canon law itself.

In all cases, however, when the procedure is *ex officio*, necessary and opportune information is requested from the ordinaries concerned, or from other persons worthy of credence.

OBLIGATION OF DECREES. 185

186. The resolutions or decrees of the Congregation of the Council which were made previous to the year 1718 have never been printed. But in the archives of the Congregation they are kept in folio volumes which are called, *The Books of Decrees*, and are so cited by Benedict XIV. and other authors who quote decisions from them. The pages of these books are numbered only on one side, so that if the decision is to be found on the unnumbered part of the folio, the words *a tergo* are added, which mean that the number given must be sought and then the page must be turned. These *Books of Decrees* are most valuable, because they contain many important decisions made from the time of the Council of Trent up to 1718, which are authentic interpretations of canon law.

Some of them have been copied by authors deemed worthy of confidence, such as Fagnan and Benedict XIV.; and others may be obtained in authenticated copies from the secretary of the Congregation, on the payment of a small fee for the copyist. But from the year 1718 the decisions and decrees issued by the Congregation on matters treated by it in folio or in print have been published under the title, *Thesaurus Resolutionum*. One volume appears each year and the average cost is about one dollar a volume. The work is most necessary for canonists, since it contains the law of the present day.

The resolutions and decrees issued on matters treated in the Congregation by the summary process are not included in this *Thesaurus*, but the principal causes thus treated and decided from 1823 to 1870 have been gathered by Lingen and Reuss and printed by Fr. Pustet.

187. There is considerable controversy among canonists regarding the authority of the resolutions made by the Sacred Congregation of the Council. They dispute as to whether these resolutions have decisive force only in the case proposed and in respect to the persons who proposed it, just as in the case of judgments rendered by a tribunal; or whether they are not rather general rules obligatory in law and conscience on all who may be in a position similar to that mentioned in the case adjudicated.

There can be no question in regard to those decrees which are issued by the Congregation with the consent of the Sovereign Pontiff and are promulgated in Rome in the usual manner of laws; for in respect to them nothing can prevent them being considered pontifical laws. The question is therefore confined to declarations or answers given to proposed cases.

188. St. Ligouri says there are two opinions in this matter and either is probable. Many hold that the replies of the Congregation are to be considered doctrinal decisions, which are indeed of great weight, so that a wise man will not recede from them unless for a very grave reason, but which nevertheless of themselves have no obligatory force except for the persons to whom they are given. Others maintain that the declarations of the Congregation have the force of law for all to whom they become known.

The solution of the question seems to depend on the object which is directly effected by the decision of the Congregation. For either it lays down a general principle by giving an interpretation of common discipline; or it applies a general principle to some particular fact with its circumstances; or finally it discerns, orders or prohibits something beyond the general law, which interpretation is called by canonists an extensive one.

In the first case the interpretation is authentic, has the force of law and must be applied to all similar cases, even if it is not promulgated in the usual way of laws; provided only the decision is authenticated by the signatures of the cardinal-prefect and the secretary of the Congregation. The reason is, that according to the more common and well-founded opinion of the learned, an interpretation which does not make new law but simply explains a law already made and promulgated, does not require a new solemn promulgation. Further, the very end which the Holy See had in view in committing to the Congregation the interpretation of general discipline, as well as the practice of the Congregation itself which constantly orders that when new doubts are proposed its previous declarations must be followed, gives a conclusive argument that the declarations interpreting general discipline are of obligation everywhere and for all. Hence, too, the former opinion mentioned by St. Ligouri, that these decisions are only doctrinal, can no longer be considered probable, because it is against the established practice of the Apostolic See, now better known than when St. Ligouri wrote.

189. In the second supposition, that is, when the decision of the Congregation applies a general principle to a particular fact viewed in all its circum-

stances, there is no authentic interpretation of law, but a judgment is rendered in a particular case. Hence it may be said with DeAngelis, that such a declaration is applicable only to that one case, as in trials, but not to similar cases so that they should be considered decided thereby. But it is nevertheless of great authority, and if the circumstances and adjuncts are the same, other similar cases may be considered prejudged, even though not decided by such a declaration.

In the third supposition, that is, when an extensive or restrictive interpretation of the general law is given, by adding to or subtracting something from the text, it has not the obligatory force of law in respect to all, unless it is promulgated like a new law or unless it is given in agreement with and to confirm the generally accepted interpretation which through custom already has the force of law. The reason is that this Congregation has not the power of making new laws, such as this interpretation would be. Hence such an interpretation to become law must be promulgated in the usual manner. *

190. Several subordinate or particular Congregations are attached to the Congregation of the Council. One of them is the special Congregation or subcommittee for RECEIVING AND EXAMINING THE REPORTS OF BISHOPS ON THE STATE OF THEIR CHURCHES. Benedict XIV. instituted this special Congregation on November, 23, 1740. The reason given is that, "since patriarchs, primates, archbishops, bishops and also inferior prelates who have quasi-episcopal jurisdiction with a distinct territory, are obliged at stated times to make a visitation *ad*

limina, and at the same time give a report to the Holy See concerning the churches confided to their care; and since they are accustomed to annex to their reports certain doubts and difficulties to which they request opportune responses, it not unfrequently has happened that these replies were delayed much longer than was right, because the Congregation to which was committed the care of examining these reports and replying to the questions contained therein was unable to do so on account of the immense amount of work always on hand." Wherefore, innumerable complaints being received from bishops in regard to the matter, Benedict XIV. to meet and overcome the difficulty, established a special committee of prelates to which this work was assigned. The prefect and secretary of the general committee or Congregation of the Council are also prefect and secretary of this particular subcommittee, and therefore it is considered merely a section of the Congregation.

191. The method of proceeding in this Congregation on the Reports of Churches was laid down by Pope Benedict XIV. when he established it. The report made by the visiting prelate is referred to the special committee, consisting of nine prelates, and read and accurately considered in its ordinary meetings. If nothing extraordinary or difficult is found in it, the cardinal-prefect and the secretary attend to the contents. But if certain doubts or difficulties of greater moment are found, they are presented by the secretary to the full committee or Congregation of the Council. Afterwards the opinions reached by both the committee of prelates and

the Congregation of Cardinals are referred by the secretary to the Holy Father and he determines what reply is to be made to the visiting prelate.

192. The visit *ad limina* referred to in the preceding number, consists in this, that each bishop at a certain stated time is obliged to visit the Sovereign Pontiff, the center and head of the Church, and make a report to him on the condition of his diocese. The time for this visit varies according to the distance of the bishops from Rome. Thus the bishops of Italy and the adjacent islands are to make the visit every three years; those of southern and western Europe every four years; those of other parts of Europe and of Africa every five years; and those of the rest of the world every ten years. The beginning of all these periods is counted from December 20, 1585, when the constitution of Sixtus V. to this effect was issued.

The time for the visit is the last year of the respective period of three, four, five or ten years; and therefore bishops, especially those of Italy, are usually not received for their visit *ad limina* in the first year of their period. In the second year they are received only rarely and because of a reasonable cause. The same is to be said of the longer periods. (S. Cong. Res. Epis. July 17, 1657.) They must make the visit, however, before the expiration of the period, that is, before December 20 of the last year of their respective periods, according to an Instruction of the Propaganda dated July 1, 1877; and neglect of this visit formerly was punished by suspension *ipso facto* incurred. This censure, however, was removed by Pius IX. because it is omitted from the constitution *Apostolicæ Sedis*. If the bishop is unable to make this visit personally, he may do it through a procurator specially appointed by him for the purpose.

193. The visit of a bishop *ad limina* consists of three acts; namely, a visit to the basilica of St. Peter and St. Paul, an audience with the Pope, and a report made orally to the Pontiff and in writing to the Congregation concerning the condition of his diocese in regard to both persons and things. The prelates of missionary countries, instead of handing their written report to the special committee of the Congregation of the Council, make it to the Congregation of the Propaganda. The report must be made in regular order, giving replies to sixty-four questions. The headings under which these questions are grouped are the following: The origin, progress and boundaries of the mission or diocese, with a map; The quality and aptitude of the missionaries or clergy; The government of the missions or dioceses; The native clergy; Institutes of Regulars; The sacred ministry and the conversion of gentiles; Churches, chapels and presbyteries; Ecclesiastical property and its administration; Things relating to divine worship; The education and care of youth; Pious institutions or societies; Feasts, fasts and abstenance; Cemeteries and sepulture; The administration of the sacraments; Abuses and necessities of the mission or diocese. If any question is inapplicable to his diocese, the bishop replies to that number by the words: "I have nothing to reply to this question."

Bishops who report to the Congregation of the

Council, according to an instruction issued by order of Pope Benedict XIII., are to reply to sixty-one questions grouped under eight headings. The first heading regards the material condition of the diocese, giving the number of churches, parishes, hospitals, colleges and the like, belonging to it. The second regards the bishop himself and his rule, while the third regards the secular and the fourth the regular clergy of the diocese. The fifth heading contains questions in regard to nuns, the sixth in regard to the seminary, the seventh in regard to confraternities and pious places, and the eighth in regard to the laity. Under a separate heading the bishop will group his requests and other information he may wish to convey.

From merely reading these headings it is evident that if exact and truthful replies are given to each question, the Holy See acquires an intimate knowledge of the condition of every diocese in the world. These reports are preserved in the Congregation and used for reference whenever necessity or prudence demands it. Likewise all papers and correspondence containing complaints in reference to dioceses are kept in the Congregation for ten years at least, and when received are placed in the respective pigeon-hole or case assigned to each diocese. These assignments are made not alphabetically but by grouping the dioceses under the ecclesiastical province to which they belong. After ten years many of these reports and papers are placed in the archives for preservation.

194. Another section or subcommittee of the Congregation of the Council, is that for REVIEWING

PROVINCIAL COUNCILS. It was established by Pope Pius IX. while he was at Gaeta in 1849. About this time many provincial councils were held throughout the world, and agreeably to the requirements of law were submitted to the Holy See for revision. It was apparent that if this work of revision was to be done by the whole Congregation in the usual way, many years would elapse before approval could be granted; and innumerable complaints would ensue. Hence Pius IX. instituted a particular committee of cardinals selected from the Congregation of the Council and to them assigned this work of revision. The cardinal-prefect and the secretary of the Congregation of the Council were made prefect and secretary of this subcommittee. Seven cardinals at present compose this subcommittee to which twenty-seven consultors are assigned. These were taken at first only from the prelates of the Roman Court, but later, at the request of Cardinal Mai, also from the regular clergy. Now twenty-one of them are members of religious orders and six are prelates.

195. The method of proceeding in this particular Congregation is this: The provincial synod which is to be examined is referred to one of the consultors, who is chosen for the purpose by the secretary with the consent of the cardinal-prefect. This consultor diligently examines all the decrees of the synod and gives his animadversions thereon in writing noting the pages to which reference is made. These animadversions are then printed and given to each of the cardinals and consultors. The consultors then meet with the secretary and give their opinions on the criticism. Later the cardinals meet and after the

secretary has submitted the opinions of the consultors, they decide on the corrections which should be made in the decrees of the provincial council and on the letter which should be written to the metropolitan regarding the matter.

196. The Congregation on ECCLESIASTICAL IMMUNITY which was instituted by Pope Urban VIII., and formerly had much work to perform, is to-day only an appendix of the Congregation of the Council. It is not known whether Urban VIII. established the Congregation orally or by a decree in Consistory or by a brief; but its work was to protect and defend ecclesiastical jurisdiction and immunity, so that this immunity might not be violated and the jurisdiction of the Church might not be usurped by secular magistrates and communities. Several cardinals and prelates constituted the Congregation. The latter were to examine and report the cases in a summary way; and then, without any judicial process but through information obtained by familiar letters sent to and from the ordinaries, apostolic nuncios and other prelates whom the business concerned, a decision was reached. The Congregation formerly met twice a month in the apostolic palace, but to-day, on account of the great changes in the civil laws of most countries, very little business is left the Congregation to do, because there is scarcely any immunity for ecclesiastical persons or things recognized by civil governments. Hence vacancies that occur in the offices of this Congregation are no longer filled; and work which would belong to it, is now done either through the office of the Secretary of State by

concordat, or through the Sacred Congregation of the Council.

197. The Council of Trent laid great stress on the obligation of residence, and enacted severe laws against beneficiaries who are absent from their benefices longer than the usual three months allowed each year. On bishops especially is urged the observance of this law; and hence also Pope Urban VIII. on December 11, 1634, instituted a special Congregation to see to the enforcement of the obligation and to examine and report to the Sovereign Pontiff the reasons for which permission is requested by bishops for a longer absence than is allowed by law. This work had been done previously by the Congregation of the Council.

Originally the CONGREGATION ON THE RESIDENCE OF BISHOPS consisted of six cardinals with the cardinal-vicar of Rome as prefect and the secretary of the Congregation of the Council as secretary, both holding these positions *ex officio*. Pope Benedict XIV., on September 3, 1746, confirmed the establishment of this Congregation and added to its duties. At the same time he decreed that it should not meet regularly, but only when some business was referred to it by the Roman Pontiff. Thus it happened that gradually much of the work of this Congregation was done by others; and to-day, though the title of a Congregation on the Residence of Bishops still remains, nevertheless the cardinal-vicar of Rome and the secretary of the Congregation of the Council are the only members of it. They both hold *ex officio*, and perform what duties may be assigned to them;

the chief of which is to receive and place before the Sovereign Pontiff requests made by bishops for leave of absence from their dioceses. Rescripts relative to these matters are forwarded by the cardinal-vicar of the city.

CHAPTER X.

THE CONGREGATION OF BISHOPS AND REGULARS; AND THE CONGREGATION ON REGULAR DISCIPLINE AND ON THE STATE OF REGULARS.

198. Among the various Congregations of Cardinals is one whose special duty is to settle affairs which concern bishops and regulars. It is called the Congregation of Bishops and Regulars, not because it is composed of them but because it has charge of affairs which concern them. At first there were two Congregations established for this work; one in regard to consultations by bishops, the other in regard to consultations by regulars. The former seems to have been established by Pope Gregory XIII., the latter certainly by Pope Sixtus V. in a brief dated May 17, 1586. Thus there was a distinct Congregation for the secular and another for the regular clergy of the Church. But since uniformity and harmony, not only in judicial decisions but also in the spirit of government, are necessary for the greatest good of the Church and the best development of both secular and regular clergy, it was deemed wise to unite these two Congregations as the most efficacious means of assuring these objects. This was done in the year 1601, and therefore the present Congregation of Bishops and Regu-

lars has all the powers which the two separate Congregations formerly had.

199. The Congregation by rule has twenty-four cardinals assigned to it, though practically the number depends on the Sovereign Pontiff. At present twenty-nine belong to this Congregation, one of whom is the prefect. The secretary is a prelate, and so also are the subsecretary, who assists the secretary, and the summista, whose duty is to prepare a compendious exposition of the causes brought before the Congregation. It has also a judge-relator, not a cleric, on whom it is incumbent in criminal causes brought to the Congregation by way of appeal, to report the state of the case to the assembled cardinals in order that they may judge whether the sentence of the lower court is to be confirmed, reversed, or modified in some way. In these causes the fiscal procurator general also participates for the purpose of defending the sentence of the episcopal court. In causes of greater moment which are not criminal, a cardinal is designated by the Sacred Congregation, whose duty is to consider and report the cases assigned to him. This cardinal is called the cardinal-relator or the Most Eminent relator in respect to these cases.

Before the time of Pope Gregory XVI. the Congregation had no consultors. But on September 5, 1834, a decree was issued by which a number were assigned to it, without, however, interfering with the previous practice of the Congregation in designating a certain cardinal to act as the Most Eminent relator for a certain cause. At present six prelates and twenty-one members of religious orders are consultors. The office of the Congregation is in the Palazzo della Cancellaria Apostolica.

200. By virtue of the constitution of Sixtus V., the Congregation of Bishops and Regulars confirmed by him has competency in all causes and business which concern bishops and the proper administration of their dioceses, excepting only those cases which involve an interpretation of the Council of Trent. Hence it is competent to receive appeals made to the Apostolic See against bishops, either by their subjects or by members of religious orders; it can also take cognizance of lesser criminal charges against bishops, to hear and terminate which it has ordinary jurisdiction; it takes cognizance also of greater criminal causes of bishops, but only by delegation of the Sovereign Pontiff, that is, the Pontiff must first know and approve the intention of the Congregation in the matter and then confirm its acts. Further, the Congregation replies to difficulties and questions which may arise in the administration of a diocese and summarily hears and decides causes respecting churches and jurisdiction whether these concern the chapter or individual persons.

Again the Congregation examines and approves or disapproves the alienation of church property, for which permission is required from the Apostolic See. Finally it assigns a vicar apostolic to a bishop who may be unable or incompetent to discharge the onerous duties of his office, and examines the causes which demand the removal of a vicar-capitular or even of a bishop, the Sovereign Pontiff being first consulted. An instance of removal of a bishop occurred not long ago in Belgium, where the bishop of Tournai was removed by a decree of the Congregation of Bishops and Regulars.

201. Cardinal DeLuca writes thus of the powers of this Congregation: "This Congregation has full power of acting even in those things which are peculiar to other Congregations; wherefore it appears to be, as Urban VIII. said, in a certain sense a universal Congregation, except for those causes which directly concern questions of faith or the formal interpretation of the Council of Trent; in other cases, though there is a Congregation of the Council, still the Congregation of Bishops and Regulars takes cognizance of what concerns the execution and observance of the council and its decrees. In the same way, although there is a Congregation of Rites, whose peculiar duty is to hear and decide controversies on precedence and ecclesiastical pre-eminence between secular and regular clerics as well as to consider the claims of laymen to participate in ecclesiastical functions, still this Congregation of Bishops and Regulars has full competency in all these causes. Therefore the exclusive right of the Congregation of Rites is limited to prescribing for divine worship and to the canonization of saints."

202. The Congregation of Bishops and Regulars, inasmuch as it is a Congregation for regulars, by virtue of the same constitution of Sixtus V., treats the affairs of all regular orders and communities. Thus it settles contentions which arise between different religious orders, or·within the same order; it examines disturbances and complaints caused by the election of a superior general or other superiors, or by their conduct in administering their office. It

permits a religious to go from one order to another of stricter observance, and takes cognizance of those who leave their monasteries. Also it considers and decides concerning the establishment and suppression of monasteries. In a word, this Congregation, has competency in all that regards the proper rule and direction of religious orders in the Church. Hence it is said to be the busiest of all Congregations and the principal one in regard to the multiplicity of its affairs, excepting the Propaganda.

203. The method of proceeding in the Congregation of Bishops and Regulars is not the same to-day as it was formerly. Hence different authors give different methods in accordance with the time in which they write.* Plettenberg says that in the year 1693 all business of the Congregation was conducted in an informal and summary way, and therefore controversies were terminated before it as before princes without the form of trial, but with only a certainty of the facts obtained through extra-judicial information. He adds that all business, even the most important, was done by this Congregation without any charge whatever, even for the necessary writings and papers relating to the causes.

204. The present method was made of obligation by a decree of September 5, 1834, at which time the working of the Congregation was somewhat re-organized and consultors were added whose duty is to examine and give an opinion on doubts and questions which may be referred to them by the cardinals.

Of the business coming to the Congregation some is of lesser importance or of urgent need. In such cases, if the cardinal-prefect and the secretary consider it better to attend to the matter without bringing it before the Congregation, after acquiring information extra-judicially and at times secretly, they determine the decision themselves. Nevertheless they use the name and authority of the Congregation in issuing the resolution and in sending it to the bishops whom it concerns or to the general procurators of religious orders, residing in Rome, if it pertains to regulars.

Again there are other matters which are proposed to the cardinals in Congregation and are decided by them, but without certain formalities which are observed in the treatment of contentious causes or of those of great importance. When matters are settled by such procedure, they are first proposed in the Congregation by the secretary, who explains in a compendious way the petitions of the parties and the documents which bear on them. After deliberation or discussion each cardinal gives his opinion, and what seems best to the majority is made the decision of the Congregation. In these meetings the secretary has no vote. They are now held in the palace of the apostolic chancery once a month on Friday, but during Lent once a week, also on Friday.

206. If the cardinals determine that the matter in hand needs more accurate treatment they order the regular method to be followed, and assign a cardinal-relator to present the case. Then the following rules enacted by the Congregation must be strictly followed:

1°. Whenever in business brought before the Congregation, either by reports of ordinaries or by appeals of parties, it seems expedient that the matter should follow the course of law, a reply is made: "Let the parties present their case before the Most Eminent —— who will examine and report it, after the opposing party has been cited and the form of the *dubium* or question has been agreed upon."

2°. All the acts which prepare the way for judgment are prepared before the cardinal-relator or his auditor, with the aid of a notary of the Sacred Congregations.

3°. Wherefore the interested party in the presence of the same auditor summons the opposing party into court to agree upon the form of doubt or question under which the matter in dispute is to be presented to the Congregation; otherwise it is taken for granted that the form which is submitted with the notice is acceptable.

4°. The Most Eminent relator or his auditor by consent of the parties arranges the wording of the doubt either as proposed or as amended; but if they cannot agree he orders them to use their right before the Congregation by means of a memorial on the matter.

5°. If the cited party fails to appear within the specified time, he is cited a second time to arrange the *dubium* or doubt and to specify the date for the meeting of the Congregation on the matter.

6°. If the party continues in contumacy, the Most Eminent relator or his auditor prepares the *dubium* and assigns the meeting wherein the cause shall be proposed, allowing however a period of thirty days to intervene; a decree on the matter is sent to the adverse party by a messenger.

7°. A copy of the claims, rights or laws which each party uses is deposited with the secretary fifteen days before the day of proposing the cause, and information to this effect is mutually given.

8°. The allegations of both parties are brought to the cardinals, to the secretary and to the secretariate of the Congregation ten days before the meeting.

9°. On the same day in the house of the auditor of the Most Eminent relator a mutual interchange of the allegations and summaries is made by the parties.

10°. The replies are made and distributed as in the preceding number, three days before the proposing of the cause.

11°. The Most Eminent relator puts into writing the resolution of the Sacred Congregation, signs it with his name and gives it to the secretary to be communicated to the parties.

12°. If within ten days the defeated party asks to be heard again, the Most Eminent relator can grant the benefit of a new hearing.

13°. Whenever by unanimous vote the matter is decided with the clause *et amplius*, or with one dissenting vote and the clause *et non concedatur*, then permission to return is not given except by the full Congregation.

14°. The cause is proposed the second time in the same manner and intervals as at first.

15°. The cause being decided, an authentic copy of the resolution is given to the winning party.

16°. The victor presents himself before the auditor of the Camera; who, merely as the executor, decrees the enforcement of the resolution of the Sacred Congregation.

207. In criminal causes when an appeal is taken to the Congregation of Bishops and Regulars the fol-

lowing is the method of proceeding as ordered by the Congregation December 16, 1834, with the approval of Pope Gregory XVI:

1°. Those convicted in criminal cases by episcopal courts are given ten days within which to appeal to the Sacred Congregation of Bishops and Regulars.

2°. The ten days will be counted, not from the day on which sentence was given, but from the day on which it was announced by messenger to the defendant or his advocate.

3°. That time having elapsed without the defendant or his advocate appealing, the bishop will execute the sentence passed by him.

4°. An appeal being interposed within the ten days, the episcopal court will at once send to the Sacred Congregation the written acts of the whole case, namely: first the process itself prepared in court; secondly, a brief of it or a compendious statement of all that came from the process; thirdly, the defense offered by the defendant; fourthly, the sentence passed.

5°. The episcopal court itself will announce to the defendant or his advocate that the appeal is to be prosecuted before this same Congregation.

6°. If no one appears, or if the acts of the appeal are negligently or maliciously protracted, a congruous time will be assigned to the Sacred Congregation, which being passed without use, the cause will be considered deserted and the sentence of the episcopal court will be ordered executed.

7°. The brief of the process which is made by the judge-relator of the Congregation, must be given to the defendant or to him who has undertaken his defense. (This judge-relator, as was said above, is not a cardinal nor even a cleric.)

8°. The allegations or defense which are to be distributed to the Most Eminent Fathers shall not be printed unless the judge-relator shall have given permission to print.

9°. The cause shall be decided on the appointed day by the Most Eminent Fathers in general assembly.

10°. The fiscal procurator general and the judge-relator shall be present at this meeting.

11°. The judge-relator shall report to the Most Eminent Fathers on the whole state of the cause; and the fiscal procurator general shall stand for the episcopal court and explain his conclusions.

12°. After this the Most Eminent Fathers will give judgment, either confirming, reversing or reforming the sentence of the episcopal court.

13°. The sentence being pronounced, it shall be sent together with all the acts of the cause to the episcopal court, that it may be executed.

14°. A revision or rehearing of the matter adjudicated shall not be granted, unless power to grant it shall have been given by His Holiness and unless there are very weighty reasons, the consideration and judgment of which pertain to the full Congregation.

208. Besides the Congregation of Bishops and Regulars, another Congregation was instituted to assist it, on August 4, 1698, by Pope Innocent XII. under the title of the CONGREGATION FOR THE DISCIPLINE AND REFORMATION OF REGULARS. This Congregation formerly had its own prefect but to-day by order of Pope Pius IX. under date of March 12, 1856, is under the cardinal-prefect of the

Congregation of Bishops and Regulars. Likewise it no longer has it own secretary, but the secretary for Bishops and Regulars performs the duties of this office. However, it has an official who is called the substitute. The work of this Congregation consists chiefly in designating in Italy and the adjacent islands monasteries or convents of men where novices and the professed of religious orders are to dwell, and also in granting permission for novices to receive the habit and make their religious profession. Further, this Congregation looks to the observance of perfect community life and can dispense from rules in regard to the internal discipline of a religious house. However, most of its work is now done through the Congregation of Bishops and Regulars. It is known to-day by the name of the Congregation for Regular Discipline.

209. Finally Pope Pius IX. in order to provide for the changed conditions of the present time in regard to regulars, on June 17, 1847, instituted a particular Congregation whose title is the CONGREGATION ON THE STATE OF REGULARS. This Congregation had the duty of preparing rules for the reception and instruction of novices, and for admitting them first to simple and afterwards to solemn vows. It also made regulations for restoring community life among regulars to the actually existing circumstances. When not long ago a vacancy occurred in the office of prefect of this Congregation on the State of Regulars, it was not filled, but Pope Leo XIII. reserved the position for himself. The secretary of the Congregation is the same who is secretary to that of Bishops and Regulars.

CHAPTER XI.

THE CONGREGATION FOR THE PROPAGATION OF FAITH.

210. For English-speaking countries the Congregation of the Propaganda is of all the most interesting, because to it the dioceses of these countries at the present time are subject. While the necessities of other dioceses making recourse to the Holy See, are tended to by the various Congregations set over questions of faith, of worship or of discipline, all the business which the faithful of missionary countries, clergy and laity, may have with the Holy See, is done and must be done through the one Congregation of the Propaganda.

The Congregation for the Propagation of Faith, as its name implies, was instituted for the purpose of propagating the Catholic faith in those regions where infidelity and heresy prevail. Pope Gregory XV. established it, June 22, 1622, by his constitution *Inscrutabili* and gave it most ample powers. He says: "We have thought it well to commit this work to the peculiar solicitude of several of our venerable brethren, cardinals of the Holy Roman Church, as by the tenor of these presents we do commit and assign. We wish that, with the help of some prelates of the Roman Church and other religious men and a secretary, they consult about, take cognizance of and treat all and every kind of business which pertains to the propagation of the faith in the whole world. We wish further, that they refer to us the more important matters which they treat, but other matters they shall decide and expedite according to their own prudence. They shall superintend all missions for the preaching and teaching of the Gospel and Catholic doctrine, and shall appoint and change the necessary ministers. For by our apostolic authority over these matters, by these presents we concede and impart to them the full, free and ample faculty, authority and power to work, carry on, treat, do and execute both the foregoing and also all and everything else which is necessary or opportune for the purpose, even if it is such that it requires a special, specific and express mention."

211. The jurisdiction of the Propaganda extends to all countries in which Catholic affairs are managed *more missionum*, after the manner of missions; or in other words, it covers fully two-thirds of the world. For church purposes the world is divided into those countries which have the ordinary hierarchy and those which have missions. The former are those which have episcopal sees and dioceses canonically erected and whose bishops have ordinary jurisdiction, so that each bishop administers his diocese not as a vicar or delegate of the Sovereign Pontiff, but as an ordinary who obtains jurisdiction by promotion to an episcopal see. The latter or missionary countries are those which lack such episcopal sees and whose ecclesiastical affairs are administered by delegates and vicars of the Sovereign Pontiff.

Such vicars apostolic usually receive episcopal consecration and a title from some ancient see, which because of infidelity or heresy no longer exists except in name; but through promotion to these ancient titles they do not obtain jurisdiction anywhere. Hence they are called titular bishops, and the jurisdiction they have in their vicariates flows entirely from the special delegation of the Sovereign Pontiff. However the most ample jurisdiction, far above the ordinary, is granted them by way of delegation for the whole tract of country assigned them as a vicariate.

212. In this way, then, church affairs are managed wherever infidels and heretics exceed Catholics in number and power, and the faithful of such countries with all their missionaries, prefects and vicars apostolic are subject to the Propaganda as their superior. But even after the ecclesiastical hierarchy has been established or restored and episcopal sees canonically erected, the Propaganda frequently retains the government of these countries. Thus in the United States, England, Ireland, Scotland, Australia, Canada, Holland and other countries, there are regularly established episcopal sees with their titles and bishops, but nevertheless all these countries are still subject to the Propaganda.

The rule is that whenever the hierarchy is established in any country, the apostolic letters, which erect the episcopal sees, decree at the same time whether or not the new sees shall be withdrawn from the jurisdiction of the Congregation of the Propaganda. If they are not specifically withdrawn they remain still subject. This is considered a special favor, because it affords them an easier, more expeditious and less expensive method of doing their business with the Holy See. Hence besides over missionary countries, the Propaganda exercises its watchfulness and authority also over others which have the ordinary hierarchy of the Church regularly established. Over all, too, it has the same ample jurisdiction and is practically the mouth of the Holy See.

213. The power of the Propaganda extends to all matters and causes, and is limited only by the one condition that it cannot enact or expedite affairs of greater importance without the assent of the Sovereign Pontiff. All ecclesiastical causes no matter what their kind, which pertain to missionary regions are subject to the jurisdiction of the Congregation of the Propaganda.

This power of the Propaganda is legislative, judicial and gubernative. For such are the words of the constitution by which it was established that it can do all and everything which it may deem expedient. Hence not only can it judicially decide all causes and controversies but it can also make laws and decrees, and can rule and govern missionaries, even the vicars apostolic, as subjects. The one limitation of this threefold power is that no grave matter shall be settled until after a report has been made of it to the Sovereign Pontiff.

From this it is evident that for the places subject to it, the Propaganda has as much power as all the other Congregations together have for other countries. Indeed it has even greater power, for it treats the business of deputing vicars apostolic in missionary countries and the election of bishops in those dioceses, which though canonically erected, are still subject to it. The Propaganda is therefore the organ through which the Sovereign Pontiff appoints these vicars and bishops; and likewise the organ through which they are removed. An instance of removal occurred in the United States on May 21, 1895. On that day the archbishop of St. Louis, by a decree of the general Congregation of the Propaganda, approved by Pope Leo XIII., was removed from the archbishopric of St. Louis because of failing mind, and assigned to the see of Marcianopolis as titular archbishop.

It may be noted that whenever a matter is sent to the Propaganda which directly concerns faith, this Congregation sends it to the Congregation of the Holy Office. Likewise if a matter pertains directly to the forum of conscience, it requests a proper remedy or solution of the question from the Sacred Penitentiary. In each case, however, the answer is usually returned through the Propaganda.

214. The decrees of the general Congregation of the Propaganda have the force and value of apostolic constitutions, whenever they are issued by the prefect and subscribed by the secretary; for such is the decree of Urban VIII. on the subject. Moreover this decree was confirmed by Pope Innocent X. on July 30, 1625; for, it being reported to the Holy See that in the Phillipine islands some missionaries asserted "that the decrees of the Propaganda made only a probable opinion and were a pure and simple declaration, and therefore the contrary of the decree could also be defended," Pope Innocent X. at once declared this opinion untenable and re-enacted that

by virtue of the constitution of Gregory XV. the decrees which are issued by this Congregation with the authority of the Sovereign Pontiff have the force of apostolic constitutions.

215. Likewise Pope Pius IX. in his constitution, *Probe*, of May 9, 1853, very distinctly meets the objection, which is sometimes urged to-day, that what is done by the Propaganda is not always the work of the Holy See. He says: "There is nothing more senseless than what these priests are reported to have scattered abroad to ensnare the simplicity of the faithful, namely, that there are many things which have been enacted, not by the Apostolic See and the Roman Pontiff, but which have been ordered without his knowledge by the Sacred Congregation for the Propagation of the Faith; and that there are some things which need not be minded because the placet of civil authority has not been given. All know that our Sacred Congregation is nothing unless the minister of the Apostolic See. Moreover it is a foul and impious assertion that the rights divinely conferred on the Apostolic See and the helm and power of supreme rule in the Church which was given by Christ the Lord, can be lessened, curtailed or prescribed by human decisions or favor." They are therefore entirely wrong who say the decrees of the Sacred Congregation of the Propaganda are not of obligation; for all its decrees are the work of the Holy See itself and have the force of apostolic constitutions. In disciplinary matters such decrees are the supreme law, and coming from proper ecclesiastical authority they demand obedience. No appeal from the Propaganda's decision is possible to

any other tribunal; but parties who feel themselves aggrieved may beg a rehearing from the Congregation itself, for its decrees are not irreformable. In the meantime, however, the decrees are of absolute obligation.

216. The Roman Pontiffs decreed that all business should be done in the Congregation of the Propaganda without any charge whatever, and in order that this might be possible they assigned such revenues and established such endowments as would enable the Congregation itself to pay all costs. From this it is apparent that the dioceses which remain subject to the Propaganda even after their canonical establishment, have a great advantage in this, that all their business with the Holy See is done without charge. The other dioceses, however, belonging to the ordinary hierarchy are obliged to pay regularly constituted fees for all documents issued and costs for all trials held before most of the other Congregations.

217. The principal work of the Propaganda is the spreading of the Catholic faith throughout the world, and particularly in missionary countries. That this might be accomplished, a college was established by Pope Urban VIII., called the Urban college or the college of the Propaganda, wherein young men born in missionary countries are received, instructed in letters, languages and theology, and then sent back to their native land to be faithful missionaries for the preservation and propagation of the faith. This college is in the palace of the Propaganda, erected on the Piazza di Spagna, by Urban VIII. for the use of the secretary and other officials

of the Congregation and for the holding of its general meetings. In the same building, but towards the other end, there is also an immense printing establishment, where documents needed for administering the affairs of the Congregation are printed, and where summaries of various causes sent to the Propaganda for final judgment, are put into type for the use of the cardinals and officials. Books on theology and philosophy, and pamphlets on kindred subjects are printed in various languages in this polyglot establishment and distributed free in missionary countries, if necessity requires it.

The beginning of this college and printing establishment was laid by John Baptist Villes, a Spaniard dwelling in Rome, who gave all his wealth and a most beautiful house to Pope Urban VIII. for this purpose. Many generous souls even to the present day have imitated his example and contributed to the great work of spreading the Gospel of Christ. (*Jus Pontificium, sub Propaganda.*)

218. Formerly in this same palace of the Propaganda, apartments were provided for missionaries who returned to Rome to inform the Sovereign Pontiff and the Congregation in regard to their missions, and to suggest means for further propagating the faith. Poor priests and bishops from other places, also, were comfortably lodged and fed in this palace during their stay in Rome on business. But all this has been completely changed, either because of a diminution of the revenues of the Propaganda or for other reasons. Even the poorest of vicars apostolic must now seek other quarters and provide for himself as best he can. In fact Rome and the Propa-

ganda have been so overrun with visiting clergymen that lately an order was issued prohibiting them from remaining longer than two months in the city without special permission of their ordinary.

219. The Propaganda has sent out and still sends out many missionaries to preach the Gospel and administer the sacraments, and for this purpose it provides them all with most ample faculties. Further than this, it has arranged an extraordinary title for their ordination, called the title of the mission, by which it takes them under its own special protection. Even in dioceses canonically erected, priests ordained *titulo missionis* still remain under this special protection of the Propaganda; and the Congregation always insists on their proper maintenance by the diocese to which they belong. In a strictly legal sense a priest ordained by this title is bound directly to the Propaganda, and indirectly to the diocese or province to which he swears to devote his services. This follows also from the instruction given by the Propaganda on April 27, 1871, in regard to the title for ordination. This instruction says that ordinaries cannot confer any orders on clerics with the title of mission unless they have a special indult from the Holy See to this effect; because there is question of an extraordinary title which is beyond the common law. Such an indult is granted for a specified time or for a certain number of ordinations.

220. The same instruction says that ordinaries may use the services of priests ordained by other titles than that of mission, and that such priests cannot be forced to change their title for that of

mission. On the contrary, the Sacred Congregation explicitly asks of ordinaries that other legitimate titles be introduced as much as possible instead of the title of mission. From this it follows that the Propaganda with the consent of the ordinary will readily grant a priest who has been ordained *titulo missionis* a dispensation from his oath and a change of title into that of patrimony. This change, however, can be granted only by the Propaganda; and the same is to be said of permission to join a religious order.

221. The oath taken by the priest who is ordained *titulo missionis* is to the effect that he will not join any religious order or community without the special permission of the Apostolic See, and that he will perpetually labor in the ministry for the good of souls under the entire direction and jurisdiction of the ordinary for whose diocese he is ordained. This oath of the priest, it should be remarked, does not give a bishop in a missionary country any more extensive power than a bishop has elsewhere. The general principles of canon law must be observed by both. Hence a bishop, at least in the United States, cannot transfer a priest from place to place merely at will without considering his merits and reputation. This is clearly settled by the latest decision of the Propaganda, addressed to the bishops of the United States, under date of March 28, 1887, entitled, "On the way of procedure in changing a movable rector." It says: "In the Third Plenary Council of Baltimore, tit. X., chap. 3, par. 1, 2, as also in the instruction of this Sacred Congregation which begins *Cum Magnopere*, for trials of clerics,

the rules and regulations were prescribed by which clerics are to be tried. It was not, however, defined and decreed in what cases the bishops were held to follow the legal process when there was question of depriving movable rectors of missions of their office, or of transferring them to another office. Now, however, the Most Eminent Fathers placed over the Sacred Congregation of the Propaganda, meeting in general assembly on the 28th of March, 1887, have decreed thus: In the case of the removal or of a total deprivation of the office of rector in punishment of crime or guilt which requires disciplining, the canonical procedure in accord with the aforesaid instruction and with the decrees of the Third Plenary Council must be followed. If there be question of the transfer of a rector from one mission to another, or even to an inferior office, the ordinaries are not bound to follow the canonical procedure; but it is necessary that there should be serious reason for such action, and full account taken of the past merits, as laid down in the Third Plenary Council of Baltimore, tit. 2, chap. 5, parag. 32. If in the case of such transfer a complaint is made to the Sacred Congregation, the Sacred Congregation will remit it to the Metropolitan, or where there is question of a Metropolitan to the neighboring Metropolitan."

222. From this decree it appears that no canonical procedure is necessary for changing a movable rector when no crime is charged. The conscientious judgment of the bishop of the necessity of such transfer is sufficient for his guidance; yet he is obliged to hold himself in readiness, on presentation of com-

plaint to his and the priest's superior to give the motives which may have induced him to make the transfer. If these motives are not clearly sufficient a reversal of the bishop's action will follow. The presumption is against transfers, and the burden of proof of the wisdom and equity of the transfer rests upon the bishop who has followed an exceptional course. The instruction of the Propaganda of 1879 clearly lays down the law and establishes the presumption in favor of the permanent tenure of the priest as against removal, when it says: "Bishops must be careful not to transfer priests from place to place against their will except for serious reasons."

223. Priests who have been removed or transferred are bound to recognize the action of the bishop, no matter how unjust it may appear. They must give up the office and can appeal only in *divolutivo*, as it is called. After a regular trial this is true even of irremovable rectors in the United States, because of the special enactment of the Third Council of Baltimore to this effect with the consent of the Holy See. Ordinarily an appeal from the sentence of a court ordering removal from an office or benefice, will stay the execution until the higher court has passed judgment. This in fact is a fundamental principle of canon law, but decree 286 of the Third Council of Baltimore reverses this principle for the United States, though not for other countries. It reads as follows: "As in many of our provinces the rectors of our churches are by law appointed as *ex officio* trustees of the churches, caution is to be used lest when it is found necessary to deprive a rector of his office, he should by appeal from the sentence stop its

execution, and thereby keep before the civil authority his position of trustee. We decree, with the consent of the Holy See, that no rector, even an irremovable one, who has been juridically removed, or deposed from or deprived of his office, shall be able to appeal against the ordinary's sentence *in suspensivo* (to suspend its execution) but only *in divolutivo*, (the appeal taking effect only after sentence in the higher court), so that he shall cease to be a trustee of the church, either forever or until such time as the appellate judge giving a final decision shall reinstate him. Therefore until the matter is finally settled, another rector or administrator with proper powers shall be appointed and the bishop shall meanwhile provide for the proper maintenance of the removed rector and the administrator."

* Equity and prudence might suggest that the law itself, which so reverses an established principle of canon law, should also specifically provide for the support of the appealing rector. Leaving the allowance for his support to the judge who condemned him gives an opening for injustice and complaints, particularly when ecclesiastical courts are not fully organized and their procedure depends entirely on the will of the bishop of the diocese.

224. The Congregation of the Propaganda at the present time is composed of twenty-seven cardinals, one of whom is appointed by the Pope general prefect and another prefect of economy. Sixteen of these cardinals reside *in curia*; the others are bishops of residential sees in various countries. There are also two secretaries, one for the Latin or general

OFFICIALS OF PROPAGANDA. 221

Congregation and the other for the Congregation on Oriental Affairs. Both of these secretaries are titular archbishops, because of the great importance of the office, and because they have to correspond frequently with bishops and archbishops. For the general Propaganda there are a large number of consultors, usually twenty-four, chosen from both the secular and the regular clergy. The assessor of the Holy Office is *ex officio* a member of the Propaganda. Five minutanti superintend as many departments and direct subsecretaries or scrittori how to arrange, digest and prepare the causes or business of the different countries for submission to the general assembly of the Propaganda. They also attend to the correspondence of the Congregation, which, however, is always signed by the cardinal-prefect and the secretary. An archivist attends to the proper record and custody of documents. The minutanti receive a salary of forty dollars a month, but the head minutante receives forty-five dollars. Some of the consultors are paid eighty dollars a year, but they hold other positions or are members of religious orders.

A commission, consisting of an archbishop as president and a prelate as secretary, together with twelve consultors, is attached to the Propaganda and subject to it, whose work is to receive and examine the reports of bishops and vicars apostolic, under the Propaganda, concerning their churches. Another commission of the Propaganda, with a cardinal president, a vice-president, a secretary and four consultors, examines the constitutions and rules of new religious institutes which are subject to this

Congregation. Further, the cardinal-prefect of economy is assisted by eight signori who have charge of various departments and make up "the administration."

When Gregory XV. instituted the Propaganda, it was composed of thirteen cardinals, two priests, one monk and a secretary. Cardinal deLuca says that in his time it was made up of a competent but varying number of cardinals and of other prelates, together with officials of a lower order. One of the prelates was secretary, and the assessor of the Holy Office and one protonotary apostolic were also officials of this Congregation.

The cardinal-prefect general of the Propaganda holds a most important position, for he is practically in charge of the church affairs of two-thirds of the world. Hence he is familiarly called the red Pope; red because he is a cardinal, and Pope because of his power and influence.

The cardinal-prefect of economy has supervision over the business affairs of the Propaganda, and looks after its endowment funds and revenues.

225. There are at the present time two divisions of the Propaganda, one for general or Latin affairs, and the other for affairs of the oriental rite. Even as early as the time of Urban VIII. and Clement IX. special commissions or committees were formed of some cardinals of the Propaganda, "On Questions of the Orientals" and "On Correcting Oriental Books." But as the eastern nations acquired freer communication with the Holy See, and as the countries of North America, particularly in our century, made wonderful progress in Catholic faith, questions of

all kinds were poured upon the Propaganda in such numbers that it was deemed best to divide the work. For this purpose on January 6, 1862, Pope Pius IX. issued a constitution establishing a new and special Congregation for the treatment and direction of all the affairs of the oriental churches or rites.

These points may be noted in the constitution of Pius IX. 1°. All the affairs which heretofore pertained to the Congregation for the Propagation of the Faith, shall be divided for the future into two classes, namely, into affairs of the Latin rite, and into affairs of the oriental rite; in such a way that the new Congregation shall treat all the affairs of the orientals, even mixed ones which either because of persons or things are connected with the Latins, unless this newly-organized Congregation shall at times think it best to refer these things to the general Congregation of the Propaganda. 2°. The new Congregation will retain the title of Propaganda, but will add, "for the affairs of the oriental rite;" and it will use the same seal as the Propaganda. 3°. The new Congregation, over which the cardinal-prefect of the Congregation of the Propaganda will preside, will be composed of a sufficient number of cardinals of the same Congregation and will have its own consultors, and a distinct secretary and secretariate with its officials. The cardinals will divide among themselves the business proper to each oriental nation, so that each cardinal in a stable way shall have in charge the causes of one or more nations as it may happen in the division. In this way each nation will always have a cardinal-relator who will be able to give the Congregation most accurate information on all affairs which belong to it.

226. Both these divisions of the Propaganda, however, constitute but one general Congregation. And although each division has its own secretary, and its own office and officials, still both have the same prefect, and all the cardinals of both divisions unite in the general assembly of the Propaganda. Further, in order to secure uniformity of action and concord in the work of propagating the faith, the offices of both divisions are adjacent to each other in the palace of the Propaganda, and the secretaries of both Congregations or divisions meet in the particular assemblies held before the cardinal-prefect, and each gives his opinion of all affairs, even those of the other division of which he has no charge.

At the present time twelve cardinals are in charge of the eastern affairs. They are assisted by sixteen consultors, four minutanti and seven interpreters.

227. There are two kinds of meetings of the Congregation of the Propaganda; the ordinary or particular and the general. The ordinary meetings are held usually every week at the rooms of the cardinal-prefect general, and at them are present only the secretaries of each division and a few minutanti and officials. In these ordinary meetings the business which has come in by letters and reports of missionaries or others, is brought up and the causes and business which must be referred to the general assembly of the Propaganda and to the Holy Father are placed aside. The other matters of lesser moment are decided and expedited by the cardinal-prefect and the secretary of the division to which the matter belongs. In these meetings also

some matters are brought up, on which it is advisable to obtain the votum or opinion of the consultors, who are selected either by the cardinal-prefect or the secretary. Ordinarily a cause is referred only to one consultor; but some are so intricate that several opinions are desirable before the matter is referred to the general assembly of the Propaganda for decision.

228. The general assembly or Congregation of the Propaganda is held usually once a month on Monday, or whenever called, in the palace of the Propaganda, and at it are present all the cardinals of the Propaganda and the secretaries of both divisions. This meeting is not secret, but open to those who may wish to attend, if they are properly introduced.

Most of the business of the Propaganda, from the nature of the Congregation, is done economically and extra-judicially. But because many questions must arise between missionaries, especially of different religious orders, which require thorough examination, the Propaganda necessarily hears and decides also contentious causes. This necessity is all the greater, now that the ordinary hierarchy is established in many countries still subject to the Propaganda. Contentious causes from such dioceses are treated in accordance with the general rules of canon law, as well as under the enactments which are peculiar to those countries.

229. All such questions, then, the Congregation decides by using the summary form of trial. And indeed up to our time the parties to a controversy could employ advocates in judicial causes, either criminal or civil, and could offer the cardinals of the

Congregation allegations and arguments prepared by them. But to-day, on account of abuses, most likely because business of great importance which should have been kept secret was divulged, it was ordered that advocates should no longer be admitted for defending causes. This, however, does not prevent parties to a controversy from preparing their side of the case in writing and being guided by a canonist in arranging their argument. The defense and argument, however, must be presented in the name of him who is a party to the cause and not in the name of his advocate as formerly. All such communications are to be offered to the cardinal-prefect, who will see that they receive proper attention. The Latin, Italian or French language must be used, not the English.

230. Matters brought before the general Congregation of the Propaganda are either reported by the secretary at the time of meeting or are printed and distributed to the cardinals several days before the meeting. In the former case the secretary verbally gives the cardinals gathered in Congregation a compendious exposition of the statements made by both parties to the controversy, as well as all documents bearing on the case. All these papers, when they were presented to the cardinal-prefect by the parties to the controversy, were carefully examined by the officials, and the points which made for each side arranged so that the secretary could easily combine them in his report to the meeting.

When the secretary concludes his report the cardinals discuss and decide the matter. A majority vote is definitive in any cause. The decision is then referred to the Holy Father and the decree which is issued mentions his assent.

231. When matters of a complicated or serious nature are in question, the cause is brought before the general Congregation *in folio* or in printed form. Such matters are usually first given to a consultor who will thoroughly examine both sides of the case as presented by the written petitions, testimony and arguments. He will then quote the laws bearing on the case and sum up the whole matter in an opinion or votum. This opinion, together with a proper synopsis of the whole cause and the dubia on which the vote is to be taken, is printed, and copies are distributed to the cardinals several days before the general Congregation. In the meantime all the cardinals study the matter for themselves, and betimes also others give them outside information. Hence they are usually prepared to give suffrage and decide the matter without much discussion in the assembly. The decree issued by the Congregation in such matters is always referred to the Sovereign Pontiff together with a report of the cause. Usually he approves at once, but he has been known to order some decrees to be modified before approving them.

CHAPTER XII.

CERTAIN RULES OF THE CONGREGATIONS.

232. Experience has proved that the institution of these Congregations in the Roman Court whereby the Sovereign Pontiff can so conveniently be assisted by the cardinals, is a most wise arrangement. The Sacred Congregations constitute so many tribunals of the Holy See and proceed in the name and authority of the Pope; and therefore each in its own province is a supreme tribunal to which all the faithful are bound to yield obedience, no matter what their dignity or position in the Church. For this reason no appeal can be taken from one tribunal or Congregation to another; but if the parties in litigation desire a re-hearing it must be had before the same tribunal, the proper permission being first obtained from it.

233. Certain criteria may be laid down for the better understanding of the workings of the Congregations. In the first place, these Congregations are tribunals of the Holy See in the external and visible guidance of the universal Church. Hence all the business transacted in these Congregations pertains to the external forum of the Church, and all petitions and recourse must be made with the name of the petitioner expressed. Affairs which belong to

the forum of conscience are referred to the Sacred Penitentiary.

The second criterion: To each Congregation a particular kind of business is assigned, as is apparent from the bull of institution and from the name itself of the Congregation. But excepting the questions which are characteristic of the various Congregations, as questions of faith for the Holy Office, of books for the Index, of interpreting the disciplinary decrees of Trent for the Congregation of the Council, excepting, then, such questions, in the course of time it has become customary for one or another of the Congregations indiscriminately to treat questions of lesser moment. In fact Innocent XII. on June 4, 1692, in his constitution, *Ut occuratur*, decreed that memorials rejected by one Congregation should not be received by another; further, if a favorable reply is obtained from this second Congregation it is declared utterly null and void. Hence when it becomes known that an application made to one Congregation has previously been made to another, a reply is made saying, "Recourse must be had to the former Congregation."

234. The third criterion: In the Sacred Congregations, business is usually not done without first hearing the ordinary of the petitioner or the superior general or provincial of the order whose members or rights may be affected by the business. For this reason, it is the practice of the Roman Court to ask from the ordinary or religious superior information and a votum or opinion on the recourse or petition which has been received.

Moreover, if the business touches some third person, in the request for information the clause is added, "having also heard those who are interested."

When a decision is reached a rescript is sent to the respective ordinary or religious superior for execution. The executor must execute the rescript himself unless it contains the faculty for subdelegation. If a rescript is to be executed against an ordinary or religious superior it is of course not sent to him, but to his superior for execution. Thus a decision given against a bishop would be executed by the metropolitan or an apostolic delegate.

235. The fourth criterion: A distinction must be made between extra-judicial and judicial business. Extra-judicial business is of greater or lesser moment. If the latter and it injures nobody, then such affairs are usually expedited by the cardinal-prefect and the secretary with one or more of the chief officials of the Congregation. And if the faculties received by the prefect and secretary cover the matter, a rescript is issued at once, otherwise application is made to His Holiness. But the graver extra-judicial matters, those which present some difficulty of law or fact requiring careful weighing of circumstances, are proposed to the general Congregation of cardinals and their opinion is asked.

Affairs of a judicial kind belong to the general Congregation and are decided by following at least the summary form of trial. The point at issue is previously determined and the doubt or doubts are proposed in a certain wording for solution. The formulæ of these doubts, if parties are contesting, are usually arranged by themselves or their advocates; otherwise they are determined *ex officio* by the secretary or his assessor. This is substantially the *litis contestio*. Hence also in judicial questions a defense of each side is always granted and considered; though this must be offered in writing, not orally, before most of the Congregations. Indeed if either party is contumacious or negligent in offering a defense for his side, it is made *ex officio*, and the reasons of law and fact in his favor are explained in it and laid before the cardinals in Congregation. Hence their decision is always made from a full knowledge of the whole case.

236. This is peculiar to the Roman Congregations: they give sentence purely and simply by replying affirmatively or negatively to the doubts proposed, or by sometimes adding *ad mentem*, which means a special disposition of the matter; but they never assign reasons for their decisions.

They represent the supreme judge and legislator in the Church, who need not explain his reasons for action. From this it follows, that it is not always sure that the cardinals are induced to give their decision on account of the reasons which are presented *in folio* by the secretary, or on account of the opinions of the consultors or the arguments of the parties and their advocates. For the cardinals themselves while studying the question before the meeting may be influenced by other motives than those offered, in deciding the matter.

It may be added that as a rule trials before the Congregations, except the Holy Office and the Index, are public. Sometimes, however, the nature of the case demands secrecy and then all concerned in such a cause, even the cardinal-judges, are bound to secrecy.

237. Certain clauses are frequently used by the Congregations in deciding matters, an explanation of which may be useful. A decision may be rendered with the clause, *et amplius*. This means that the matter having been fully examined and the decision being unanimous, the cause will not be heard again. The full Congregation only can grant a re-hearing when this clause is attached. *Et non concedatur*, means nearly the same, that is, a re-hearing will not be conceded.

If a negative reply is given to a petition, a mild refusal is put in the words *non expedire*, it is not expedient. A more forcible refusal is *nihil, relatum, lectum*.

Nihil, or nothing, means that the petition was not admitted, it being entirely incongruous. *Relatum* and *lectum*, mean that the petition was read but not admitted. *Non proposita*, means that the Congregation prefers not to reply. *Reponatur*, means that a reply is not given, but the petition is placed in the archives. *In decisis* or *in decretis*, means that this same petition, having been once presented and refused, the matter has been decided and will not be re-opened. *Gaudeat impetratis*, means, let the petitioner be satisfied with what he has already obtained. *Spectare ad episcopum*, is a clause which means that the petitioner should apply to the bishop who will follow the canonical requirements in the case, but he cannot act according to his own will. *Facto verbo cum sanctissimo*, means that the Congregation not having full authority in the matter, referred it to the Sovereign Pontiff.

Ad mentem, is often added to a decision and means either that the Congregation gives or explains its decision by private information sent to a person whose authority is to be saved from a public rebuke, or that an explanation is added to the decision itself in case a sentence which should be given according to strict law is modified in this special case because of certain equities. *Delata*, means that the matter is deferred to another meeting, either because there is no time to hear it, or because further information is required. *Delata ad primam* or *primam post proximam*, means that the matter has been deferred to the next or the first after the next meeting. *Post aquas*, means that the matter has been deferred to the meeting after the autumn rains. *Post agnos*, *post reges*, *post cineres*, mean respectively after Easter, after Epiphany, after Ash Wednesday.

238. Experience teaches that the Congregations, or at least some of the officials connected with them, take considerable time in concluding matters referred to them. Some give one reason for this delay, others another. As an instance of such delay, it may be mentioned that some consultors take over a year before they report on a cause referred to them. In the meantime most valuable interests are confused and not unfrequently jeopardized. Are the consultors responsible? Must they do so much other work that such important causes are but secondary to them?

Again it is very noticeable that among all the employes of the various Congregations, and even of the Propaganda itself, which deals with all English-speaking countries, there are very few, scarcely any, who know the English language,—a language which is used all over the globe and by more people than any other living tongue. The Latin, Italian and French are the only languages allowed before the Congregations. Why not allow all or none but the Latin exclusively? Have not the great political changes freed the Roman Court from any special obligations in this respect?

Having such and other facts in mind, many of the bishops of France in the Vatican Council issued this request (Martin collect. edit. 2, page 156) concerning those who are to be chosen for the Sacred College of Cardinals and the Roman Congregations and tribunals: "In the Sacred College of Cardinals and in the Roman Congregations and tribunals would that there were associated with most learned men, also many practical men, of those, namely, who are accustomed and long have had a hand in managing various ecclesiastical affairs; such are bishops, their vicars-general and officials, parish priests, the rectors of religious houses, missionaries in infidel countries." Another request of the same bishops tended to this, that the cardinals and the principal officials of the Roman Court should be taken from all nations.

CHAPTER XIII.

THE TRIBUNALS OF JUSTICE; THE ROTA, TREASURY APOSTOLIC, SIGNATURE OF JUSTICE.

239. From early times, yes, from the very beginning of the Church, the Sovereign Pontiff was surrounded by a large number of clerics who were to perform certain ecclesiastical or courtly duties and were called chaplains of the sacred palace. These chaplains were consulted by the Pontiff in causes for which it did not seem advisable to call a Consistory of the cardinals. Frequently, therefore, they were commanded to examine and report to him on particular matters, and thus became known as the councilors and referees of the Pope. Just as the cardinals in the course of time were assigned to different Congregations charged with the conduct of certain affairs, so likewise these clerics constituted three tribunals of justice in the Roman Court. These are the Roman Rota, the Reverend Apostolic Treasury, the Signature of Justice.

240. THE ROMAN ROTA, or the auditory of the sacred palace, is known to be of very ancient origin, but the precise time of its establishment cannot be ascertained. When after the days of Constantine peace was established in the Church, the Roman Pontiffs chose learned men from all nations of the Christian world for chaplains, and assigned to them

for examination and report the causes and controversies which came to the Roman Court from every nation. These chaplains or auditors were deputed not to pronounce judgment but only to hear and report causes. From their reports and replies sprang the decretals which Raymond of Pennafort, one of the auditors of the Rota, by order of Pope Gregory IX. compiled into the corpus of canon law.

241. Later, however, when the business of the Apostolic See increased and the Sovereign Pontiffs became engrossed with more important affairs, the faculty of not only hearing but also deciding cases was conferred upon the Rota; and under Pope John XXII. and his successors certain rules and statutes were laid down for its guidance in conducting the business committed to it for judgment.

Thus in the course of time this sacred tribunal became very eminent, and not only did the Popes refer to it the more important causes brought before the Holy See, but even emperors and kings gladly transferred to it controversies which in any way concerned them. Consequently it is not surprising that the tribunal of the Rota became more renowned than all other tribunals of the city and the world, both because of the integrity of its judges and because of the wisdom, method and authority of its judgments.

It is called the Rota because the auditors, seated in a circle, by turn examine controversies. The decisions of the Rota have very great weight in determining similar causes, and are eagerly sought by canonists; they are not, however, of obligation on anyone but the parties to the cause at issue. The

Rota must follow the law strictly in its decisions; while the Roman Congregations may sometimes modify their decisions by dispensing from the law to a certain extent, because they are participants of the Pope's power.

242. The judges of the Rota are called auditors, because when formerly they only heard cases, this name was given them, and now when they also decide controversies the primitive designation is retained. Before the time of Pope Sixtus IV. the tribunal of the Rota consisted of an indeterminate number of auditors; but this Pontiff ordained that for the future there should be twelve, neither more nor less. The senior auditor of the twelve presides over the tribunal and is called the dean of the Rota. At present there are only five auditors.

243. The Rota takes cognizance only of those causes which are committed to it by the Sovereign Pontiff. Usually these are not criminal, but civil causes which have been referred to the Holy See. The tribunal as a body has jurisdiction over all causes referred to it, even though each cause is assigned to a different judge by special commission. One peculiarity of the Rota is that if a cause is decided by it in the first or second instance, an appeal is taken to the same court in the third instance. This will not appear so strange when it is recollected that causes before the Rota are usually not judged by all the auditors, but by one on the vote of four others. Each cause brought in is assigned to the auditor whose turn it is to receive one. He is called the proponent of the cause, and in making his decision and passing sentence is bound to follow the votes

of the four auditors who sit next to him on the left. He himself has no vote, although he renders the decision. When therefore a cause comes up again on appeal, it rarely happens that it is committed to the same auditors. Sometimes, however, the commission reads that the cause must be judged by all the auditors. Then there can be no appeal to any other tribunal, but only a re-hearing by the Rota, if sufficient new evidence is produced to warrant such an order. A recourse may be had to the Pope from a decision of the Rota, because the Rota does not issue pontifical sentences.

244. The Rota at one time had very extensive jurisdiction in civil causes, especially for the pontifical states, and was used as a supreme court. This is one reason why causes from the universal Church began to be seldomer referred to it. Another is that with the increasing number of Congregations of Cardinals and their better acquaintance with law, the cardinals began to treat many causes that formerly went to the Rota. With the loss of the temporal power came the withdrawal of all civil causes from this tribunal; so that to-day the auditors of the Rota are assigned to other work than the hearing and deciding cases. Most of them are appointed to the various Congregations of Cardinals as consultors.

Still the college of auditors even now preserves its existence as a tribunal for the special assistance of the Sacred Congregation of Rites. The auditors collectively decide by a deliberative vote the worth of a process for the beatification or canonization of servants of God. Also, the Rota as a tribunal, is authorized to decide questions of precedence which may arise between ecclesiastical persons, and which being referred to the Congregation of Rites, are by the cardinal-prefect of the Congregation sent to the Rota to be examined and definitely decided.

245. The auditors of the Rota are chosen from various nations and hold their office for life, unless they resign or are deprived of it because of crime. Three of the auditors are selected from the city of Rome, one from France, one from Austria, two from Spain and the others from different parts of Italy. Whenever a vacancy occurs it is filled from the city or country whence the retiring auditor was selected. There are so many formalities necessary for the reception or admission of an auditor, that the appointee is apt to lose all patience. Likewise the expenses are so great that few covet the position or at least the admission to the circle or Rota.

246. Each auditor is obliged under pain of excommunication to be incurred *ipso facto* to preserve secrecy in regard to all votes given not only by himself but by his associates; and he is obliged to a like secrecy in regard to all matters which are treated collectively by the Rota. This is the decree of Urban VIII. The auditors are each allowed the help of a canonist who is called the auditor of study. He thoroughly examines each case and assists the auditor in preparing decisions. Another assistant is also allowed each auditor. Both of these assistants, however, are bound to the same secrecy as the auditor himself, and before beginning work must make an oath before the auditor to preserve secrecy in regard to the designated matters.

247. The judges of the Rota, besides being judges of causes, are at the same time chaplains and sub-deacons to the Sovereign Pontiff, and as such have a special office to fulfil in sacred functions. The office of auditor is therefore twofold, ministerial and judicial. Whenever the Pope solemnly celebrates, the auditors by turn serve him as sub-deacon; two of the older auditors assist the Pope to vest and unvest, and two others hold up the edges of his vestments. The others, in *cotta* and rochet remain near, ready to perform the duties assigned by the master of ceremonies according to the solemnity of the occasion. When the Pope does not celebrate but only assists at Mass, then the dean and the four senior auditors assist as above at the vesting and unvesting. The last auditor brings in the chalice. The auditors of the Rota have the right to wear a purple cassock and a hat bound with the same color. They may also use the *cappa* and *mantelletta* in various functions, and everywhere and in presence of everybody are allowed to wear the rochet.

248. Not unfrequently the auditors of the Rota are chosen bishops or archbishops or are sent as apostolic nuncios to kings and emperors. At times an auditor who has been made bishop desires to retain for a while the office of auditor, and in the meantime rule his diocese by a vicar. In such a case he is not called an auditor, but locumtenens. The reason is that as bishop he is the brother of the Pope and cannot therefore be his chaplain. For this reason he ceases to be an auditor strictly speaking and is called locumtenens of that office.

249. THE REVEREND APOSTOLIC CAMERA OR

TREASURY is another tribunal of justice in the Roman Court. Just as the Pontiff was accustomed to commit juridical causes to his clerics, so likewise did he commit to them the different cases which occurred in the administration of the public treasury, and in contentious jurisdiction regarding fiscal affairs. But for a long time the power of one official, the cardinal-chamberlain, who had great authority as the presiding officer of the Apostolic Treasury, interfered with the establishment of a separate tribunal for the examination and determination of causes arising out of financial matters.

250. The cardinal-chamberlain was very prominent and formerly had a number of administrative officials subject to him, chief among whom was the governor of the city of Rome, also called the vice-chamberlain. The treasurer and the auditor general of the Apostolic Camera were likewise under the power of the cardinal-chamberlain. To the auditor general of the treasury, however, much of the power of the cardinal-camerlengo was transferred, so that he possessed full jurisdiction in criminal affairs, the right to execute pontifical briefs, and authority over the officials of the curia. The power of the cardinal-camerlengo having gradually been restrained, not only did these three administrative officers become independent of him, but the whole treasury department acquired a tribunal of its own.

251. When first established, this tribunal consisted of twelve associates, but now consists of nine. Each one of these is the head or chief of a certain department of administration, and as such constitutes a particular tribunal from which an appeal may be

taken immediately to the general tribunal of the treasury.

As regards the universal Church mention should be made of the fact that fiscal matters may be brought before the auditor of the Camera or Treasury in the second instance and then to the full or general tribunal of the Camera in the third instance. The auditor of the Apostolic Camera is even at this day the executor of apostolic constitutions and decrees of the Sacred Congregations.

252. THE SIGNATURE OF JUSTICE at the present time is a college of clerics which is presided over by a cardinal-prefect and whose work is to examine and report to the Sovereign Pontiff on various petitions for justice which are presented to the Apostolic See. These petitions are either signed and granted by the Pope or referred to judges for trial. Hence the term *signature*. From the time of Innocent VIII. affairs of mere favor were separated from those of justice, and Sixtus V. deputed thirty referees to report on affairs of justice. Of these thirty, twelve enjoy the privilege of voting on questions brought up, and they are called voting referees. Alexander VII. constituted these referees into a college. The Signature of Justice on account of its work of reporting directly and immediately to the Pontiff has obtained the authority of a supreme court or court of cassation. At present the Signature of Justice has six voting prelates and seventy-four referees. The prefectship is vacant.

CHAPTER XIV.

THE TRIBUNALS OF FAVOR; THE SIGNATURE OF FAVOR, THE DATARY, THE SACRED PENITENTIARY.

253. Besides the tribunals of justice there are in the Roman Court three tribunals of grace or favor; the Signature of Favor or Grace, the Datary and the Sacred Penitentiary.

THE SIGNATURE OF FAVOR is a tribunal for the examination of various matters of favor and for reporting on them directly to the Sovereign Pontiff. After Pope Innocent VIII. separated the two kinds of petitions, those of justice from those of favor, this tribunal was established to report to His Holiness on the matter of the petitions for favors which were addressed to the Holy See. It takes cognizance only of extraordinary, not ordinary matters. These extraordinary matters the Pontiff reserves to himself, and after consulting the Signature of Favor concerning them, renders a decision. Very often he does not consult even this tribunal, but having advised with his own auditor, announces his decision and grants or refuses the petition.

254. The Signature of Favor is in a certain sense a forum of equity against the excessive rigor of the laws in some particular cases. For while the laws may strictly demand certain things, these demands

may be remitted by way of favor by the Sovereign Pontiff. The petitions for favors, however, are usually subjected to strict examination, and for such examination this tribunal was established. A cardinal-prefect is assigned to the Signature of Favor, but his office is only titular. Besides the twelve voting referees of the other signature—that of justice—the auditor of the treasury, the treasurer, the datary, the dean of the Rota, the regent of the chancery, the auditor of His Holiness and three other participating referees constitute the Signature of Favor, when fully organized.

255. The Signature of Favor or Grace examines petitions for extraordinary favors asked from the Holy See. The TRIBUNAL OF THE DATARY, however, attends to ordinary petitions, and grants petitions and dispensations concerning matters which are reserved to the Pontiff in the external forum. Formerly the Datary and the Apostolic Chancery were one and the same tribunal, but in the course of time, because of the pressure of business, they were divided into two tribunals. Though the precise time when the Datary was established, or when this division took place, cannot be ascertained, still it is certain that in the year 1216 when Honorius III. ascended the pontifical throne, the Datary already existed. The Datary is so called from the fact that papal concessions or favors were properly dated and the date registered by an official of the pontifical court. He needed several assistants and thus in the course of time this whole department of the chancery was separated and made a distinct tribunal.

256. The favors which are granted through the

Datary are: The conferring of benefices which are not consistorial, the reservations of pensions from benefices, concessions of prelatial insignia such as the right to use the *cappa magna*, dispensations in irregularities, matrimonial dispensations and such like public favors.

Pope Benedict XIV. in his constitution, *Gravissimum*, of December 6, 1745, determined what favors and business should be granted and done through the Datary, ·what through the Secretariate of Briefs and what through the Sacred Penitentiary. In the same constitution he assigned to the Datary authority over all concessions for which a tax is to be paid to the chancery, or for which some compromise is to be made to the Datary.

257. These taxes or assessments for favors granted by the Apostolic See have been in vogue for centuries and also have been sanctioned by general councils of the Church. The revenues thus received through the Datary are partly spent in paying salaries to the officials of the tribunal itself, partly in paying the salaries of officials connected with other tribunals and with the Congregations of Cardinals. What is left is devoted to pious works. The salaries received by some of these officials are meagre indeed. Some of the Monsignori who hold prominent positions receive only thirty dollars a month, and are supposed to spend the time between 10 o'clock a. m. and 4 o'clock p. m. in their offices.

258. The officials of the Datary are: 1°, The datary who is the head of the whole tribunal. If he is a cardinal, as is usually the case, he is called the pro-datary, because the position of datary is not a

cardinalitial office; 2°, the sub-datary; 3°, the prefect of the office which is called "through death;" 4°, the prefect of the office which is called "concession;" 5°, the general administrator of affairs to be compromised; 6°, his substitute; 7°, the treasurer of the datary; 8°, the prefect of requests granted; 9°, the reviser of matrimonial dispensations; 10°, the second reviser of petitions on benefices; 11°, the first reviser of the same; 12', the official for matters sent; 13°, the substitute for the sub-datary; 14°, the substitute for the official "through death;" 15°, the official for briefs; 16°, the substitute for the reviser of matrimonial dispensations; 17°, the reviser of accounts or taxes; 18', the writer of bulls to be issued secretly; 19°, the keeper of petitions and of the register of bulls; 20', the official for collating extracts from briefs and bulls; 21°, the notary of processes for promotion to cathedral churches; 22°, the accountant; 23°, the notary; 24°, about thirty inferior officials. Except the cardinal-pro-datary, the sub-datary, the prefect of favors granted and the notary for promotions to cathedral churches, all these officials are signori and not clerics.

259. The name of datary is supposed by some to be given the head of the tribunal, because formerly he dated the dispensations and other favors granted by the Sovereign Pontiff. Others say he is called datary, because he has so much to do with granting these favors. The Pope, however, and not the datary grants all favors.

Originally the office of datary was filled by a prelate and not by a cardinal. Hence when it began to be filled by a cardinal, he was called pro-datary, lest the cardinalitial dignity might seem lowered by filling an office formerly held by a prelate. For the same reason, when a prelate who is nuncio to a court must remain there for a time after he becomes a cardinal, he is then called no longer nuncio, but pro-nuncio.

260. In everything that is done through the Datary, the cardinal pro-datary represents the Pope; so that everything done by him in his official capacity is as valid as if done by the Pope personally. At the death of the Pontiff the jurisdiction of the cardinal-pro-datary expires. And then all the petitions and favors not yet expedited, even though granted, are placed in a sealed case and given into the custody of two prelates. This transfer is made usually at the first meeting of the cardinals after the death of the Pontiff.

The sub-datary assists the cardinal-pro-datary and supplies his place even in regard to the matters which must be referred to the audience of the Holy Father. He signs briefs and copies, and holds the first place among all the officials after the cardinal. He lives in the palace of the Datary and is usually a domestic prelate.

261. The office of the official "through death," means the office of the official who has charge of those matters coming to the Datary because of a vacancy through death. Such matters relate especially to benefices vacant through the death of their incumbents. Many benefices are reserved to the Holy See, and much of the detail work connected with them is done under the direction of this official.

Every day, in the morning, there is a meeting of the Datary, at which the cardinal-pro-datary, the sub-datary and the official "through death" are present. The cardinal, with the consultive vote of the sub-datary and the official, weighs and determines the business of the tribunal. The matters to be referred to the Sovereign Pontiff are arranged, and later the same day are presented for the assent of His Holiness; because he and not the cardinal-pro-datary grants the favors of the Datary. They are then expedited through the proper officials.

261. THE SACRED PENITENTIARY is a tribunal of the Roman Court established especially for the forum of conscience, that through it the Holy See may give absolution from sins and censures specially reserved to it; that, moreover, it may grant dispensations from vows, from the obligation of reciting the office, from occult impediments and irregularities, and that it may decide doubts of conscience for those whose anxiety induces them to apply for an authoritative solution.

262. Not a few of the learned trace the institution of this tribunal, or at least the idea of it, back to the time of St. Cornelius and St. Cyprian, when certain priests were specially commissioned to absolve those Christians who unfortunately had fallen away from the faith because of the raging persecution, and who wished to be restored to the bosom of the Church. They say also that the dignity of the major penitentiary which for many years past has been conferred only on a cardinal, was instituted by Pope Benedict II. From his time up to the reign of Pius IV. the power and jurisdiction of the tribunal and of the cardinal were very great, so that not only matters of conscience and occult impediments and

irregularities, but also public impediments came under the competency of this tribunal. Pope Pius IV., however, and especially Pope Pius V., restricted these faculties; and later Pope Benedict XIV. re-arranged the whole tribunal, so that now it dispenses only in occult impediments and irregularities, and decides cases of conscience properly referred to it. In the case of the poor, however, it grants all, even public dispensations, gratuitously, which otherwise would have to be obtained from the Datary and for which the usual tax would be charged.

263. The persons who constitute the Penitentiary are: The major penitentiary, the regent, the theologian, the datary, the corrector, the sealer, the canonist, four procurators or secretaries and four ordinary writers. Besides these, there are three minor penitentiaries who hear confessions in the basilicas of St. John Lateran, St. Peter and St. Mary Major, for which they use faculties granted them by the major penitentiary. There is also a chaplain or guard of the Penitentiary, an archivist or an assistant sealer who helps the sealer.

All these persons have a life tenure, and except in the case of legitimate deprivation, their offices are not supposed to be vacant unless through free resignation or through promotion to the cardinalate or to a bishopric requiring residence, or through transfer to another office of the same Penitentiary. Each prelate connected with this tribunal—they are all prelates—before taking office makes oath that he will faithfully and gratuitously execute his office, that except his salary he will accept no money from any one, even if gratuitously offered, and that he will inviolably keep secret the cases, persons and business of the Sacred Penitentiary.

264. The major penitentiary, according to the constitution of Benedict XIV., is to be at least a cardinal-priest of the Holy Roman Church, who is a master in theology or doctor in canon law. He shall be chosen by the Roman Pontiff and appointed by letters in the form of a brief. He shall personally exercise his office, but if absent or impeded for some cause approved by the Pontiff, he himself shall appoint another cardinal with the aforementioned qualifications to take his place. The cardinal thus appointed pro-penitentiary shall fulfil this duty himself and in his own name expedite letters. If during a vacancy in the Holy See, the cardinal penitentiary should die, a cardinal pro-penitentiary shall be chosen by the majority of the cardinals and shall serve until the election of the new Pontiff.

The chief duty of the major penitentiary is to carefully use the faculties granted him. During Holy Week he is to hear confessions and grant indulgences in the three great basilicas of Rome; in St. John's on Palm Sunday, in St. Mary's on Wednesday, and in St. Peter's on Thursday and Friday. Finally he is to assist the Roman Pontiff in his agony, and give him spiritual aid and consolation.

265. Of the other officials, the regent, the theologian, the datary, the canonist, the corrector and the sealer, must be priests of conspicuous learning and integrity. They shall be selected with great care by the major penitentiary, and after being presented to the Roman Pontiff, if they deserve his confirmation, shall be admitted to their offices by letters

patent of the major penitentiary countersigned by one of the secretaries. The offices of the procurators and secretaries shall be filled by concursus, held under the direction of the regent and the corrector, who shall, moreover, diligently inquire into the life and character of the applicants for the positions, during the six days which must elapse before the office can be filled. The appointees shall be entitled to their offices on receiving letters patent of the cardinal penitentiary.

266. The regent according to ancient custom is one of the auditors of the Rota or sacred palace. His duty is to direct the affairs of the tribunal, and diligently examine all matters brought before it. Nothing can be undertaken by the secretaries without his assent, even if there is no difficulty in the case. In doubtful matters he consults the cardinal penitentiary, and later these matters are decided in the signature or meeting of the officials which is held on stated days. But in routine cases the regent examines and expedites the petitions in a meeting of the procurators held each week at his order.

The corrector is to examine and correct the letters prepared by the secretaries, and if necessary cause them to be re-written, so that they may be in proper style, clean and without erasures when transmitted to the parties to whom they are addressed. The datary affixes at the bottom of the letters the place, day, month, year of the Christian era and of the reigning Pontiff when the petitions were granted.

267. The theologian consultor is a member of the Society of Jesus, and his duty is to give his opinion, in writing if necessary, on difficult cases or petitions

which are referred to him by the cardinal or the regent of the tribunal. The canonist, also, when requested by the cardinal or the regent shall give his opinion on cases referred to him. The sealer shall examine and if found properly written affix the seal of the tribunal to all letters sent out by the Penitentiary. He shall also have charge of the archives and registers of the tribunal, and in this duty may have the assistance of the pro-sealer. This latter official shall have charge of the revenues of the tribunal.

268. The procurators or secretaries shall carefully examine all letters received, and if the case permits, make digests of them. Then they shall refer all to the cardinal or to the regent and make no reply whatever without his order. They shall prepare all replies according to the set forms adopted in the Penitentiary. In this and in keeping the records they shall be assisted by four writers or copyists. The duty of the chaplain, who shall be a priest, or at least a cleric in major orders, is to act as janitor or guard to the hall where the meeting of the officials of the Penitentiary is held; and to give proper notice of these meetings to the various members of the tribunal.

269. The faculties of the major penitentiary are very ample and cover most cases of conscience. But if he has no faculties, he can always receive them by word of mouth from the Pontiff, and therefore it is not necessary for anyone to inquire whether or not the Sacred Penitentiary has faculties for such or such a case. In regard to all doubts in the matter of sins the cardinal penitentiary has unlimited jurisdiction.

All dispensations, absolutions and other favors are

granted by this tribunal absolutely gratuitously. The names of the persons for whom favors are requested need not be mentioned, but an address must be given whereto a reply should be directed. The English or any other language may be used in the application, but the reply will be made in Latin.

270. The case must be clearly stated and the true reason given for the recourse, for if the true reason is concealed and a false one given, any dispensation founded on it will be null and void. Fictitious names may be used; but the case itself must be stated truthfully. A confessor may apply to the Sacred Penitentiary for absolutions and dispensations which the bishop has faculties to grant. And at times on account of circumstances it is advisable to do so, particularly if there is danger of the seal of confession being infringed, or of the bishop in some way becoming acquainted with a matter which should be kept absolutely secret from him.

When application is made to the Penitentiary in such a case, mention had better be made of the reason for not applying to the bishop of the diocese. The envelope containing the letter should be directed to: The Most Eminent Cardinal Major Penitentiary, Rome, Italy. The letter should begin with the words: Most Eminent and Most Reverend Sir. The etiquette of the Roman Court requires that all letters sent to cardinals should be commenced about half way from the top of the first page. At the bottom of the letter the address to which a reply should be sent is added in these or similar words: May your Eminence deign to direct the reply to——.

271. Careful attention should be given to the for-

mulas used in the reply from the Penitentiary. Ordinarily the dispensation or faculty for absolving is sent to the person applying for it, but it can be applied only by a confessor, who, however, may be selected by the person himself. At times also the reply contains the condition that the confessor to apply this dispensation or to use this faculty for absolving, "must be a master, that is, licentiate or doctor, in theology or a doctor of canon law." In such a case no other confessor can use the faculty. Further, a person who has only honorary degrees, except they be from the Pope, is not considered competent in such cases nor does he fulfil the required condition.

272. Except in occult cases, the Sacred Penitentiary does not grant dispensations unless the applicants be poor. In such circumstances this tribunal grants dispensations also for public impediments. From reserved sins and censures, however, it grants absolution, whether they be hidden or public; with this difference, that if the cases be secret it grants the necessary faculties to the confessor, but if the cases be public, it sends the necessary faculties to the ordinary of the diocese from which the application came.

The faculties of the major penitentiary for the external forum expire with the death of the Roman Pontiff; but those for the forum of conscience are perpetual and continue also during a vacancy in the Apostolic See. All decisions of the Penitentiary are issued in the name of the major penitentiary, not of the tribunal.

273. It is customary for the tribunal of the Penitentiary to use many peculiar abbreviations in its replies.

PECULIAR ABBREVIATIONS.

That such abbreviations may not be misunderstood, and necessary conditions thereby be omitted, an explanation of the most frequent ones is inserted:

archiepus	archbishop
alr	otherwise
als	otherwise
absoluo	absolution
aplica	apostolic
autte	authority
appbatis	approved
cardlis	cardinal
canice	canonically
cen	censures
Xtus	Christ
confeone	confession
coione	communion
consciæ	conscience
discreoni	discretion
dnus	lord
ecclæ	church
effus	effect
exit	exists
ecclis	ecclesiastics
epus	bishop
excoe	excommunication
fr	brother
frum	brother
gnali	general
humoi	of this kind
humilr	humbly
infraptum	undersigned
irregulte	irregularity
igr	therefore
lia	license
ltima	legitimate
lræ	letters
lite	licitly
mrimonium	matrimony
magro	master
mitaone	mercy
mir	mercy
nulltus	not at all
ordio	ordinary
ordinaoni	ordination
Pp	pope
pr	father
pontus	pontificate
ptus	aforesaid
ptur	is preferred
pntium	present
pbter	priest
poenia	penance
poenaria	penitentiary
poe	can
pror	procurator
qtnus	in as far as
qmlbt	in some way
qd	which or what
relari	regular
relione	religion
Roma	Roman
sntæ or stæ	holy
saluri	salutary
sentia	sentence
spealtr	specially
supplibus	supplications
spualibus	spiritual
tn	nevertheless
tm	only
thia or theolia	theology
tli	title
venebli	venerable
vræ	your

CHAPTER XV.

THE TRIBUNALS OF EXPEDITION; THE ROMAN CHANCERY, THE SECRETARIATE OF BRIEFS, THE SECRETARIATE OF STATE, THE SECRETARIATE OF MEMORIALS.

274. The tribunals of expedition in the Roman Court are those through which apostolic letters are issued. Chief among them is the APOSTOLIC CHANCERY, through which in proper form pontifical bulls and apostolic letters regarding matters treated in the Consistory are expedited. The Chancery prepares and expedites these bulls and letters according to the petition signed by the Pope in the Datary, if there is question of benefices, or of matrimony, and according to the consistorial schedule signed by the Pope in the Secretariate of Briefs, if there is question of consistorial affairs, such as appointments to bishoprics or similar important matters.

275. The chief officials of the Chancery are: 1°, The cardinal vice-chancellor, who is also the summista; 2°, the regent, and 3°, the sub-summista, both of whom are prelates. Then there are others who are not prelates, viz.: 4°, the substitute of the summista; 5, the president of the lead seal; 6°, the sealer; 7°, the notary secretary; 8°, the keeper of the chancery, 9°, the substitute for contradictory claims. Attached to the Chancery is a college of seventeen

prelates, abbreviators of the larger room (parco), so called from the place where they gather and perform their duties. Three of these seventeen prelate abbreviators are acting and fourteen supernumerary. Six signori are substitutes for them. With the exception of the prelates mentioned above, all the Chancery officials are signori, not clerics.

276. The name and office of chancellor is most ancient in the courts of secular princes. In the Roman Court the office itself is very ancient, but the name seems to have been introduced only about the year 850. From the first ages the Roman Pontiffs had about them some clerics who wrote and expedited letters in their name. St. Jerome testifies that he thus assisted Pope Damasus. Still these clerics were not called chancellors, but went by the name of notaries, regionaries and librarians. In the ninth century, however, the word chancellor was introduced, derived as some say from the fact that the chancellor cancelled every letter with a line drawn through it, or, as others assert, from the grate behind which he sat and gave audience.

277. Bonaface VIII. is said to be the first Pope who committed to a cardinal the office of chancellor of the Apostolic See. The cardinal, however, is not called chancellor but vice-chancellor, because formerly this was not a cardinalitial office, and a depreciation of the cardinalitial dignity is supposed to be thus avoided.

The cardinal vice-chancellor, as regards office not dignity, is greater in the Roman Court than anyone except the Pope, for he carries the sceptre of justice. He presides over the protonotaries, the officials in charge of the archives, the auditors of the Rota, the secretaries and other officials. He is judge in those things which concern the expediting of bulls, and signs all apostolic letters on every matter, except those sent out over the seal of the fisherman. He first approves them with the letter L, which means that he has read them, and on the opposite side with the letter R, which means that he orders them entered in the register. Further, the cardinal vice-chancellor acts as secretary to the Consistory and writes the decrees made therein regarding the titles of cardinals, promotions to bishoprics and other matters, and then sees that these decrees are properly arranged in the Chancery and sent to those promoted in Consistory.

278. By the death of the Roman Pontiff the jurisdiction of the cardinal vice-chancellor at once expires, and the pontifical seal of which he has charge is broken before the cardinals at their first meeting after the death of the Pope. The cardinal vice-chancellor is created vice-chancellor and summista by two separate bulls expedited in the Consistory after the election of the new Pope. As vice-chancellor, the care of the chief affairs of the Apostolic See devolves upon him, especially of those things treated in Consistory. Hence when a Consistory is to be celebrated, on the day previous, he receives from the auditor of the Sovereign Pontiff or the national cleric of the Consistory, the consistorial folia, or the compendium of the preconizations. For it is his duty, as notary of the Sacred Consistory, to record these provisions, as well as all other acts of the Consistory, in the Chancery.

Likewise it is his duty to draw out into full form these and similar decrees issued by the Pope in Consistory. He also testifies in writing to these consistorial decrees, and on his testimony to their truth, the consistorial schedule is drawn up in the Secretariate of Briefs to which schedule the Pope affixes his signature, and in accordance with which the bulls are afterwards expedited from the Chancery.

270. All apostolic letters issued over the lead seal are signed by the cardinal vice-chancellor. Even appointments to bishoprics, although assured by the aforementioned consistorial schedule signed by the Pope himself, must nevertheless be made valid by the bulls drawn up by the officials of the Chancery. The cardinal, acting as summista of the Chancery, oversees ths expediting of all bulls sent out by the office. From this summary of his work, the great power and immense influence of the cardinal vice-chancellor are apparent. But on the other hand, the great watchfulness which the duties of his office entail upon him makes his position most trying and delicate.

280. The office of regent of the Chancery was established in the year 1377, when Pope Gregory XI. left Avignon in France and returned to Rome. Cardinal Manturcus at that time was vice-chancellor, and backed by Charles V. of France, refused to return to Rome with the Pope, but remained at Avignon. Gregory XI. preferred to tolerate his action rather than proceed against him. But in order to have the duties of the office fulfilled, he created the regent of the Chancery to take the place of the cardinal in his absence. Hence the regent

holds the first place in the Chancery after the cardinal vice-chancellor. He distributes the documents to the different abbreviators, so that they may make minutes of them. He signs each bull with the first letter of the name of the vice-chancellor. He also places the letters L and C near the middle and end of each bull, to signify that it has been read and corrected. Then he gives the document to the prefect of the lead seal who attaches the seal to it in the usual way. The office of regent of the Chancery formerly was a venal one, as were also many others, so that they who obtained them might sell their positions to others. But Pope Pius VII. abolished this custom in regard to the whole Chancery. All offices are now filled by appointment.

281. The bulls by which greater benefices, such as bishoprics, are conferred, must be countersigned by one of the notaries participating in the Roman Court in order that they may be valid.

The substitute for contradictory claims, when appointed, takes the place of a tribunal which formerly existed in the Chancery for the settlement of such claims. When opposition was made to appointments or other favors granted by the Apostolic See, the officials of this tribunal examined and reported the matter with their opinion thereon to the cardinal vice-chancellor. Such contests, however, being now very rare, one official, called the substitute for contradictory claims, is able to attend to all such cases under the direction of the cardinal and regent. Lately the work of this official, when there is any, is performed by others, and the office is left vacant.

282. The business of the Apostolic Chancery is done

according to certain rules, seventy-two in number, which were first established by Pope John XXII., and are re-enacted by each Pope the day following his election. These rules are specially in regard to benefices, dispensations and other favors. By them the Sovereign Pontiff declares what benefices are reserved for his own disposal, (Rules 1 to 11); by them he revalidates letters of favor or justice granted by his predecessor during the year preceding his death and not yet presented to their executors (Rule 12); further, he recalls certain favors or faculties which have not yet had issue and which it is deemed best to submit to re-examination (Rules 13 to 15); he lays down the method to be followed in granting benefices, that justice may not be denied, and that fraud on the part of applicants may be precluded and contests avoided (Rules 17, 48, 55, 68); again by other rules he determines what must be expressed in grants of dispensations, indulgences and other favors that the will of the granter may be clearly manifested (Rules 16, 49, 54); he also precludes the abuse of extending the grant beyond its limits (Rule 52) and of it interfering with the rights of others unless they are specially mentioned (Rule 18). In like manner he ordains by Rule 70 that the cardinals of the Holy Roman Church are not supposed included in any apostolic constitution unless they are specifically mentioned. By Rule 71 he also ordains that the rules of the Chancery shall not be supposed annulled or derogated from by any constitution or other pontifical enactment unless these rules are specifically mentioned in such enactment. Lastly by Rule 72 he determines the power given to the vice-chancellor and to the regent of the Chancery. The Chancery follows these rules exactly and they are in themselves of obligation on the whole Church.

283. Besides the Apostolic Chancery where bulls are expedited in regard to consistorial and important church affairs, there is another tribunal for expediting letters which concern affairs of lesser moment. This is called THE SECRETARIATE OF BRIEFS. Formerly the Chancery, Datary and Secretariate of Briefs were all united; but after the Datary was made a distinct tribunal, a second division was found advisable and the Secretariate of Briefs was also made independent. This Secretariate was brought about because the Sovereign Pontiffs were accustomed, with the aid of a cardinal, to attend to these minor concerns themselves and expedite them in the form of a brief. The cardinal who acted as secretary for these matters was usually one most familiar with the Pope and therefore was called the "cardinal nephew." In time the "cardinal nephew" required assistants, and thus the special tribunal for expediting the minor concerns of the Holy See was established distinct from the Chancery. It still retains the marks of its institution, for its seal is the fisherman's ring, which is the private seal of the Pope as compared with the lead seal which may be called the seal of state.

284. The Secretary of Briefs is always a cardinal, and his position is most important and influential. He hás charge of expediting indults for indulgences attached to crucifixes, beads and images, and for establishing private oratories with the privilege of saying Mass and keeping the Blessed Sacrament in

them. The Secretariate of Briefs also issues many rescripts of grace which are granted by the Datary; for the Datary receives and examines petitions, grants the favor asked, but sends the matter either to the Secretariate of Briefs or to the Chancery to have it forwarded to the petitioner.

Although Pope Benedict XIV. in 1745 determined just what matters should belong to the Datary and what to the Secretariate of Briefs, still it may safely be said that all provisions, favors, absolutions, dispensations which are granted by the Pope, and which are not sent out directly by certain Congregations, or by bulls of the Chancery, are expedited in the form of briefs by the Secretariate of Briefs.

A prelate is the substitute for the secretary, besides whom there are an assessor, six minutanti, a prelate archivist, a keeper and an accountant. The office is at Number 8, via S. Appolinare.

285. The Chancery, the Datary and the Secretariate of Briefs are all near each other; so that any matter which by mistake has been sent to one office can easily be transferred to another where it properly belongs. No concern need be felt, lest the rescript be issued by the wrong tribunal, for the officials in charge are fully conversant with the faculties they possess.

The original draft of every rescript or brief is preserved in the archives so that there may be no question raised regarding its validity, and no chance for fraud to go undiscovered if notice is sent to the tribunal that expedited the rescript.

The Secretariate of Briefs also issues letters concerning those matters which the Pope refers to the

Signature of Justice or of Favor for examination and report.

286. The Apostolic See has relations not only with the universal Church, in religious matters, but also with the civil governments of the nations of the world. Even now, when it has lost its temporal power, these relations are still intact with many governments. Matters which concern the temporal power of the Pope and his relations with other rulers, are transacted through THE SECRETARIATE OF STATE. The Secretary of State is always a cardinal of prominence and diplomatic ability. His office, or secretariate, is in the Vatican palace, near the apartments of His Holiness. He has a number of assistants, all subject to him and receiving orders from him alone. Among them is a substitute, seven minutanti and three archivists.

Besides civil affairs in which the Holy See is concerned with the nations, ecclesiastical affairs in which these nations are interested are treated through the Secretary of State. Hence apostolic nuncios sent to kings and emperors report to the Secretary of State, and receive their appointment and recall through his office. Ambassadors of nations also treat with the Holy See through this office. With the loss of the temporal power much work and prestige has been taken from the Cardinal-secretary of State, but his position is nevertheless most important.

287. THE SECRETARIATE OF MEMORIALS has no cardinal-secretary at the present time but a prelate acts as his substitute. It has attached to it two minutanti, a summista, and a protocolist. Its office

is in the Palace Mignanelli, near the Piazza di Spagna.

There is also a prelate secretary for letters to princes and another for Latin letters, both of whom have their office in the apostolic palace. All these secretariates are called palatine, because immediately connected with the apostolic palace. Their names express the work they do.

CHAPTER XVI.

ADVOCATES, NOTARIES, AGENTS, IN THE ROMAN COURT.

288. Those who constitute the Roman Court are called curials, and therefore cardinals, prelates and judges are all comprehended in this name. Common usage, however, has restricted the term, so that it includes only those subsidiary persons who are attached to some tribunal, or act for interested parties, as advocates, procurators, notaries, solicitors and agents. Most of these curials are not clerics.

The members of the Roman Court are assigned to various tribunals, so that all who live at Court fill at least one office. Thus all the cardinals make up the Consistory at which the Pope presides. Again the various Congregations set over particular matters are composed of a number of cardinals, one of whom is prefect, and of several prelates and inferior officials. In a similar way, the administration of the lesser tribunals is committed to prelates assisted by officials of various grades.

289. Life at the Roman Court is therefore not a sinecure; it is made up of onerous duties and constant work. With innumerable petitions from every nation of the world, with frequent appeals or recourse against the judgment of inferior tribunals on

most important and complicated questions, it is evident that many persons are required to properly perform the work. Whether questions could be decided quicker with a re-arrangement of the various tribunals and an infusion of foreign blood, as suggested in the Vatican Council, is a matter beyond the competency of this treatise.

290. The curials, according to the common use of this term, are either officials assigned as assistants to various tribunals of the Court, or persons who act in these tribunals for interested parties who have procured their services.

Chief among the curials are ADVOCATES. They are lawyers whose business is to lay down the law, or furnish a legal opinion in such a way that it may be the foundation of a judicial sentence. Advocates are either practical or titular. Some of them are prelates and with others who are signori constitute colleges, such for instance as the college of Consistorial Advocates. To them the matters of the Consistory are frequently referred for a legal opinion. Seven of these consistorial advocates, called participating advocates, constitute the academy of jurisconsults.

291. Practical advocates, who are not prelates, undertake for a stipulated fee to assist parties in trials before a judge or before the Congregations. Not everyone is allowed to practice before the Roman Congregations, but only they who are regularly admitted. Titular advocates are those, who, having passed the regular examination and obtained their degrees, nevertheless instead of practicing, prefer to do certain judicial work, such as assisting

judges to study causes and prepare decisions. Not unfrequently also these titular advocates are appointed consultors for the various Congregations. They examine the cases referred to them, give an opinion on the facts, quote the laws which apply to the matter, even if they have been overlooked by the parties themselves, and thus present a votum to the Congregation which is usually accepted as the basis of its decision.

292. PROCURATORS are persons who represent litigants before the Court and appear in their stead. They receive compensation for their services, paid by those whom they represent. Twenty-four of them constitute a peculiar and privileged college, similar to the college of advocates. Formerly these procurators had the exclusive right to represent litigants before the tribunal of the Rota; but later certain others, called Rotal Procurators, were also allowed to represent litigants before this tribunal after complying with stated prescriptions of law. From this second class, the college of procurators then also began to fill its vacancies. The procurators who represent parties before other tribunals are called simple procurators. Procurators, like the principals for whom they act, generally employ the services of an advocate to assist them in their contest before the tribunal or Congregation that hears their cause.

293. NOTARIES are persons whose work is to prepare documents and instruments in judicial causes. They, like advocates, are either practical or titular. Active notaries, or those in practice, either perform work in the various tribunals to which they are reg-

ularly attached, or have offices in different parts of the city, so that they may be easily reached by private individuals who need their services. There is a college of notaries specially attached to the tribunal of the Rota.

All notaries of the Roman Court are supposed to know how to draw up documents and instruments required in tribunals. No priest can act as a notary public, except such work is necessary that he may obtain a living. Titular notaries are those who lend their services to other notaries until they themselves happen to obtain the position of notary public.

294. Besides advocates, procurators and notaries there are also SOLICITORS or AGENTS connected with the Roman Court, who act for private parties and are paid by them for all services rendered. These agents are employed by bishops and others, either temporarily or perpetually, to look after their interests in Rome. Whenever any work is to be done or information obtained, these agents or solicitors go to the various Congregations or tribunals, urge the requests of their employers and generally succeed in getting what they seek.

295. Solicitors or agents are recognized by the Roman Court to such an extent that it is quite necessary to do business through them and not by letter. They urge matters and spend money in accordance with the directions of those whom they represent. When dispensations, faculties, or other favors are to be obtained from the Datary or some Congregation, they prepare the application, call for the rescripts, pay the tax if any is required and forward the letters to their employers. A careful, prudent,

active agent, who stands well with the officials of the various Congregations and tribunals, is a great help to bishops and other persons who have business in the Roman Court and cannot attend to it personally. The charges of these agents do not seem extravagant; but a little extra money induces them to urge cases more strenuously, and helps to preclude the excessive delays which are so annoying to the American character.

PART THIRD.

PRELATES, LEGATES, VICARS APOSTOLIC, PROTONOTARIES.

CHAPTER I.

PRELATES OF THE ROMAN COURT.

296. After the cardinals, prelates hold the first place in the Roman Court. They in general are called prelates who are preferred and placed over others in honor and jurisdiction. Patriarchs, primates, metropolitans, bishops, are prelates properly so called, because they take precedence by virtue of their office and have ordinary jurisdiction over inferiors. All other prelacies are merely an imitation and participation of this episcopal jurisdiction, and pre-eminence is granted their incumbents only by special privilege of account of the office they fill.

These prelates participate in episcopal jurisdiction either by virtue of a title recognized and contained in the law, or because of a special and express delegation from the Sovereign Pontiff. The former are called abbots or inferior prelates, the latter are known as vicars apostolic. By ecclesiastical institution both these classes have ordinary jurisdiction in contentious matters and are therefore really prelates. In a broad sense any cleric who has the care of souls may be called a prelate, as is proved by *Cap. Tua Nos. 4, De Clerico Aegrotante*; and in the same way those who have greater prerogative without jurisdiction, such as parish priests, deans of chapters, archpriests are known as prelates. But in the usual acceptation of this term, none but them who have ordinary and contentious jurisdiction over others may be called prelates.

297. A parish priest has no such jurisdiction; his is confined to the internal forum, that of conscience. A rural dean, likewise, has no jurisdiction in contentious matters, nor any authority whatever over the clergy of his district. Neither has he any precedence over them except only in those acts wherein he is the delegate of the bishop. "Any custom to the contrary is an abuse." *Zittelli, Apparatus Juris Can, page 147; Craisson, Manuale, No. 634.* The Sacred Congregation of Rites in at least sixteen decisions, given to different countries and made of universal application, has decreed that, "a vicar forane or dean by reason of that office has no precedence in choir, in sessions, in processions and in other acts and ecclesiastical functions over other parish priests, canons and priests older and more worthy than himself; but the vicar or dean must stand, sit and walk in the place of his reception and dignity, just as if he were not a vicar forane or dean, both with the cotta and without it, *notwithstanding any*

DEANS HAVE NO PRECEDENCE. 273

and every order of the bishop to the contrary; except only in those congregations or conferences which are held each month by order of the bishop, in which as the delegate of the bishop he should precede all, but not, however, in the procession, Mass and other acts which take place before or follow the conference." And in another decree, intending to eliminate even the custom, the same Sacred Congregation ordered the observance of the above decree, "notwithstanding any and every custom to the contrary." *Ferraris, sub verbo Vicarius.*

Neither the Second nor the Third Plenary Council of Baltimore (II. Conc. No. 74; III. Conc. Nis. 27-40,) contains anything which should be held to disagree with these decisions. On the contrary all these decisions having been made after the establishment of deans by St. Charles Boromeo—whose statutes are quoted in the Baltimore Council as the foundation for its decrees, or rather suggestions— these Baltimore decrees should therefore be interpreted to harmonize with the explicit ruling of the Sacred Congregation which binds the universal Church.

298. Besides the prelates and inferior prelates mentioned above, there are in the Roman Court certain officials who by the express will of the Sovereign Pontiff are decorated with the title and dignity of prelates. Those who obtain this dignity have a great prerogative, so much so that they can by ordinary or delegated power act for the Roman Pontiff.

To obtain a prelacy by right in the Roman Court. it is necessary for the candidate to make studies covering a period of years, and have an annual income of at least a thousand dollars. Pope Benedict XIV. established a pontifical academy for noble ecclesiastics wherein ecclesiastical diplomacy and political science are taught, and from which students are graduated into prelatures.

299. Besides these ecclesiastics who earn their dignity, there are a large number of others whom the Sovereign Pontiff decorates with the title and dignity of prelate, either because of the offices they fill in the various Congregations and tribunals of the Roman Court, or because of the favor and honor he wishes to bestow on the recipients or their friends. Thus it happens that many prelates of the Roman Court live away from Rome and never even see the Court to which they belong. Their prelacy, as such, gives them no jurisdiction over clergy or laity, but only dignity and precedence according to the class of prelates to which they belong. From this it will be noticed, that, like the cardinals, Roman prelates are a special institution peculiar to the Roman Court.

300. Precedence is strictly observed in the Roman Court, and its rules are applicable to the universal Church. After the Pope, the cardinals of the Holy Roman Church take precedence over all without any exception. Even if they have not the episcopal character, nevertheless because of the sublime dignity of their office, they rank before all bishops, archbishops, primates, patriarchs and legates of the Apostolic See. This seemed hard to Henry, archbishop of Canterbury, primate of England and legate-natus of the Holy See; and accordingly he refused precedence to John Kemp, archbishop of

York, who had been created cardinal by Pope Eugene IV. This refusal occasioned the celebrated letter of Pope Eugene IV., mentioned in the first part of this work, wherein he treated extensively the cardinalitial dignity and assigned it the highest place in the Church, next to the papacy.

Later, in the year 1449, the archbishop of Gneisen, the primate of Poland, contended for the prerogative of place with Cardinal Sbigneo, the bishop of Cracow, but Pope Nicholas V. again decided in favor of the cardinal. Precedence among the cardinals themselves is regulated by the order of cardinal-bishop, cardinal-priest or cardinal-deacon to which they belong and seniority in creation.

301. After the College of Cardinals, the college of patriarchs, archbishops and bishops who are assistants at the pontifical throne comes next in rank in the Roman Court. This college consists at present of nine patriarchs, sixty-four archbishops and eighty-nine bishops of residential or titular sees in different parts of the world. To be made an assistant at the pontifical throne is a special favor, and gives precedence in papal ceremonies over those of equal rank in the hierarchy. In other respects seniority of promotion for archbishops and of consecration for bishops is the criterion of precedence. No distinction is now made on this point between the incumbents of residential and of titular sees.

302. There are eighty-six titular archbishoprics and four hundred and thirty-four titular bishoprics which the Holy See is accustomed to confer, in order that the persons thus promoted may fill important offices in the Roman Court, or act as auxiliary and

coadjutor bishops to the incumbents of residential sees throughout the world. Besides these, the Propaganda has two titular archbishoprics and twenty-seven titular bishoprics which, with the consent of the Sovereign Pontiff, it confers on persons subject to it, who are to act as coadjutors, or who have resigned their residential sees in missionary countries.

From the titular archbishops thus promoted by the Holy See, apostolic nuncios and delegates are chosen for various countries, and the secretaryships of the more important Congregations of Cardinals are filled.

303. After the college of patriarchs, archbishops and bishops who assist at the pontifical throne, the vice-chamberlain of the Holy Roman Church, the two princes who assist at the throne, the auditor general of the Reverend Apostolic Camera, the treasurer and the major-domo of His Holiness take precedence in the order mentioned. To them succeed in the order of promotion and consecration the archbishops and bishops, both residential and titular, of the Church throughout the world. Following them comes the college of protonotaries apostolic according to the order of their admission, first they of the number participating and then the supernumaries like to those participating. There are seven of the former and two hundred and six of the latter scattered throughout the different countries of the world.

After the college of protonotaries come the commendator of the Holy Spirit, the regent of the Apostolic Chancery, the abbot general of the regular canons of the Lateran, the abbots general of the monastic orders, the generals and the vicars general of the mendicant orders.

304. The prelate auditors of the Roman Rota come next, followed by the domestic prelates of the Camera, the domestic prelates voting and the referees of the Signature of Justice, the prelate abbreviators of the Larger Room of the Chancery and the domestic prelates who do not belong to the foregoing colleges. Of these last there are at present two hundred and twenty-four, most of whom live outside of Rome and have received this prelacy as a favor to themselves or their friends. All these are addressed as "Right Reverend." Then come the private chamberlains participating and the officers of the noble pontifical guard, none of whom are clerics.

The Very Reverend supernumerary private chamberlains, of whom there are six hundred and thirty in the different dioceses of the world, then take rank, followed by three hundred and twenty supernumerary private chamberlains of the sword and cape who are not clerics. Next to them come the two hundred and twenty Very Reverend chamberlains of honor in *Abito Pavonazzo*, and two hundred and five Very Reverend chamberlains of honor living outside of Rome.

Then come four chamberlains of honor of the sword and cape, and one hundred and eight supernumeraries, none of whom are clerics. There are, moreover, six private chaplains and forty-eight honorary private chaplains, besides ninety honorary chaplains who reside outside of Rome. Two private clerics, six common chaplains with twelve supernumeraries complete the pontifical family, all of whom may participate in papal ceremonies, and are properly addressed "Very Reverend."

305. All the clerics mentioned above are prelates of the Roman Court, and as such have personal preeminence in any and every diocese of the world. They are in dignity and therefore capable of receiving and executing papal commands. Pontifical letters may be addressed to them, but rarely are they sent to any of the inferior clergy.

The vicar general of the diocese wherein these prelates live, even though not a prelate, takes precedence over them all, because he is in dignity on account of his office, and, through communication of certain rights, by law participates with the bishop in ruling the whole diocese. Because, however, Roman prelates according to their grade have personal pre-eminence, a petition was introduced in the Vatican Council requesting that the honorary titles and privileges of the Roman Court, such as of chamberlains, protonotaries, missionaries apostolic, should not be conferred on priests living outside of Rome, unless their ordinaries were first consulted.

306. It may not be useless to give the approved forms used in the Roman Court in addressing prelates and inferior clergy; for a knowledge of them may preclude the confusion and embarrassment which are often experienced in this matter.

The Pope is entitled "His Holiness;" a cardinal, "His Eminence." A patriarch is called, "His Excellency the Most Reverend." A primate or archbishop is entitled "Most Reverend," and in Latin, "*Illustrissimus et Reverendissimus.*"

Apostolic delegates and nuncios are addressed according to their rank as archbishop, with the addition, generally, of apostolic delegate or nuncio. A bishop is called "Right Reverend," and in Latin, "*Illustrissimus et Reverendissimus*," the same as an archbishop. Abbots or inferior prelates having jurisdiction are entitled "Right Reverend", and in Latin, "*Reverendissimus*."

Protonotaries apostolic and domestic prelates of the Pope are called "Right Reverend" or "Monsignor," and in Latin, "*Reverendissimus*." In Rome the title "Monsignor" is given to all prelates above these classes, except to cardinals and abbots. It is also given to private chamberlains and chaplains of the Pope, although in English these are entitled "Very Reverend," and in Latin, "*Admodum Reverendus*." Administrators of vacant dioceses, vicars general, provosts, archpriests, canons of cathedral chapters, heads and provincials of religious orders, and priors of priories are by right entitled to the appellation "Very Reverend." By courtesy some others, such as priors of monasteries over which abbots preside, rectors and local superiors of religious houses, presidents or heads of seminaries, are properly addressed "Very Reverend."

Doctors of divinity or of law, vicars forane or rural deans, presidents of colleges, diocesan consultors, examiners of the clergy, chancellors or secretaries of a diocese, fiscal procurators and others along with simple priests, have no claim to be styled "Very Reverend." These and all others in priest's or deacon's orders should be styled simply "Reverend."

CHAPTER II.

LEGATES OF THE APOSTOLIC SEE.

307. An apostolic legate is one who is chosen and sent with power to some eminent person or to a certain province in order to administer spiritual affairs. He can be sent to represent either the person of the Pontiff or the Apostolic See. Whatever may have been former usage, to-day all legates are sent in the name of the Holy See, and therefore their power assumes the nature of ordinary jurisdiction and continues even after the death of the Pontiff who commissions them.

The right to send legates for spiritual affairs into any and every part of the world is a necessary consequence of the primacy of the Sovereign Pontiff. The Roman Pontiff has ordinary and immediate jurisdiction over the whole flock of Christ, both pastors and people. Therefore not only may he teach and guide this flock on extraordinary occasions, and through the local bishops, but his duty of primacy implies that he should constantly have a watchful care over the universal Church of which he is the bishop. Still the Roman Pontiff is not the only bishop in the Church; there are also local bishops set over particular churches. Both these bishops have ordinary jurisdiction over the same people, which though concurrent is nevertheless not conflicting. While the authority of the Roman Pontiff is supreme, still it does not absorb or destroy that of the bishop set over a particular diocese. Each local bishop has his proper work, for which he has full and efficacious authority.

308. It is precisely this double jurisdiction that insures unity in the Church. The vivifying spirit of the primacy, penetrating not only the chief but every member of the body of Christ, is the cause of the wonderful vitality and harmony of action which distinguish the Catholic Church from every other organization known to man. The obligation of carefully watching, feeding and guiding the Church in every portion of the world, necessarily implies and gives the Sovereign Pontiff the right to do through others what he cannot perform himself. Hence Pope Pius VI. writing on nunciatures to four German archbishops says that, "the Roman Pontiff fulfils the apostolic duty of caring for the universal flock by delegating ecclesiastical men, either permanently or temporarily as he judges best, and ordering them to take his place in distant regions and there exercise the same jurisdiction which he himself if present would exercise." Hence apostolic legates are sent to exercise the authority of the Sovereign Pontiff in as far as it is communicated to them. They are not sent to grasp and exercise the authority of local bishops. On the contrary, just as the ordinary jurisdiction of the Sovereign Pontiff and of the local bishop are concurrent and harmonious, so also must the authority of apostolic legates and the authority of local bishops mutually sustain each other.

309. The apostolic right of sending permanent

legates with ordinary jurisdiction was strenuously opposed in the year 1787 by four archbishops of Germany, those of Cologne, Mayence, Salzburg and Treves. They protested against the establishment of an apostolic nunciature, and in letters addressed to Pope Pius VI. and to their suffragan bishops claimed that, "they had fulfilled all their duties as pastors of the churches over which they had charge, and therefore the Pope was not justified in extending to their churches the extraordinary rights of the primacy; and consequently, as the Pope had no right to send legates, so they were in no way obliged to receive them and permit the exercise of their powers to the detriment of their own ordinary jurisdiction over the flocks divinely intrusted to their watchful care." *Responsio super Nunciaturis, Cap. 18, No. 6.*

Pope Pius VI., however, in reply to their pretensions issued his celebrated letter *On Nunciatures*, in which he teaches, "that the Roman Pontiff has a right to have some persons, particularly in distant places, who may represent him in his absence; who may exercise jurisdiction and authority conferred upon them by permanent delegation, and who, in a word, may take the Pontiff's place." Moreover, he teaches that, "the Roman Pontiff has this right by the very reason and nature of the primacy; by the constant discipline of the Church even from the first ages; by the authority of ecclesiastical and imperial laws, and by the common opinion of canonists and lawyers, especially Germans and Protestants."

310. In the early history of the Church we find two kinds of pontifical legates, the apocrisarioi or responsales, and the apostolic vicars. The former

were sent to the emperors at Constantinople, and later also to other princes; the latter, or apostolic vicars, were delegated to act for and represent the Roman Pontiff in certain countries of the world. The original and chief duty of the apocrisarioi was to treat with the emperor or prince concerning a matter of interest to the Roman Pontiff, and to deliver to the Pontiff the reply received. Their position was of great importance and highest honor; but from extant documents it cannot fully be shown that these legates had ordinary and permanent jurisdiction in spiritual matters.

311. Although Hincmar, a writer of the ninth century, says: "The ministry of the apocrisarius began at the time when Constantine the Great erected his throne in his city which before was called Bizantium; and thus the responsales of the Roman See as well as of other principal sees kept watch in the palace in regard to ecclesiastical affairs;" still the earliest documents extant in regard to the apocrisarioi are contemporary only with the Council of Calcedon held in the year 451, a century and a quarter after the removal of the emperor to Constantinople. These documents are letters of Pope St. Leo in which he appoints Julian, bishop of Cos in the Archipelago, his representative to the Emperor Marcian, "because he was a man brought up by the Holy See and imbued with its spirit and doctrine."

In the Migne collection, letters 111, 112, 113 of Pope St. Leo concern this appointment of the apostolic legate to the court of Constantinople. Bishop Julian receives his appointment in letter 113, while his credentials are given in letter 111 addressed to the emperor, and in letter 112 a strong recommendation is made in his favor to the Empress Pulcheria. The pontifical letter to the emperor commends Julian, and requests that he be received and properly treated; "for," says the Pope, "confident of the sincerity of his faith I have delegated to him my office against the heretics of the time."

312. In this way special legates were appointed from time to time, but while a shadow of imperial power remained in the West, and while Theodoric and other Gothic kings were dominating Italy, there was no special reason for having apocrisarioi in Constantinople; in fact it was more necessary for the Popes to have them in the courts of the western conquerors. In the meantime, however, the bishop of Constantinople acted as apocrisarius for the Roman Pontiff, until a disagreement arose because of the schism of Acacius. Later, however, when the Emperor Justinian conquered the Goths and subjugated the greater part of Italy, Pope Agapetus sent one of his deacons, named Pelagius, to Constantinople to remain in the imperial palace and act as apocrisarius and nuncio. The Pope himself while in Constantinople had seen the advantage of having such a legate residing permanently at court, especially after Rome again had come into possession of the emperors. In a few years the power of the apocrisarius at Constantinople became illustrious and a stepping-stone to the papacy. For Pope Virgilius was succeeded by Pelagius, and later Pelagius II. was succeeded by Gregory the Great, whom he had sent as apocrisarius to Constantinople. Gregory in turn sent his legate;

but soon he was obliged to prohibit him from assisting at the Mass of the patriarch of Constantinople unless the latter reformed. For this reason it happened that the apocrisarius of the Pope was withdrawn from court, and for a while none of the Roman clergy could be induced to go to Constantinople, because of the abuse received by former legates.

313. Under Phocas, Pope Gregory the Great was persuaded to send a legate named Boniface whom he ordained deacon for the purpose. This legate afterwards succeeded Pope Sabian, who himself had been apocrisarius under Pope Gregory but had been recalled because of the exasperating conduct of the Emperor Mauritius. An interruption again occurred after Pope St. Martin was ignominiously treated by the Emperor Constantine, the Monothelist, and it continued until Constantine Pogonatus, having restored the integrity of Catholic faith in the East, begged Pope Leo II. to restore former relations and send a legate "to live in the imperial city and to act for and represent the person of His Holiness in doctrinal and disciplinary and all ecclesiastical affairs." In response the Pope sent as apocrisarius a sub-deacon who had been one of his legates in the Œcumenical Council held at Constantinople in the year 680, in which the Monothelites were condemned. This request of the emperor insinuates that the legates of the Pope at Constantinople had ample and permanent jurisdiction.

The fury of the Iconoclastic emperors soon again interrupted friendly relations so that no papal legates resided in the imperial court thereafter, except once in the year 743 under Constantine Copronymus. But when later the western empire was revived under Charlemagne, the apocrisarioi or nuncios again appeared.

314. The second kind of pontifical legates known to the early church are the vicars apostolic. From the first ages the Roman Pontiffs had their vicar in Illyria, usually the bishop of Thessalonica, who in their name exercised jurisdiction over all the bishops and archbishops of that country. This vicariate must be of very ancient origin, for it is mentioned as an ancient institution by Pope Innocent I., when in the year 412 he appoints Rufus his vicar and states that he does this in imitation of his predecessors. Even before this he had written to Bishop Anysius, the apostolic vicar whom Rufus succeeded, a letter confirming his appointment as vicar, which he says had been made by his predecessors, Damasus, Siricius and Anastasius. Hence Pope Damasus is said to have established this vicariate. *Collectio Holstenii, pg. 45.* In the same way St. Sixtus III. in the year 431 writes that, "he has given his vicar, the bishop of Thessalonica, nothing new, but only the same that his predecessors had given to the predecessors of the vicar."

315. Moreover in all these letters the Roman Pontiffs write "as primates of the universal Church," and refer to the obligation incumbent on them of caring for the whole flock of Christ. The jurisdiction also of the apostolic vicar was most ample both in gracious and contentious matters; for he had the right to visit churches, to examine and approve candidates for the episcopate, to examine and consecrate metropolitans, to convoke councils and send

their acts to Rome for confirmation, to give metropolitans leave of absence, to receive reports concerning what bishops and priests were doing, to receive and forward petitions to the Holy See, to hear in the first instance all major causes, to hear and decide all controversies between bishops, and finally to judge all and every cause which one might have against a bishop. *Super Nunciaturis Cap. 8, No. 53.*

These faculties of the apostolic vicar of Thessalonica were so ample that they comprehended every cause; and as they covered every cause so they included all the faithful and all bishops and metropolitans. Moreover the sanction of excommunication was attached to disobedience and contumacy, though it was scarcely necessary to apply it, since the bishops recognized and obeyed the delegated authority of the apostolic vicar. If later some applied to the Emperor Theodosius and asked him to change the vicariate to the see of Constantinople, neither their action nor that of the emperor had any effect; for the Roman Pontiffs continued delegating the bishop of Thessalonica as their vicar.

316. Very similar to the vicariate of Illyria was that of Arles in Gaul, whether we consider its name and title, or the time and reason of its institution. It was established by the Popes as primates of the universal Church, and for the reason that they were unable personally to visit and care for such a distant region. The letters of Pope Hilary in the year 461 and of Pope Symachus in the year 498, addressed to the bishop of Arles, suppose at that time the long-continued establishment of the vicariate with ample

jurisdiction over both the faithful and the bishops and metropolitans.

In the fifth century Pope Simplicius made Zeno, the bishop of Seville, his apostolic vicar for all Spain; and in the year 514 Pope Hormisdas added Portugal to the vicariate of Seville already established with ample powers.

The same Pope Hormisdas made St. Remigius, the archbishop of Rheims, his vicar apostolic for the territory which was subject to Clovis. St. Boniface, the apostle of Germany, was commissioned by Gregory II. an extraordinary vicar apostolic, but after he established the sees of Cologne and Mayence, by three succeeding Popes he was made vicar apostolic with ordinary and permanent authority over all Germany.

317. The vicariate of Sicily is of equally ancient origin; but this difference may be mentioned regarding its vicars apostolic: in the other vicariates a resident bishop was usually chosen by the Roman Pontiff, but in regard to Sicily not unfrequently a cleric was sent from Rome to act as vicar apostolic and have full jurisdiction over all bishops. Thus St. Gregory the Great sent a sub-deacon named Peter to act as his vicar and committed to him the right to rule all the churches of Sicily as vicar of the Apostolic See.

The apostolic legation in Sicily, which was called "*regia monarchia,*" endured through all changes to the time of Pope Pius IX. But he by a constitution made in 1864, and published October 10, 1867, entirely abolished the legation with its judge, ministers and officials and assigned a method of trial for the causes formerly brought before it.

318. The vicariates in the course of time became weakened, though they were still continued or revived between the ninth and fifteenth centuries. That of Sicily continued, while that of Arles, which had depreciated, was restored in the year 1056 when Rambold, the archbishop, was made vicar of Pope Victor II. and in that capacity presided over the Council of Toulouse. But if the vicariates became rarer, primacies became more frequent; so that, because the metropolitans of certain sees had again and again been appointed apostolic vicars, these sees became primatial and acquired the rights of vicariates. Such primatial sees were known as "legations-born" and their incumbents were "legates-born" of the Apostolic See. Legates-born were the bishops of Arles, Lyons, Narbonne, Toledo, Mayence, Salzburg, Treves, Bremen, Prague, and others, such as the bishops of Canterbury and York in England and of Piza in Italy. These legates signed themselves, even in administering their dioceses, "Apostolic legates by the favor and mercy of the Apostolic See."

319. Permanent legates of this kind received extensive delegated power from the Holy See and took precedence over all other metropolitans, who in fact were ordered to obey them as they would the Pope himself. Since they represented the Roman Pontiff, they were at first considered judges of appeal, and later also began to hear greater causes in the first instance, so that an appeal from their decision lay only to the Apostolic See. *Legati-nati* were obliged to send messengers to Rome each year for instructions, and they themselves were supposed to visit the Apostolic See every three years.

Their power, however, was so ample, that, wielded as it sometimes was by unworthy men, many abuses ensued. The jealousy of the ordinaries also made difficult even the proper exercise of their authority. In fact so strong was the opposition thus developed, particularly in the eleventh and twelfth centuries, that the Holy See was obliged to send extraordinary legates *a latere* to calm the minds of the metropolitans and temporarily satisfy their jealousy; because when a legate *a latere* entered a province all power of legates-born was in abeyance and continued thus until the extraordinary legate left again for Rome.

320. These extraordinary legates were sent from Rome not unfrequently at the request of the legates-born, who professed to need their help and counsel. Thus Pappo, the archbishop of Treves and legate-born of the Apostolic See, about the year 1038, begged Pope Benedict IX. to send him a legate *a latere*. Legates *a latere* were always sent with most ample powers, both gratious and contentious; and as a rule even from antiquity such legates were sent by the Roman Pontiffs to preside in their name over œcumenical councils.

The bishops, either through jealousy that others less powerful in temporalities, were nevertheless set over them in spiritual authority, or because they desired greater freedom, became more and more alienated from the native apostolic legates, so much so that Drugo, the bishop of Metz, in the year 844, forced by many vexations, resigned his position of vicar or legate, "lest being an offense to his brethren and fellow priests he might introduce a schism into Holy Church." The same occurred in the primacy of Lyons and in the primacies or legations of other kingdoms, especially in Germany, where emulation was so strong that the bishops declared they would receive no legate except he came from Rome direct. For a similar reason Bruno, the archbishop of Treves, in the year 1120, visited Pope Callixtus II. and begged him to free the province of Treves from the power of every legate, except legates *a latere*. Arnold, also, the archbishop of Cologne, in the year 1157, requested of Eugene III. that his province should be subject to no primate or legate-natus, but only to Holy See or a legate *a latere*.

321. For such reasons the power of native legates was allowed to wane, and soon to cease entirely. The consequence was that innumerable causes which formerly had been heard and decided by the native legates, as vicars of the Apostolic See, could now be heard in no court save that of Rome. Legates *a latere* were sent only for particular business and for a short time; therefore they could decide but few such causes on appeal. The delay, the trouble, the expense of making a journey to Rome had never before been put upon litigants, except in rare and graver causes. For from the first ages of the Church, as was said above, apostolic vicars residing in the provinces and later *legati-nati* heard and decided nearly all causes on appeal from the diocesan or metropolitan courts.

322. Again, therefore, the bishops complained, and with them princes and people. They had destroyed the native tribunals, but could not bear the consequences of their act. Rome was obliged to

find a remedy; and it found one. For the Apostolic See, after all its endeavors to exercise the primacy through native vicars apostolic had failed, again introduced the former practice of sending from Rome to various countries certain persons agreeable to secular princes and placed in ecclesiastical dignity, in order that they might act as apostolic vicars with ordinary and permanent jurisdiction, and thus represent and take the place of the Roman Pontiff.

"The metropolitans were unwilling that anyone of themselves should have the right of perpetual precedence, and their personal ambition and mutual jealousy were therefore the cause and the reason why the Roman Pontiffs in order to fulfil the duty of primacy, from the fifteenth century to the present day, have sent from their own Court to Germany, France, Spain, Portugal and other kingdoms, nuncios foreign to the country and attached to no party, but placed in dignity and acceptable to the reigning princes. Thus ordinary nunciatures were established at Catholic courts and in chief cities." *Pius VI. Super Nunciaturis, No. 132.*

323. With the establishment of these nunciatures the power and office of legates-born ceased, so that nothing is left to former primatial sees but the name. The bishops of Cologne, it is true, and Salzburg, Prague and Greisen still retain the title by consent of the Holy See, but it gives them no jurisdiction.

To-day therefore all legates of the Holy See are *legati missi* or sent from Rome. They are of two kinds; cardinal legates *a latere*, and nuncios or delegates. Legate is a general term which comprehends every person sent by the Apostolic See to execute a command. When formerly legates-born existed, any legate sent from Rome, whether a cardinal or not, was called a legate *a latere*, which meant sent from the side of the Sovereign Pontiff. But to-day the term legate *a latere* is used only when a cardinal is sent on a certain extraordinary mission. Such a mission was that of Cardinal Caprara to Napoleon Bonaparte, for the re-adjustment of ecclesiastical affairs in France. In earlier times cardinals were often sent as legates *a latere* to preside at general councils held outside of Rome.

324. Nunciatures or legations are of two classes. Those of the first class are at the capitals of greater nations and are such as immediately prepare the way to the cardinalate; so that legates are usually not recalled from them except to receive the purple. Such are the nunciatures of Austria, Hungary, France, Spain, and Portugal. To these nunciatures we may add the American legation, if the words of Pope Leo XIII. receive their full meaning; for he says in his Enclyclical to the American bishops dated January 6, 1895, "When the Council of Baltimore had concluded its labors the duty still remained of putting, so to speak, a proper and becoming crown upon the work. This We perceived could scarcely be done in a more fitting manner than through the due establishment by the Apostolic See of an American legation. Accordingly as you are well aware We have done this. By this action, as We have elsewhere intimated, We have wished, first of all, 'to certify that in our judgment and affection America occupies the same place and rights as other

states be they ever so mighty and imperial." These words would scarcely be true if the American legation is not considered one of the first class; and the Holy Father's judgment, "that America has the same place and rights as other states be they ever so mighty and imperial," would scarcely have full force if the apostolic delegates of the American legation were recalled to assume a nunciature, while the nuncios of Austria, France, Spain or Portugal are recalled only to receive the cardinalitial dignity.

325. If legates are sent to the courts of emperors or kings of greater countries they are called nuncios; but if sent to courts of lesser rank or to cities where there are no courts they are called internuncios. Holland and Brazil have internuncios. Belgium and Bavaria, however, like the greater nations, have nuncios. A new departure seems to have been made in regard to republics, which were scarcely known when nunciatures were established. Representatives of the Apostolic See sent to republics usually are called delegates apostolic, and if in addition to spiritual affairs they represent the Pontiff in civil matters, they are called delegates apostolic and envoys extraordinary. Such legates represent the Holy See in Columbia, in Equedor, Bolivia and Peru, and in San Domingo, Haiti and Venezuela. One delegate extraordinary, it will be noticed, represents the Holy See in three countries.

326. The nunciatures are under the Cardinal-secretary of State and receive instructions through him. The legations in the countries of South America, as well as the countries themselves, are

under the Sacred Congregation for Extraordinary Ecclesiastical Affairs which is intimately connected with the Secretariate of State. The position of the American legation seems not yet fully settled, for while it is nominally under the Propaganda, still it depends more directly on the Vatican than on this Sacred Congregation. Neither have its limits been exactly determined.

The greater legations, Austria, France, Spain, Portugal and the United States, besides the legate have each an auditor and a secretary, appointed to them by the Holy See. Bavaria, Belgium, Brazil and Holland each have an auditor but no secretary. The other legations have only the delegate apostolic. These legations are supported directly by the Holy See, so that, as Pius VI. says to the bishops of Germany, there may be no complaint made on the score of expense or abuse. *Super Nunciaturis, No. 139.* The sum of $6,000 annually is allowed the apostolic delegate to the United States.

The nations which have representatives at the papal court to-day are Austria-Hungary, Bavaria, Belgium, Bolivia, Brazil, Columbia, Ecuador, France, Hayti, Monaco, Peru, Portugal, Prussia, Russia, San Domingo, Spain. Mexico at the present time is re-establishing relations with the Holy See.

Besides the American legation, which, dating from January 24, 1893, is the latest one established, there are seven other apostolic delegations depending on the Sacred Congregation of the Propaganda. These are: Constantinople, established May 6, 1887; Egypt and Arabia, October 9, 1888; Greece, April 29, 1892; Oriental India, March 15, 1892; Mesopotamia, Kurdistan and Armenia Minor, April 4, 1884; Persia, February 13, 1881; Syria, August 19, 1890.

The Apostolic delegation to Oriental India is quite similar to that of the United States. It is placed over eight archiepiscopal and twenty-two episcopal sees. Like that sent to the United States it was established by His Holiness, while the other delegations were established by the Propaganda with the sanction of the Pontiff. None of these delegations represent the Holy See in civil matters; their faculties and jurisdiction are confined to spiritual affairs. For this reason they are all called apostolic delegations, whatever may be their power and influence. The legations to the United States and to Oriental India are placed over archbishoprics and bishoprics properly established, but the other apostolic delegations are placed over apostolic vicariates and prefectures, all of whose incumbents have delegated, not ordinary jurisdiction. Because then the legations to the United States and to Oriential India were to be placed over bishops having ordinary jurisdiction, the Sovereign Pontiff himself established them, by virtue of his primacy over the universal Church.

CHAPTER III.

THE POWER OF APOSTOLIC LEGATES.

327. The nunciatures and legations of the present day succeed the legates-born and the vicars apostolic and apocrisarioi of previous ages. Legates of the present day, however, have not the extensive faculties possessed by those of former times; but nevertheless like them they have permanent and ordinary jurisdiction in the regions over which they are placed.

One great and notable difference in the policy of the Apostolic See in regard to legates is this: while the legates-born were always natives of the country where they exercised apostolic authority in the name of the Roman Pontiff, and while the apostolic vicars were nearly always bishops of the province over which they had delegated jurisdiction; at the present day nuncios and delegates apostolic are strangers and have no episcopal see in the country to which they are sent as legates.

328. The experience acquired by the Church from the ninth to the sixteenth centuries will undoubtedly be sufficient to last for several ages to come. Legates of the Holy See, who were bishops of the country wherein they exercised jurisdiction were failures, because of the jealousy of other bishops against them, and because when necessity required

severe measures against some of their brethren they were either from sympathy or from fear unequal to the occasion. They could stop neither simony nor incontinence; nor could they protect the Church against the encroachments of the civil power on which too often they depended for their temporalities. Again they were likely to be partisans or to serve their own interests and those of their residential see, rather than the interests of justice and the dictates of a broad and generous policy which alone could satisfy Christendom.

The apostolic delegate to the American church, it may therefore safely be said, will never be the bishop of a residental· see in the United States. Moreover in the light of history it is doubtful whether he will ever be an American; for human nature is the same to-day as it was fifteen centuries ago. The jealousy of good men is not less in America to-day than it was in Illyria in the fifth century and in Europe in the tenth. Inferior officials, assistants or assessors, may properly be natives and residents of the country wherein a legation is established; for they can bring a knowledge of peculiar circumstances and a spirit of nationalism to the legation, which combined with the vivifying life and Catholic spirit of a legate fresh from the Holy See, cannot fail to produce the happiest results; but the legate himself will be an impartial stranger.

329. Legates sent from the Holy See are either *legati non-judices* or *legati judices*. The former are those sent to perform some special duty, which being done they return to Rome. Such legates are sent, for instance, to carry the biretum to a newly-created

cardinal who lives away from Rome. They are usually called ablegates, and have no ordinary jurisdiction in the country to which they are sent.

Legate-judges are those who have ordinary spiritual jurisdiction in the country to which they are sent. Legates *a latere* and nuncios or delegates apostolic have such ordinary jurisdiction in the countries confided to them; and this jurisdiction does not expire through the death of the Pope who appoints them, even though they have not yet assumed their office. The reason is that they are commissioned and sent by the Apostolic See which never dies. Ordinary jurisdiction is essential to the office of an apostolic legate, that is, his jurisdiction must be, morally speaking, universal or extending to all causes and persons of a certain territory or society. A jurisdiction which extends only to certain particular causes or persons is a delegated not ordinary jurisdiction. The ordinary jurisdiction of an apostolic delegate comes from his office and dignity, not from special delegation.

330. This can best be understood by recalling examples known to Americans. Archbishop Spalding was appointed apostolic delegate to preside over the Second Plenary Council of Baltimore. In the same way Archbishop Gibbons was made apostolic delegate for the Third Plenary Council. They had full authority over bishops and archbishops in all that pertained to the council, but their jurisdiction ended with the completion of its work. Again, Monsignor Satolli was sent as the Pope's representative to the opening of the Catholic University of America; his position was that of an ablegate, not

a judge-legate, and having performed his mission he returned to Rome. Later he was sent as an ablegate to represent the Holy See at the World's Columbian Exposition in the fall of 1892; but at the same time he was commissioned as a special apostolic delegate in regard to several causes and controversies which had been referred to Rome. On January 24, 1893, the American legation was established, and Monsignor Satolli being appointed delegate apostolic, thereby from this office and dignity acquired ordinary jurisdiction over the bishops, clergy and Catholic people of the United States in all spiritual affairs. From this it is evident that the term, apostolic delegate, is rather a general one, and the power it represents can be judged only from the position of the legate, whether he is a special legate or the incumbent of a permanent legation, or from the letters of appointment. For as Pirhing says, "the power of an apostolic legate, both as to extension and restriction depends absolutely on the will of the delegating Pontiff; in nearly the same way as the power of a vicar general depends on the will of the bishop appointing him."

331. All legates having ordinary jurisdiction can sub-delegate to others causes within their competency. Such delegation, however, expires with the death or recall of the legate, unless the cause has been begun at least by citation.

When the Pope has specially delegated a certain cause to anyone, an apostolic legate cannot interfere. The reason is, that a special mandate derogates from a general one, and "a special delegate of the Pope in the cause committed to him is greater than the legate of the Pope." *Smalzgruber, tit. 30, lib. I. Decret.* Hence in such a case, the legate cannot call the matter before himself, nor can he annul the sentence of the special delegate, nor receive an appeal from his sentence. Thus a controversy which a metropolitan by special delegation has heard before the advent of a legate, cannot be reviewed by the legate, but only by Rome itself. Moreover a cause which has once been heard in Rome, if only on an interlocutory point, cannot be heard by an apostolic delegate.

332. Legates of the Apostolic See are competent judges in the second instance in regard to all ecclesiastical causes of the whole province or region committed to them. Before the Council of Trent they could hear causes also in the first instance, but this power was then withdrawn. Hence before the Council of Trent an apostolic legate had concurrent jurisdiction with all the ordinaries existing in his province, even in regard to judging controversies in the first instance. In other words a litigant was free to begin his case either in the diocesan court or before the apostolic legate; for when there is more than one ordinary judge, the complainant has the choice of courts.

But this competency of apostolic legates in the first instance was withdrawn by the Council of Trent in these words: "All causes which in any way pertain to the ecclesiastical forum, even regarding benefices, shall be heard in the first instance only before the ordinaries of places. Legates, even those *a latere* and nuncios, whatever their faculties, shall not presume to impede or trouble bishops in the aforesaid causes." Hence unless legates are authorized by a special faculty since the Council of Trent they cannot hear and decide causes originating in a diocese between clerics or laymen, or causes of a bishop against clerics of his diocese. When parishioners, therefore, make complaints against their pastor to the apostolic delegate, such complaints are usually forwarded to the ordinary of the diocese wherein the complaint originated.

333. If, however, a cleric, as complainant, has a cause against his own bishop, the apostolic legate of the country may hear it in the first instance. Such a cause does not pertain to the diocesan court. The bishop cannot judge his own cause, and the diocesan tribunal cannot judge the bishop. Neither can *arbitri necessarii* be selected for such a case.

Moreover the jurisdiction of the metropolitan in the first instance in purely civil causes in which a cleric, as complainant, sues his bishop, is doubtful, and will remain so, because Rome has declined to decide the question. On January 20, 1893, the Sacred Congregation of the Propaganda to whom the question was referred on appeal, replied: "Since it is controverted among canonists, the Sacred Congregation does not wish to decide the question by its sentence." This decree was approved by the Holy Father on February 10, 1893.

The jurisdiction of the metropolitan over his suffragans in such a case being doubtful, practically it is useless. Such cases must therefore be brought in the first instance either before the Apostolic See or before its legate. If brought before the Apostolic See the case will be remitted to its legate or a special delegate will be appointed. An example of such a case might occur, if a bishop declined or neglected to repay a sum of money which he had borrowed from one of the priests of his diocese. The apostolic legate is the ordinary superior of the bishop and has competent jurisdiction.

334. Legates according to the present law do not hear causes in the first instance, unless these causes having been begun, are not terminated in the diocesan court within two years. In the second instance, however, or on appeal, legates have full jurisdiction; so that a litigant may appeal from the sentence of his ordinary either to the metropolitan or to the apostolic delegate.

It may be noted, that at the present time, the American legation does not hear causes in the third instance, or as a court of last resort. Thus a cause begun in a diocesan court, then heard on appeal in the metropolitan court, cannot be heard by the apostolic legate, but only by Rome. This, however, is expected to be changed, so that the legation may be a supreme court. Further, it may be noted that a regular appeal does not lie to Rome against a decision or sentence of the apostolic delegate, but only a recourse to the Holy See. For sufficient reasons a rehearing may be granted by the legation itself without such recourse.

335. Suspensions *ex informata conscientia* may on recourse by the suspended cleric, be examined by the apostolic delegate at the American legation without the necessity of a recourse to Rome. When recourse is made against such a suspension, the legation writes to the bishop for his reasons, and the matter is then carefully examined and the suspension re-

laxed if the reasons alleged do not seem sufficient, or the suspension sustained if it is founded on proper testimony.

Again the legation is used as a tribunal of interpellation. Ordinaries consult with the apostolic delegate as to the proper method of proceeding in certain cases, so that, following his directions, there may be no danger of them going wrong and being reversed on appeal. Such interpellation, however, should contain a clear and complete statement of the case, not a partial one, else reversal will likely follow.

336. An apostolic legate, although he is the superior and ordinary judge of the bishops and archbishops residing in his province, nevertheless since the time of the Council of Trent by ordinary law cannot proceed against their crimes.

It is true that Smalzgruber says: "A pontifical legate can and should reform the morals and correct the vices even of bishops and archbishops who are in his province, because he is their ordinary judge and superior in power." *Tit. 30, De Legato.* But this, it seems, should be understood of the common law as it existed before the Council of Trent. For that council reserved the greater criminal causes of bishops to the Holy See, and the lesser ones to the provincial council. Whence according to ordinary law an apostolic delegate has no jurisdiction in such matters. Criminal charges against bishops must therefore be filed with the Holy See, which may then commission its delegate to examine and report the matter. The ordinary duty of the legate himself requires him to report such cases.

FACULTIES OF LEGATES. 305

According to *Session 24, chapter 20, De Reformatione*, "legates are not to proceed against clerics, or other ecclesiastical persons, unless a demand first has been made on their bishop and he has been negligent." Any offence, however, committed by a cleric or other person against the apostolic legate himself renders such offender directly amenable to punishment by the legate.

But while an apostolic delegate may not by his ordinary commission proceed against even the minor personal crimes of bishops, still he may insist on their remedying all defects in the administration of their dioceses. If he meets with refusal, instead of dealing out censures, the usual procedure at the present time is to refer the matter to Rome, whither the recalcitrant bishop soon is quietly called to explain his conduct.

337. A general rule regarding the power of legates is that a legate can do in his province or region whatever a bishop can do in his diocese, an archbishop in his province and a primate in the region over which his primacy extends. This general rule, however, has no application in those matters which the canons, the Council of Trent or the apostolic constitutions expressly reserve to ordinaries.

Further, according to Pirhing, *Tit. 30, De Legato*, "a legate can do all that the Sovereign Pontiff can do except only those things which are reserved to the Sovereign Pontiff as a mark of his singulär privilege or prerogative; because these things are not comprehended in the general office and mandate of legation unless they are specially mentioned." Whence it follows that a legate cannot transfer bishops from one see to another, nor divide or unite bishoprics, nor depose bishops nor accept their resignations. Neither can he authorize the alienation of church property.

338. In all these matters, however, he not only may but is required to make reports to the Holy See. Likewise in the filling of episcopal sees, a legate has not a little influence. Apostolic nuncios, even where they have but little jurisdiction, as in France, nevertheless draw up for the Holy See the canonical information in regard to those nominated by the government to the episcopacy.

Likewise the canonical process in regard to candidates recommended for episcopal sees in the United States at one time or another passes through the legation.

In the same way letters sent by the Holy See to the whole episcopate are forwarded to the apostolic delegate for execution. Petitions to the Holy See if forwarded through its legate and with his recommendation are generally granted. Further, according to a special brief of the Holy Father, the Peter's pence, collected in the various dioceses of the United States, is to be sent to the apostolic delegate that by him it may be forwarded to Rome.

339. According to common law apostolic legates may validly assist at marriages even where the Council of Trent has been promulgated. They cannot, however, either approve confessors or confer orders unless at the request of bishops.

Legates can enact for the entire province or region over which they are placed, permanent statutes, i. e., such as will remain in force even after their legateship has expired. They can, moreover, by virtue of their general commission and without any special authorization of the Pope, convene a provincial or even a plenary council; but the acts of the council must be sent to Rome for approval. They can also visit the churches and institutes of the country to which they are sent, in order to eradicate and destroy what is contrary to the laws of the Church.

Finally the office of an apostolic legate may be summed up by saying, it is his right and duty to exercise supreme inspection in ecclesiastical affairs, to procure the observance of the apostolic constitutions, to restrain abuses, to correct depraved morals and defects, to foster concord and fidelity to the Sovereign Pontiff and to report to the Holy See what he thinks will be conducive to the good of the Church.

340. Cardinal legates *a latere* according to common law have certain rights and privileges greater than other legates. As soon as a cardinal legate *a latere* leaves Rome he can assume the insignia of his office and conduct himself as a legate even before he reaches the province to which he is sent. On his return he puts off his insignia only on entering Rome or the city where the papal Court resides. During all this time, even outside his province, he can absolve those excommunicated for laying violent hands on clerics. A legate can do this only within his province. Moreover while he is present in his province, all other legates cannot use the insignia of their office or exercise jurisdiction. The reason given is that a cardinal legate, being nearer to him, more nearly represents the Pontiff.

Again legates *a latere* have jurisdiction over those

exempt from episcopal jurisdiction, except only in some matters specially reserved to the Pontiff. Hence they can hear and decide the controversies of exempt clerics, notwithstanding their privilege of exemption. But other legates by virtue of their general commission have no faculties over them who are exempt from episcopal jurisdiction. By special delegation apostolic legates may receive such faculties, and as a matter of fact, the American legation has exercised jurisdiction over those ordinarily exempt.

341. Cardinal legates *a latere* concurrently with ordinaries may confer benefices. This rule, however, has many restrictions, for they cannot confer episcopal sees, whether elective or not. Neither can they confer regular or collegiate churches, nor the greater dignities of cathedrals if these are elective. Benefices which are in litigation or which are specially reserved to the Sovereign Pontiff are also outside their jurisdiction.

When a cardinal asserts that he is sent as a legate *a latere* he is to be believed without being required to show his letters of appointment. In regard to his powers he is not obliged to show his delegation, except as to extraordinary faculties which he has received in addition to those conferred by law on cardinal legates.

A nuncio or apostolic delegate, however, is obliged to make his faculties known, both in regard to those given him by common law and those specially conferred; otherwise he need not be acknowledged.

342. As soon as a cardinal legate makes his appointment known officially, he takes precedence, in his province, over all bishops, archbishops and pri-

mates, so that he occupies a higher throne in the church, and exercises pontifical rights and gives the blessing even in the presence of the diocesan bishop. He has precedence also over all other cardinals, even if they are his seniors and of a higher order. Cardinal legates, therefore, receive the highest honor, for they directly and immediately represent all the authority of the Apostolic See. Further, they can celebrate pontifically in the cathedral of an archbishop even without his permission. This a nuncio or apostolic legate cannot do, according to a decision of the Sacred Congregation of Rites.

When a legate is present in a city, its bishop cannot bless the people nor use the mozzetta or the rochet uncovered. Still he can do so in his cathedral if the legate is not present, or if he consents. *S. Cong. Concilii, 2 Oct. 1601.*

343. The power of an apostolic legate ceases with the completion of the work for which he was sent or with the expiration of the time for which he was appointed. His power also ceases when he leaves his province with the intention of not returning. But a legate to whom several countries are committed may go from one to the other, all the while retaining complete jurisdiction over them all. In fact he may summon causes of one country to be heard by him in another within his jurisdiction. Also by death or recall all power of a legate ceases and all sub-delegations become void if the causes are not yet begun. Finally, when a cause or business matter is brought before the Sovereign Pontiff himself every legate is prohibited from touching it further.

344. All nuncios and apostolic delegates have ordi-

nary jurisdiction over the clergy and people of their entire province; but some have more jurisdiction, others less. Their faculties depend entirely on their brief of appointment and delegation. The practice of the Roman Court to-day, especially in regard to nuncios, is to specifically determine their faculties. Lequeux says: "The nuncio at Paris exercises no act of jurisdiction except when canonical information is to be sent to the Holy See regarding the nominations made by the government to vacant bishoprics. His work is to manage the business of the Pontiff at the French court, to watch over the integrity of faith and the observance of the canons, and to inform the Sovereign Pontiff respecting all affairs of greater moment."

Nevertheless apostolic nuncios are not simply diplomatic envoys; they have also authority over the faithful of the kingdom to which they are sent. For this is specifically taught by Cardinal Jacobini writing as Secretary of State in the name of the Pontiff to Monsignor Rampolla, then nuncio at Madrid: "Nuncios have no other authority than that which is communicated to them; but their briefs of appointment show that they have not merely a diplomatic mission, but an authoritative one over the faithful and over all religious matters."

345. When legates are appointed with the faculties which pertain to them by law without any other enunciation or specification, then they have all the jurisdiction which has been mentioned in the preceding numbers as the common law jurisdiction of nuncios and apostolic delegates. By subsequent delegation they may receive other faculties, but

these do not limit but rather extend their jurisdiction.

Thus the American legation has all the extraordinary faculties which the bishops of the country have received up to the present time, regarding matrimonial dispensations and other matters contained in Form I, and Forms C, D and E, and the delegate can sub-delegate them throughout the country, if prudence, charity or necessity requires such action.

From this it is evident that the gracious jurisdiction of the apostolic delegate to the United States is very extensive, and when it is considered that during the first two years of its existence the legation treated over seven hundred and fifty contentious cases of various kinds, the position of the legate will be acknowledged not a sinecure.

346. The apostolic delegate to the United States has the full and unlimited common law jurisdiction of apostolic legates. His brief of appointment gave him without limit, "all and singular the powers necessary and expedient for the carrying on of the apostolic legation." The brief by which Pope Leo XIII. appointed Monsignor Satolli apostolic delegate was dated January 24, 1893, and is the following:

"Venerable Brother: Holding you in very special affection, We by our apostolic authority and by virtue of these present letters, do elect, make and declare you to be apostolic delegate in the United States of America, at the good pleasure of ourself and this Holy See. We grant you all and singular the powers necessary and expedient for the carrying on of such delegation. We command all whom it concerns to recognize in you as apostolic delegate the supreme power of the delegating Pontiff; We command that they give you aid, concurrence and obedience in all things; that they receive with reverence your salutary admonitions and orders. Whatever sentence or penalty you shall declare or inflict against those who oppose your authority We will ratify, and with the authority given Us by the Lord will cause to be observed inviolably until condign satisfaction be made, notwithstanding constitutions and apostolic ordinances or any other thing to the contrary."

These are great powers and the consummate wisdom, prudence and skill with which they have been exercised by Monsignor Satolli more than justify the Pope's selection of the first American delegate apostolic.

347. The American legation is ecclesiastical not diplomatic. The Holy Father commissioned his legate to the Catholic church in the United States, not to the United States government. In his encyclical of January 6, 1895, addressed to the archbishops and bishops of the United States of North America, Pope Leo XIII. himself gives the reasons why he established the legation. These are his ever-memorable words:

"When the Council of Baltimore had concluded its labors, the duty still remained of putting, so to speak, a proper and becoming crown upon the work. This, We perceived, could scarcely be done in a more fitting manner than through the due establishment by the Apostolic See of an American legation. Accordingly, as you are well aware, We have done this. By this action, as We have elsewhere intimated, We have wished, first of all, to certify that in our judgment and affection America occupies the same place and rights as other states, be they ever so mighty aud imperial.

"In addition to this We had in mind to draw more closely the bonds of duty and friendship which connect you and so many thousands of Catholics with the Apostolic See. In fact, the mass of the Catholics understand how salutary our action was destined to be. They saw, moreover, that it accorded with the usage and policy of the Apostolic See. For it has been from earliest antiquity, the custom of the Roman Pontiffs, in the exercise of the divinely bestowed gift of the primacy in the administration of the Church of Christ, to send forth legates to Christian nations and peoples. And they did this, not by an adventitious, but an inherent right. For, upon the 'Roman Pontiff Christ has conferred ordinary and immediate jurisdiction, as well over all and singular the churches, as over all and singular the pastors and faithful'.

"Since he cannot personally visit the different regions and thus exercise the pastoral office over the flock intrusted to him, he finds it necessary from time to time, in the discharge of the ministry imposed on him, to dispatch legates into the different parts of the world, according as the need arises, who, supplying his place, may correct errors, make the rough ways plain, and administer to the people confided to their care increased means of salvation.

"But how unjust and baseless would be the suspicion, should any exist, that the powers conferred on the legate are an obstacle to the authority of the bishops. Sacred to us more than to any other, are the rights of those 'whom the Holy Ghost has placed as bishops to rule the Church of God.' That these rights should remain intact in every nation, in every part of the globe, We both desire and ought to desire, the more so since the dignity of the individual bishops is by nature so interwoven with the dignity of the Roman Pontiff that any measure which benefits the one necessarily protects the other. 'My honor is the honor of the universal Church. My honor is the unimpaired vigor of my brethren. Then am I truly honored when to each one due honor is not denied.'

"Therefore, since it is the office and function of an apostolic legate, with whatsoever powers he may be vested, to execute the mandates and interpret the will of the Pontiff who sends him, far from his being of any detriment to the ordinary power of the bishops, he will rather bring an accession of stability and strength. His authority will possess no slight weight for preserving in the multitude a submissive spirit; in the clergy, discipline and due reverence for the bishops; and in the bishops, mutual charity and an intimate unison of souls.

"And since this unison, so salutary and desirable, consists mainly in harmony of thought and action, he will no doubt bring it to pass that each one of you shall persevere in the diligent administration of his diocesan affairs; that one shall not impede another in matters of government; that one shall not pry into the counsels and conduct of another; finally, that with disagreements eradicated and mutual esteem maintained, you may all work together, with combined energies, to promote the glory of the American churches and the general welfare.

"It is difficult to estimate the good results which will flow from this concord of the bishops. Our own people will receive edification; the force of example will have its effect on those without, who will be persuaded by this argument alone that the divine apostolate has descended, by inheritance, to the ranks of the Catholic episcopate.

"Another consideration claims our earnest attention. All intelligent men are agreed, and We ourselves have with pleasure intimated it above, that America seems destined for greater things. Now, it is our wish that the Catholic Church should not only share in, but help to bring about, this prospective greatness. We deem it right and proper that she should, by availing herself of the opportunities daily presented to her, keep equal step with the Republic in the march of improvement, at the same time striving to the utmost, by her virtue and her institutions, to aid in the rapid growth of the states. Now, she will attain both these objects the more easily and abundantly in proportion to the degree in which the future shall find her constitution perfected.

"But what is the meaning of the legation of which we are speaking, or what is its ultimate aim, except to bring it about that the constitution of the Church shall be strengthened, her discipline better fortified? Wherefore, We ardently desire that this truth should sink, day by day, more deeply into the minds of Catholics—namely, that they can in no better way safeguard their individual interests and the common good than by yielding a hearty submission and obedience to the Church."

CHAPTER IV.

VICARS APOSTOLIC.

348. Since the Sacred Congregations of Cardinals and legates of the Holy See take the place of the Roman Pontiff, in a certain sense they can be called, and sometimes are called, vicars apostolic. But this term is used in a stricter sense and to-day almost exclusively of another kind of ministers, whose help the Sovereign Pontiff uses to exercise his jurisdiction and fulfill his mission in various parts of the world.

349. From remote antiquity the Apostolic See was accustomed to designate some bishop in each of the principal regions of the Catholic world, to take the place of the Roman Pontiff and to preside as vicar of the Apostolic See over the other bishops and metropolitans of that region. Ordinarily this duty was committed to one of the archbishops of the region, and in fact so regularly to the archbishop of a certain see, that at his death the Sovereign Pontiff made his successor the apostolic vicar. Hence such vicars apostolic little differed from those who later were called legates-born. But to-day, when vicars apostolic are mentioned, very different persons from these are understood. Neither is the cardinal-vicar of Rome a vicar apostolic in the usual acceptation of the term, although he really takes the place of the Roman Pontiff in administering the diocese of Rome.

350. A vicar apostolic, as the term is used to-day, is a cleric deputed by the Apostolic See to exercise pastoral authority in a certain region, not in his own name, but in that of the Roman Pontiff. As to their power of ruling, vicars apostolic do not necessarily differ from ordinary bishops of places; for as a bishop in regard to his diocese is a true pastor with jurisdiction in the internal and external forum, so is a vicar apostolic the same in the region committed to him. In fact the vicar receives not only the same, but even greater faculties than the bishop. The difference between them consists in this: the bishop rules his flock in his own name, and, though subject to pontifical authority, nevertheless is not merely a vicar of the Pope. On the contrary a vicar apostolic administers his region not in his own name, but in that of the Sovereign Pontiff.

351. Some vicars apostolic have not received episcopal consecration, while others have received it and are titular bishops of non-residential sees. The episcopal character is not necessary that one may be a vicar apostolic, but it is conferred when thought useful for the better administration of the vicariate.

There are two classes of vicars apostolic; those who are deputed for regions in which there are no canonically erected episcopal sees or dioceses, and no ordinaries who rule as regular pastors; and secondly, those who are appointed to rule a diocese either during a vacancy, or when the see is not vacant, but the bishop for some cause is unable to administer it.

352. The former class of vicars are nominated by the Sacred Congregation of the Propaganda and confirmed by the Roman Pontiff, through whom

they receive their faculties and commission. No informative process regarding the state of the church or diocese is necessary, for the reason that no dioceses are canonically erected.

If the person to be made vicar apostolic is present in Rome or in Italy, or if there are two men in Rome who can testify to his fitness, an informative process concerning his qualities must be made before the auditor of the Apostolic Treasury. But if the candidate is not in Italy and two witnesses cannot be found, it is sufficient that he be judged fit by the Propaganda. This is the constitution *Gravissimum*, of Benedict XIV. dated January 18, 1757. When, therefore, an informative process regarding the qualities of the candidate has been made and found satisfactory; or when on the recommendation of the Propaganda, the Pope has consented that he be appointed vicar apostolic, letters of appointment conveying jurisdiction are sent him, with instructions regarding his consecration as a titular bishop.

353. Ordinarily in these letters the administration of a vicariate is conferred upon him with all faculties which are necessary or expedient. This general delegation gives him the same jurisdiction that a regularly appointed bishop has in his diocese. In addition, by other letters he usually receives more generous faculties.

Although the Holy See does not consider that vicars apostolic are ordinaries, still because by delegated power they are truly pastors and superiors of the clergy and people committed to them, it follows that they have all the faculties which are necessarily connected with the rule and administration of a vicariate both in the internal and external forum. In other words they have legislative, judicial and coercive power over persons, and administrative power over the property of the vicariate, so that no bishop or other ordinary, even if he have metropolitan, primatial or other dignity, can interfere in the regions committed to the care of vicars apostolic. On the other hand, neither may the vicar transgress the boundaries of his vicariate and exercise jurisdiction in any other country.

354. From the fact that vicars apostolic are not diocesan bishops, it follows that they have no cathedral churches and therefore no competency in what pertains to cathedral chapters. Hence vicars apostolic cannot name honorary canons or confer the insignia of capitulars upon their missionaries. (S. Cong. Prop. Nov. 27, 1858.) From the same principle it follows that vicars apostolic cannot have vicars general, such as by a general commission can receive the faculties which the law assigns to this office. Still nothing prohibits them from selecting some competent person to assist them in administering the vicariate, and from giving him special faculties even with the right of sub-delegating.

355. The whole obligation of a vicar apostolic in the exercise of his office is contained in this: that he preserve the Catholic faith where it has taken root and have a care for the faithful whom he finds; and secondly, that he announce Christ to infidels and endeavor to bring heretics and schismatics back to the bosom of the Church. In order to perform these duties properly he is under the obligation of preaching, of residing in his vicariate and visiting it, and of

making a visit *ad limina* or to the Holy See. It may be noted that a vicar apostolic, not having an episcopal see, may reside in any place in his vicariate; but he is obliged to remain within its limits and not to leave, even to go to Rome, without permission of the Sacred Congregation of the Propaganda.

The visitation of the vicariate may be made through other missionaries, and the visit *ad limina* may be made through a procurator sent for the special purpose or appointed in Rome. Moreover, the vicar is to appoint some one to take his place in case of death and delegate to him all the faculties he possesses. This delegate in case of the vicar's death will administer the vicariate as the delegate of the Apostolic See until other provision is made.

356. The episcopal dignity has many privileges. Some of these are common both to titular bishops and to those of residential sees; others are peculiar to the latter. A vicar apostolic, therefore, who is a titular bishop, has the privilege of a portable altar, of saying Mass or having it said in his private chapel one hour before sunrise and one hour after noon, of choosing any approved priest for his confessor, and of being subject immediately to the Holy See. But because he is not a diocesan bishop, in using pontificals he cannot act as a diocesan; that is, he cannot erect a throne in any church, or use a seventh candle on the altar; neither is his name to be mentioned in the canon of the Mass.

357. Besides vicars there are also prefects apostolic in missionary countries. When the Holy See sends a band of missionaries to a certain region it usually appoints one of them superior over the others,

and gives him special faculties which he can use as the necessity or utility of the mission requires. This superior is called the prefect of the apostolic mission or the prefect apostolic. Generally he is not a bishop, but as a priest he has unusual jurisdiction, which sometimes includes the power of administering the sacrament of confirmation.

In conferring these faculties and sending forth these missionaries to preach, the Roman Pontiff exercises his primacy or supreme authority, and he does this independently of bishops. Moreover, punishment is attached to any act which may impede the missionaries who go forth with such faculties; and if bishops without just cause endeavor to prevent the exercise of them, the missionaries may nevertheless persist, but should at once inform the Sacred Congregation of the misunderstanding.

358. From this case it will be noticed that there are two classes of prefects apostolic; those who are in charge of a territory over which no titular or other bishop has charge, and those who are sent into the territory which is under the jurisdiction of a vicar apostolic or bishop. In the latter case, prefects are obliged to show their letters patent and faculties to the bishop or his vicar as soon as they reach their destination, in order that there may be no question of their authority. The bishop's consent is necessary in order that they may use the faculty of saying Mass twice a day, and that they may administer parochial sacraments, such as matrimony and extreme unction. Their other faculties they may use without the bishop's consent, except that they cannot consecrate chalices or altar stones unless

where there is no bishop, or he is distant over a two day's journey. However, if a grave and urgent cause makes such action necessary or advisable, the bishop may limit or even suspend the use of all these faculties. In such an event he must immediately inform the Sacred Congregation and state the reasons which governed his action. The apostolic prefects, not only in such a case, but also as a regular duty, are bound to report to the Propaganda the progress of their missions.

359. The vicars apostolic mentioned above are they who are appointed in missionary countries; there are also others appointed to govern dioceses in the name of the Sovereign Pontiff where the hierarchy has been established canonically. These may be appointed to rule a diocese during a vacancy, or when the see is filled, but the bishop cannot exercise jurisdiction for one or another cause.

During a vacancy the following reasons induce the appointment of a vicar apostolic to rule the diocese until the see is again filled: If the bishop died through violence, if the chapter does not agree in selecting a vicar capitular, if the one elected by the chapter is unlearned or otherwise unfit, if the vicar capitular is called to Rome, if the see has been vacant long or is likely to be so, or if any other grave reason suggests the appointment.

360. The vicar apostolic is sent by the Sovereign Pontiff with a brief, or by the Sacred Congregation of Bishops and Regulars with letters signed by the Pontiff. Such a vicar apostolic can do all that a bishop can do, except to use pontificals, and he therefore has all the jurisdiction of a bishop. In addition

to this ordinary power not unfrequently he receives other special faculties.

Moreover, his jurisdiction does not lapse with the death of the Roman Pontiff who sends him; and further an appeal from his judgment is taken to the metropolitan, not to the Holy See, as would be necessary in case he were an apostolic delegate.

A vicar apostolic appointed to rule and administer a diocese is usually not a bishop, but if appointed over a vicariate in missionary countries he generally is consecrated. The reason for the different policy is that the vicar appointed over a diocese will remain in charge but a short time, while an apostolic vicar in missionary countries receives a permanent appointment.

361. Various causes render necessary the appointment of a vicar apostolic over a diocese which has a bishop. Some are: If the bishop governs badly, if he is sordid, if he is old or suspended from his jurisdiction, if he is to be tried or called to Rome, if he does not reside in his diocese, if the good of the church requires it, if the bishop is unfit or unable to rule and administer the diocese. The causes for which a vicar apostolic may be appointed can be reduced to this one; namely, when there is a grave reason, either with or without the fault of the bishop, that he should be removed from the administration of the diocese, and if at the same time the cause is not such as to entail deposition and again for other reasons it is not expedient to appoint a coadjutor bishop.

362. When in such a case a vicar apostolic is appointed, the exercise of all jurisdiction belongs to

him and the bishop may not interfere in any way. Hence it belongs to the vicar to hold a concursus and designate the more worthy candidate for a parish; it belongs to him also to admit candidates to orders.

When a vicar apostolic is in charge, the bishop can have no vicar general; but the vicar apostolic cannot proceed against the one who was vicar general for any acts performed when he was in office. Neither can he interfere in any civil or criminal or mixed causes which concern the bishop, unless under special direction from the Holy See.

The vicar apostolic uses his own seal, but he is allowed only the honor bestowed on the vicar general of a bishop.

363. When a bishop, for the causes mentioned above, is to be suspended or removed from office, an apostolic administrator is sometimes appointed instead of a vicar. Such an administrator is a titular bishop, and has the privileges of his episcopal office as well as delegated jurisdiction to rule and administer the diocese in the name of the Sovereign Pontiff. Thus when Napoleon Bonaparte was exiled from France, his uncle, Cardinal Fesch, was removed from the metropolitan see of Lyons by the Pope, and a titular bishop was sent to rule it as an apostolic administrator.

CHAPTER V.

PROTONOTARIES APOSTOLIC.

364. During the first centuries of the Christian era when persecution raged most furiously against the Church of God, the glorious acts of confessors of the faith and the heroic sufferings of Christian martyrs were not allowed to go unrecorded. Popes Clement I. and Antherus I. chose certain men, noted for their piety, prudence and zeal for religion, and deputed them to act as notaries in the city of Rome and wherever the cross of Christ was acknowledged. Their work was to put in writing and preserve the names of those who suffered martyrdom, and the circumstances in which it occurred, as well as to bear witness to the courageous words of the persecuted Christians and the blindness and hardness of heart of pagan tyrants.

Seven of these notaries were appointed for the city of Rome, one for each region or district; and because of their dignity and the honor in which they were held, and also to distinguish them from other notaries, they were called proto or first notaries.

365. When the persecutions ceased the office of protonotary did not cease; its work only was changed. For Pope Julius I. assigned to these men the duty of carefully recording all decrees and enactments concerning faith and discipline, and all

matters which were deemed worthy of being handed down to posterity. In this way it happened that the office of protonotary became most illustrious, and in the course of time was enriched by numerous privileges. Pope Sixtus V. increased the number of protonotaries in the city from seven to twelve, and at the same time enlarged and confirmed their privileges and assigned them large revenues wherewith to keep up the dignity of their illustrious position.

366. To these notaries who were called *participating*, others were added in different regions of the Christian world whose work in their regions was similar to that of the protonotaries in Rome. The participating protonotaries formerly were allowed to sell their office so that the buyer succeeded the seller in the College of Protonotaries. But this venality was abolished about the year 1793, and in place of the revenues which had been assigned to the college, an annual pension was paid to each member.

In the pontificate of Gregory XVI. there were only two protonotaries, and with their death the college of participating protonotaries would have become extinct, had not this Pontiff restored it. This he did in his constitution of February 7, 1838, by which he decreed that the number of participating protonotaries should again be seven and that their ancient privileges and splendor should be restored.

367. Many authors distinguish only two kinds of protonotaries, those of the number participating and those *ad instar* or supernumerary. Bouix, however, and others contend that supernumerary protonotaries should be divided into those *ad instar* and those merely titular or honorary. He quotes the consti-

tution, *Cum innumeri*, of Pius VII. in support of his second division and mentions the restricted privileges of titular protonotaries. The *Gerarchia Cattolica*, however, gives only two classes, protonotaries *de numero*, or those participating, and protonotaries supernumerary, like to those participating. Titular protonotaries may have been omitted by the compiler, because they do not belong to the pontifical family.

Protonotaries, no matter what their class, should be secular clerics, at least twenty-five years of age and doctors in theology and in both canon and civil law. They have authority to draw up and legalize every kind of writing, both public and private, and to certify to any and all documents so as to make them legal testimony both in and out of court.

One participating protonotary always belongs to the Congregations of the Propaganda and of Rites, in which latter Congregation the protonotary frequently takes the place of the secretary in drawing up the process of canonization or beatification. Again they act as referees in the Signature of Justice and the Signature of Favor, and prepare a report on the matters submitted to them, giving the facts in the case, the petition of the orator and the objections of those opposing the petition.

368. Pope Sixtus V. enumerated and confirmed the privileges of the college of participating protonotaries. Among these privileges he gave them the right to confer the doctorate. Pius IX., however, on February 9, 1853, restricted this general faculty so that they can confer degrees only in theology and law, not in philosophy and the other sciences. At present, therefore, they can confer the doctorate in

theology on four persons each year and the doctorate in law also on four persons each year, but only on the following conditions: They can confer the doctorate only on persons present in Rome; a report must previously be made to the Sovereign Pontiff on each candidate for degrees; an examination of the candidates must be held by at least five protonotaries, and if so many cannot assist, then professors of the Roman archigynasium are to be called in to supply the requisite number; the examination is to be conducted according to the constitution of Pope Leo XII.; each year a report regarding the degrees conferred is to be made by the aforementioned protonotaries to the Sacred Congregation on Studies; and another report containing the names of those receiving degrees is to be placed in the archives of the Roman College.

369. Sixtus V. gave the college of protonotaries the privilege of creating notaries, and of legitimizing illegitimate children so that they could inherit property. But Pius IX. took away both these faculties, and allowed them to create only one honorary protonotary each year, and even this faculty was not to be exercised until after the special consent of the Sovereign Pontiff had been obtained for each case.

Further, Sixtus V. made participating protonotaries the familiars of the Pope and domestic prelates; and as such they have a right to the revenues of their prebends even though absent. He exempted them from the jurisdiction of ordinaries and made them subject immediately to the Holy See, so that no bishop can pass or execute sentence upon them. This privilege was confirmed by Pope Pius IX.

Moreover participating protonotaries can use pontificals, outside of Rome, even in cathedral churches with the consent of the bishop if he is present. They also may wear a violet cassock and mantelletta, and the rochet in public functions, and use a black hat bound with violet and decorated with rose-colored tassels. To these privileges may be added that of a portable altar and a private oratory. Formerly these protonotaries had precedence over bishops, and consequently over all prelates, as Cardinal Petra shows; but Pope Pius II. about the year 1460 ordained that precedence both in Court and out of it thereafter should be given to bishops, even those not yet consecrated, over the notaries of the Pope, commonly called protonotaries. At present they precede all other prelates, except only bishops.

370. Protonotaries *ad instar* or supernumerary are in a lower grade; but they have many privileges, a copy of which is always sent by the secretary of the college to a newly-appointed protonotary. These privileges are: 1°. Protonotaries *ad instar* are familiars of the Sovereign Pontiff and domestic prelates, but they are subject to the jurisdiction of their ordinary. 2°. They use the rochet, cappa, mantelletta and mantelone in pontifical processions. 3°. They wear mourning at the death of the Pontiff and put on violet at the announcement of his successor. 4°. In pontifical processions they immediately follow the bishops who are assistants at the throne, but they precede bishops who are not assistants, because these wear only the mantelletta. 5°. In the papal chapel they have their place just back of the Most Eminent cardinal-deacons, in the

rear. 6°. If participating protonotaries are wanting, they assume their place and duties, so that they also enjoy the privilege of sitting on the bench of the bishops after the last, if there is only one protonotary. 7°. Outside of Rome on solemn feasts they can wear all pontificals, having obtained the consent of the ordinary. But in celebrating they must recognize certain restrictions. 8°. In Rome and out of it, formerly they preceded all canons and dignitaries, except bishops, both in collegiate and in cathedral and patriarchal churches. But now outside of Rome, in church and in processions they yield precedence to vicars general, to canons of the cathedral assisting as a chapter, and to abbots. 9°. In as much as they are protonotaries they are also referees of both Signatures, that of Justice and that of Favor. 10°. They have the right to use the pontifical and semi-pontifical hat, ornamented with silk rose-colored cords and tassels; and they wear these cords also on their every-day hat. 11°. They have the indult of a private oratory, to be visited and approved by the ordinary, in which even on more solemn feasts, in the presence of their relatives living with them and their servants, they can celebrate Mass themselves or have it celebrated by any approved priest, either a secular or a member of a religious order. 12°. In the same oratory they may have the stations of the cross and gain all indulgences attached to them. 13°. In the absence of the protonotary, Mass can be said in the oratory provided some one of those mentioned in number 11° is present, and provided the protonotary has not changed his domicile or wishes to use the privilege of this oratory in some other place.

In saying Mass privately protonotaries *ad instar* are not allowed any marks of distinction over simple priests.

371. Protonotaries *ad instar* began to be appointed only a short time before the pontificate of Sixtus V. At first they were few, but now the number of supernumerary protonotaries *ad instar* is two hundred and seven, many of whom live outside of Rome. They are created only by the Sovereign Pontiff. The canons of the three great Roman basilicas, those of St. John Lateran, of St. Peter, and of St. Mary Major are all protonotaries of this class.

When a supernumerary protonotary is to be created outside of Rome, the execution of the apostolic letters of appointment usually is committed to his bishop, and at the same time a *folio* is sent giving instructions and the form necessary for conferring the insignia. The ceremony generally takes place after high Mass. As part of the ceremony, just previous to the conferring of the insignia, the candidate takes an oath to fulfil the duties of his office and makes a profession of faith. The ceremony is then closed with the singing of the *Te Deum*.

372. Although merely titular or honorary protonotaries are of earlier origin than protonotaries *ad instar*, still they have not as many privileges, particularly since Pius VII. in the year 1818 restricted them considerably. Honorary protonotaries are allowed to wear a prelatic habit outside of Rome, consisting of a cassock without a train and of a small cape, called mantelletta, both of which must be black. They may use a rochet under the cape in public

prayers and other church services. The use of purple stockings and rabbi is prohibited them; these as well as the band of their hats must be black.

Further they are not allowed to celebrate pontifically or in any way different from other priests; hence they should vest in the sacristy, not wear a ring, not use more than two candles, not have more than one server.

373. Honorary or titular protonotaries take precedence, if in prelatic habit, over all clerics, priests, and even canons taken singly, but not as a college; they do not, however, precede prelates of the Roman Court, vicars general, vicars capitular and abbots.

They can draw up acts for the canonization or beatification of saints, unless there is in the same place a participating protonotary. They can also be chosen conservators for religious orders, synodal judges, apostolic commissaries, and are fit to be selected by the Sovereign Pontiff judges for ecclesiastical and beneficial causes. A profession of faith may be made before them by those bound to it, and pensions can be transferred legally in their presence. Moreover by common law the benefices they hold, when vacant, can be conferred only by the Apostolic See.

The chief points of difference between protonotaries *ad instar* and honorary protonotaries are, that the former are familiars of the Pope and have rank in the Roman Court, the latter are not members of the pontifical family; the former have a right to a private oratory, the latter have not. Again protonotaries *ad instar*, with the consent of the ordinary, on solemn feasts can wear pontificals, such as the mitre; but titular protonotaries have no such privilege. Both these classes, however, are under the jurisdiction of the diocesan ordinary like other clerics.

---

374. The Roman Court is the most ancient in the world; for it had gathered the experience of several centuries before any of the secular courts known to-day had begun to exist. It is the most splendid, and still the most democratic; for the son of a peasant may reach the pontifical throne as well as a prince who has the prestige of wealth and noble blood. The members of this Court are bound together, not by family ties, but by those of religion.

The head of the Church, in his lonely, abstemious life, is an exemplar for all who are honored with membership in the Roman Court. Religion, it is true, has a human side as well as one which is divine. It is neither truthful nor wise to claim absolute perfection in anything that depends even partially on human nature. Hence no one claims immunity from imperfections for the entire Roman Court. But what is evident, is that these imperfections, originating in human weakness, have not acted upon it as upon other courts. Other courts have been destroyed thereby; the Roman Court still remains, and to-day is brighter and stronger than in the centuries of the past. Humanity and diplomacy have not done this. The vivifying, ever-present assistance of Divinity is the only possible explanation of the long-continued existence of the papacy and the Roman Court.

www.ingramcontent.com/pod-product-compliance
Lightning Source LLC
Chambersburg PA
CBHW021158230426
43667CB00006B/462